IN YOUR MIDST

THE STORY OF
THE BENEDICTINE SISTERS OF PERPETUAL ADORATION

SR. DOLORES DOWLING, OSB

. . . We have asked the Lord who is to dwell in the tabernacle and we have heard His command to any who would live there . . .
—Prologue to the Rule of Benedict

Dedicated

to my sisters past and present
whose story this is; and to our
families who made the story
possible.

Special thanks are due Sr. Audrey Jones who initiated, Sr. Maureen Truland who encouraged, and Sr. Karen Joseph who saw this book to completion. Also to Srs. Gertrude Gross and Romanus Penrose who proofread the pages, as well as Pat and Jim Chenot for all their careful work on the word-processor.

Cover design: Sr. Denise McMahon

Contents

Chapter One

Despite a wind that seemed determined to hurl him back down the mountainside, the pilgrim climbed stubbornly on. Lashed by the blinding snow of a winter blizzard, he could barely see the outline of the great monastery crowning the peak before him. At last he reached the gate. A few more weary steps and his half-frozen fingers were fumbling for the bellrope. Quickly the door was opened to him. "Enter in the name of the Lord! God be praised for his protection! What do you seek, brother, in this storm?" "Peace!" was the laconic answer.

Legend has it that this pilgrim was Dante some time in the early years of the 14th century.[1] Another legend from a century later in Switzerland marks the beginning of the story of the Benedictine Sisters of Perpetual Adoration. Zwingli was the chief reformation figure in Switzerland in the early years of the 16th century. Wherever he went, a wholesale destruction of altars, sacred vessels, pictures and images followed. In 1528, one such wooden statue of the Virgin and Child had been consigned to the flames. Watching this, a shepherd lad named Zumbuel suddenly darted toward the fire, snatched the statue and made off with it. He later claimed that the statue rose toward him out of the flames. In the spring, he brought his treasure with him to the mountains at the foot of the Musenalp. There he placed it in a hollow tree, saying his prayers before it as he watched his sheep. When fall came and it was time to return to his own village, Zumbuel could not budge the statue from the tree. Some of his friends came to help him, to no avail. Then they called on the pastor of Stans. His luck was no better. It was only when the people promised to build a small chapel there that the tenacious Madonna allowed herself to be plucked from the tree. First, a little wayside shrine of local stones was made for the statue. Later in 1565, a chapel was built to accommodate the pilgrims who began to come in ever larger numbers. By 1688, a still larger chapel was needed.[2]

At the head of the Nidwalden Valley in Canton Unterwalden, the ancient Benedictine Abbey of Engelberg occupies a commanding position. Founded in 1082, it grew to have considerable jurisdiction over towns and villages in nearby areas during the Middle Ages. Much of this was curtailed by the rapid spread of the Reformation in the 16th century. The Abbey's influence was further destroyed by the effects of the French Revolution and the French invasion of Switzerland which resulted in the dissolution of many Swiss abbeys. Napoleon's Constitution in 1803 restored some of the abbeys, but re-introduced state control of the church. As the 19th century progressed, this church-state tension was to have its effect on the destiny both of the Engelberg monks and the Benedictine Sisters.

The village of Maria Rickenbach, not far from Engelberg, has one of the loveliest, if more inaccessible, sites in all Switzerland. It sits on a green plateau with the towering Musenalp behind it, looking out over the valley of Engelberg and up to the Nidwalden Alps, the Stanzerhorn and the cloud-circled Mt. Pilatus.

It was to Maria Rickenbach that two young Swiss women came for the first time in 1853. Both belonged to a diocesan religious institute in Baldegg, Canton Lucerne. Both wished to belong to a community devoted to perpetual adoration of the Blessed Sacrament and were disappointed that their institute continued only to teach, along with looking after orphans and old folks. Sr. Vincentia Gretener, the older of the two, had come to Maria Rickenbach for her health, with Sr. Gertrude Leupi as companion. While the former's health improved in the fresh air and sunshine, the latter was fascinated by the story of the miraculous statue in the small church of Maria Rickenbach.

Praying before this treasured image, Sr. Gertrude had what a chronicler[3] calls a vision in which the Virgin told her that she was to be a superior of a Benedictine community here at Maria Rickenbach, a community devoted to perpetual adoration, where children would be taught the truths of the Catholic faith and prayer would be offered for sinners. According to this chronicler, Sr. Gertrude was no stranger to visions, having had more than one as a child. A bright, precocious youngster and a resolute young woman, she had entered religious life despite the opposition of her family. Interior messages from Christ and his Mother had often comforted her, while devotion to the Blessed Sacrament greatly attracted her.

Both these devotions, to the Sacrament and to Mary, were flourishing at this mid-19th century period. In 1846, in neighboring southeast France, two peasant children of LaSalette claimed to have experienced an apparition of the Mother of God in which she pleaded for repentance for widespread religious apathy. In 1854, Pope Pius IX defined the dogma of the Immaculate Conception. In 1858, at Lourdes in southwest France, Bernadette Soubirous claimed eighteen apparitions of the Lady who called herself by this title.

In 1856, a French priest, Peter Julien Eymard, founded the first adoration society for men in France. A few years later he established the Peoples' Eucharistic League. In far-off Canada, a cloistered contemplative community of Sister Adorers of the Precious Blood was founded at this time. Nocturnal adoration societies were springing up and pilgrimages being encouraged to places where eucharistic miracles were commemorated.

Sr. Gertrude was a deeply prayerful, intelligent woman, one attuned to the religious culture of her time. Eucharistic piety then, as it had since the seventeenth century, centered around the tabernacle rather than the altar. Eucharistic theology was preoccupied with questions of the real presence. During the eucharistic action, attention was focused on the elevation of the Host rather than on the people assembled together to share this holy meal. Corporate understanding of the Eucharist had been lost, with the altar subordinate to the tabernacle and the "throne" of exposition. The style of the court was adapted to the veneration of the Eucharist: Christ was said to "hold court" and was to be treated with the exacting ceremonial due an earthly ruler.[4]

Both Srs. Vincentia and Gertrude left Maria Rickenbach more than ever determined to find a religious life centered on the adoration of the Blessed Sacrament. With the help of Sr. Gertrude's confessor, Fr. Anselm Villiger, a monk of Engelberg, they were able to speak to the Abbot of Engelberg. He allowed them to continue running the orphanage at Engelberg, without renewing their annual vows with the Baldegg institute. It was not long before other young women began coming to the orphanage, attracted by the kind of life the two sisters hoped to live.

It was a difficult enough life, for now the two were separated: Sr. Vincentia at Gauglera in Freiburg and Sr. Gertrude at Engelberg. There was little time for any kind of religious training; incessant work was needed just to care for the old folks at Gauglera. The director of this home was fearful of government opposition if he allowed any time for novitiate instructions. Still the two sisters persevered and on Holy Thursday, 1857, both Sr. Vincentia and Sr. Gertrude made simple vows as Benedictines, though neither had had a monastic novitiate.

Sr. Vincentia had the larger group of novices at Gauglera. She realized it was time to move, time to begin a community devoted to perpetual adoration, along with some form of active ministry. Sr. Gertrude, still at Engelberg, would have preferred perpetual adoration alone, as she did not feel that the two could be successfully combined.

Through her brother, Sr. Vincentia was able to rent an old farmhouse, called Staefeli, about a three-minute walk from the Maria Rickenbach shrine. With her novices she took possession of this house in 1857, despite the fact that its isolated location in a hamlet of

3

scarcely fifteen families made any kind of caring for the sick or orphans rather unlikely. Within two weeks the first six sisters had begun perpetual adoration, kneeling in the shrine church from five in the morning till nine in the evening. At night they knelt in a room in their farmhouse whose window faced the chapel.

Not everyone in the area appreciated the sisters. The anti-clerical spirit of the times provoked a good deal of opposition. This, combined with hard work and the severe winter, broke Sr. Vincentia's health. She sent to Engelberg to ask for Sr. Gertrude as her assistant. The latter arrived at Maria Rickenbach in May, 1858, and by August had been elected superior, as Sr. Vincentia wished to resign. Sr. Gertrude's was a more endearing personality than Sr. Vincentia's. More supple and sensitive to others, she combined firmness with tact, a considerable resourcefulness with drive. Sr. Gertrude also enjoyed the active interest and support of Fr. Anselm Villiger, now prior of Engelberg Abbey.

In May, 1859, Fr. Anselm directed an appeal to all the bishops, pastors, and religious institutes of Switzerland, asking for funds to help this young community at Maria Rickenbach to build a convent for the thirteen sisters who were now very crowded in the old farmhouse. At this time the community also numbered two novices and three postulants. One of these was to be the future foundress of the Benedictines of Perpetual Adoration in America: Anna Elizabeth Felber. Only sixteen at this time and not strong, she was determined, and deeply devoted to the Blessed Sacrament. Novice Elizabeth's father was a school caretaker; her mother had died when she was very young. Always ready to help, humble, tenacious and a skilled embroiderer, she was to become the subprioress later when she had made vows. It was in 1860 that she and the others received the traditional Benedictine habit as a gift from the Abbess of Sarnen. Now garbed in the black habit, scapular and veil, with the white coif, the sisters and their neighbors felt themselves to be real Benedictines.

Prior Anselm's appeal for funds, begging tours made by the sisters from village to village and farm to farm, a raffle, a spiritual association of Perpetual Adoration in which a donor could be enrolled for the offering of five francs: all these brought in enough money to start construction on the new convent in 1862. Every piece of equipment, every stone and pipe, had to be carried up the mountain on the backs of skilled mountaineers or patient mules. Yet by July of 1864, the chapel could be consecrated, and on August 28th, the sisters were able to take possession of their new home.

For the next two months Prior Anselm remained with the community as spiritual director, organizer, and for all practical purposes, novice director. He drew up the order of the day, set up the Exercises of St. Gertrude in German as the office the sisters were to pray, divided into the customary monastic hours. The time of meditation was arranged, as well as that for the rosary; the hours of adoration were carefully prescribed. The indefatigable prior also set up the meals, work and recreation schedule. His instructions about eucharistic devotion are typical of this time: "Interiorly united with the sacrifice of Jesus, the sisters prepare themselves during Mass for the reception of Holy Communion."

The sisters were very poor. To support themselves they did some weaving, made church vestments, collected herbs from the mountains for medicine and had an Association of Perpetual Adoration. Their diet was meager. Prior Anselm worried about them. Gradually things improved, though a careful economy was always necessary. Before long they were able to build a small academy and take in some thirty or forty boarders whom the sisters taught. A laundry, woodshed and house for the chaplain were completed in 1865.

The following year Prior Anselm was elected abbot of Engelberg. Now it was he who received the sisters' annual vows, who gave them the annual retreat and who, in 1866, drew up a set of statutes for them which he hoped would explain and illustrate the ancient rule of Benedict, while promoting monastic regularity and discipline for the young community.[5] A mixture of paternalism, genuine concern for the sisters, good sense and unconscious humor, these statutes reveal much about the religious culture of the day. The Mother Prioress is to do nothing without the agreement and advice of the Father confessor. When at a loss, she is to ask his advice. On the other hand, the Abbot was liberal in his regulations for receiving communion. At a time when weekly reception was considered advanced, he advocated few limits for communion or the sacrament of penance. The sisters are allowed to sing songs "in Latin or any other language during a low Mass." The novices are not to be overwhelmed with work, and recreation is to be outdoors for all as much as possible. But this time of recreation is not to be used, says the Abbot sternly, "for gossip or womanish tattling." No sister is to attempt to account for the time another may spend in the confessional.

The Mother Prioress is to explain things clearly at Chapters, to listen to the advice and opinions of every sister and to abide by the decision of the majority. The various officials of the community receive some excellent and detailed instructions. The director of postulants is to be gifted, tender-hearted and careful. The portress is to be friendly, obliging and careful. During the summer months the sister in charge of the vestry is to see that the beds are brought into the sun once or twice. The cook is told that, without having to work at it very strenuously, she will have occasion to practice most of the virtues, especially patience. Faithful servants are indispensably necessary to the temporal prosperity of the monastery, but the cellarer is charged to see to it that the workmen abstain from visiting saloons and from all nightly excursions. While the community may have the necessary domestic cats, these may never be taken to the sisters' bedrooms.

In these statutes Abbot Anselm dealt only with the three vows of poverty, chastity and obedience. There is no mention of the specifically Benedictine vows of stability and conversion. This may have been due to the fact that he considered the sisters to be Oblates of St. Benedict, in distinction from the cloistered Benedictine nuns. Whether this was to protect them from possible consequences at a time when the Swiss government was inimical to religious orders, or was owing to their lack of dowry and enclosure, is not clear.

NOTES

1. Dorothy Sayers writes of this tale in the introduction to her translation of: *Dante: The Divine Comedy, I: Hell* (Melbourne, London, Baltimore: Penguin Books, 1949), p. 39.

2. The centenary brochure of the Maria Rickenbach convent, *Garden Enclosed,* published in 1957, gives an outline of this legend.

3. A sketch of the life of Mother Gertrude is found in *Sr. Gertrude Leupi,* by Moritz Jager (Kanisius Verlag, 1974), translated by Alexander Leutkemeyer, O.S.B., p 105.

4. Johannes H. Emminghaus describes the eucharistic devotion of the medieval and subsequent periods in his book, *The Eucharist: Essence, Form, Celebration* (Collegeville, Minnesota: the Liturgical Press, 1978), pp 81, 88.

5. There is a partial German handwritten copy of these Statutes in the archives of the Benedictine Sisters of Perpetual Adoration, along with a typed English translation of the complete work.

Chapter Two

In all its centuries of existence, the abbey of Engelberg had never made a foundation. But in December, 1872, when Abbot Anselm received an offer of land for a Benedictine foundation in Missouri, U.S.A., he was willing to consider it very seriously. One of the by-products of the Franco-Prussian war of 1870–71 had been the end of the papacy's temporal power. This was now the era of *kulturkampf,* a time of considerable church-state tension in Germany, Austria, and Switzerland. Pius IX's "Syllabus of Errors," with its condemnation of pantheism, naturalism, nationalism, socialism and freemasonry had alienated many Protestants. Bismarck, the German empire's chancellor, was angered by the pontiff's claim to complete independence of the church from state control, and his defense of the temporal power of the papacy. The definition of papal infallibility in 1870 further incensed him. A spirit of anti-clericalism and nationalism was very much abroad. The Swiss federal constitution of 1873 was revised to prohibit the establishment of any new Catholic dioceses or monasteries without the consent of the government. Jesuits and other religious orders were expelled.

It was time, thought the Abbot, to act. Swiss monasteries might well need a refuge elsewhere. In January, 1873, the monastic chapter of Engelberg Abbey voted to accept Bishop Hogan's proposal. Engelberg would make its first foundation in America. Nor did the Abbot forget the sisters at Maria Rickenbach. They, too, might need a refuge. Already, the Daughters of Charity, along with the Little Sisters of the Poor, had been driven from Geneva. If Engelberg's foundation in far-off Missouri was successful, the monks would invite the sisters to make a similar foundation there. In fact, the monk chosen to begin the American foundation was Frowin Conrad, O.S.B., who had been chaplain at Maria Rickenbach for a year.

Bishop Hogan's offer of land for a foundation had a history traceable to Reading, Pennsylvania. In the spring of 1855, the so-called "Irish

Riot" broke out during the construction of the Lebanon Valley Railroad. Unemployment, which was to strike the entire nation in 1857, was already felt in Reading. Day laborers in the iron industries, the coal mines, and the railroads were hardest hit. There were ongoing disputes between the German and Irish. Some of the more successful Catholic leaders of the community, men like the German Anthony Felix, the Irishman, Owen O'Reilly, and Fr. James Power, the recently appointed pastor of St. Peter's in Reading, got together to see if these disputes could be settled by negotiation rather than violence. One of the first suggestions was to resettle some of the Irish laborers and their families farther west.[1]

By their second meeting Anthony Felix, Owen O'Reilly, with his son-in-law, William Brady, and Fr. Power had a plan to resettle some of the Irish workmen on land offered by the government for such colonization in the midwest. With some financial support from the Reading community, Fr. Power with Felix and O'Reilly, were in St. Joseph, Missouri, by November, 1856. The only priest in the area, Fr. Thomas Scanlon, suggested that, due to the Platte Purchase, there were still large tracts of land available in Nodaway County, about fifty miles north of St. Joseph. At this time, the city of St. Joseph itself numbered around six thousand people and was growing rapidly. The Pony Express had originated there during the recent California gold rush.

While Fr. Power stayed in St. Joseph with Fr. Scanlon, Felix and O'Reilly went to the land office in Plattsburg, Missouri, and were able to buy only 120 acres of land which was up for sale in Nodaway County. It was to take a Senate investigation of the General Land Office in Washington, D.C., before their right to buy the tracts they wanted could be established. Behind all this was probably the fear of more northern sympathizers settling in a slave state, as Plattsburg was one of the most militant centers of pro-slavery in Missouri.

Led by William Brady, an Irish-born, level-headed, resolute, thirty-five year old, a group of Irish settlers left Pennsylvania in March, 1858. The railroad had not been completed past St. Louis, so a river boat took them up the Missouri River to St. Joseph. Here a good many of the original group chose to remain where they could be sure of work, religious services and schools for their children. Undaunted, William Brady, with twelve adults and several children, bought four yoke of oxen, several covered wagons, and a supply of provisions to start overland for Nodaway County, following the meandering course of the Platte River. On April 28, 1858, they arrived in the general area of their new home. It had taken them four days to cover a distance of fifty miles. The men built the 12' × 15' cabins that would have to suffice for the time being, since the soil had to be prepared for planting. None of the settlers had any practical frontier experience on this prairie land covered with stumps, tough roots, and stones.

It was a very discouraged group that Fr. Power visited in October, 1858. The loneliness and lack of religious services was the chief complaint. Worse was to come in 1859: sickness, death, fear of the abolitionist raids from Kansas, and near-starvation plagued them. During these turbulent years before the Civil War, violent feuding was commonplace along the Missouri-Kansas border. During the war, both Union and Confederate troops in that area were rag-tag bands, often with only vague sanctions from either army. Much of the fighting was the guerilla-type. The notorious Jesse James and the Younger Brothers were part of this scene. During the years of the Civil War, missionary work in western Missouri came to a virtual standstill, although the indomitable Fr. Power did manage to visit his colony some twelve times between 1861 and 1864.

After the war, Fr. Power returned to settle permanently in the colony. He had always dreamed of a religious order for the settlement, preferably a stable, monastic one. First he tried the Cistercians of New Melleray, Iowa, but they could not help him. Next he wrote to Abbot Boniface Wimmer of St. Vincent's in Pennsylvania. The Abbot was favorable to this request, but the archbishop of St. Louis was not. Then in 1868, the western half of the state of Missouri was separated from the Archdiocese of St. Louis, and became the diocese of St. Joseph with John Joseph Hogan, a close friend of Fr. Power, as the new bishop. Bishop Hogan, himself a missionary for many years, recognized the desperate need of the colonists for priests. On his return from the first Vatican Council, he agreed to appeal to the Abbot of St. Meinrad's for priests to take over the colony of what was now called Conception. This abbey was of German origin. While the original Conception colony had been composed of Irish families, since the Civil War the new colonists had been almost all German, following the general pattern of Catholic immigration throughout the midwest after the war. Bishop Hogan had an offer of some valuable property near St. Joseph which might serve as a missionary center and also as a good location for a seminary. Abbot Martin Marty of St. Meinrad's did not feel he had enough monks to spare any for a Missouri foundation, but immediately suggested that the Bishop apply to the Abbot of Engelberg in Switzerland, whom he knew to be considering just such a foundation.

The monk chosen by Abbot Anselm to cross the Atlantic with Frowin Conrad, O.S.B. was Adelhelm Odermatt, O.S.B. They arrived at St. Meinrad's in Indiana in May, 1873, to find that Abbot Martin had sent his prior, Fr. Fintan, ahead of them to Missouri to scout out the land. He had accepted not the original offer of Bishop Hogan, but one from Fr. James Power of 260 acres of land at Conception, Missouri. He described it as one great rolling prairie whose horizon reminded him of the ocean.

Having learned something about frontier life in America from the veteran missionary Abbot Marty, Frs. Frowin and Adelhelm came to

Missouri in September. The colony at Conception then numbered about one hundred families. There was a small church and rectory, with work beginning on a monastery. Fr. Frowin promptly moved into the rectory and set about learning his new parish, while Fr. Adelhelm was placed in charge of the parish at Maryville. Forty years old at this time, Fr. Frowin was slight of build, patient and persevering, with a Swiss solidity of temperament. His companion, Fr. Adelhelm, was only twenty-nine, more mercurial in disposition, given to swift enthusiasms and impatient of delay.[2]

American Catholicism at this time remained European in its values and customs, dependent on the continental tradition in most things. As wave after wave of immigrants continued to arrive, the problem of inserting a monarchical institution into a basically democratic society increased. As far as monasticism in America was concerned, new pressures were continually weighing on a very ancient way of life. Monastic life in Europe had been that of a limited geographic space, circumscribed by a daily schedule of prayer and work that was not subject to continuing change or adaptation. The new communities being founded in the United States soon discovered that such a stable and confined community atmosphere was conducive neither to the culture nor the type of work they were being called to carry out.[3] American bishops were desperately in need of priests for the ever-increasing flow of immigrants. Boniface Wimmer, O.S.B., Abbot of St. Vincent's in Pennsylvania, felt this as a personal obligation. Abbot Martin Marty of St. Meinrad's in Indiana traveled ceaselessly, seeking Benedictine men and women for the Indian missions. Both envisioned American monasticism as a response to the real needs of the church at this time, while also believing that they were true to the ancient tradition of the monk-missionary.

From the beginning, then, there was a built-in tension between the contemplative tradition and the apostolic activity needed in the new land. In 1864, a decree from the Congregation of Bishops and Regulars stated that all sisters in America, with the exception of a few Vistandine communities, must take simple vows. Among the reasons behind this decision was probably the request of American bishops to have sisters staff schools in their dioceses, a work very difficult under claustral restrictions then imposed on those in solemn vows.[4]

Added to the strong missionary impulse in America was the need for education. German Catholics in particular had a high regard for learning. The European liberal arts tradition was pursued in the Swiss and Bavarian monasteries and passed on to the rather different climate of America. German-born monks and sisters considered the idea of a school as part of the Benedictine presence in this country. The American bishops, for their part, regarded the early monks and sisters as educators who would encourage vocations by building seminaries and schools. This had its inevitable consequences. There was too much work for the monks and sisters to spend long hours in extended periods of choral prayer. Thus began the tension between mission and education versus monastic detachment from the world. It led, in the framework of American pragmatism and pluralism, to a certain freedom and self-sufficiency on the one hand, and to a subjective individualism on the other. Vocations came from the schools. So with dogged determination and faith, the early monastic founders in America responded to the needs of the frontier. They were willing to risk adapting previous monastic experience to a new culture. Not one tradition, but a rich variety of traditions, had wide impact on the United States. These early founders were not about to repeat the failure of 14th century Benedictinism to respond to the needs of the times.

For all of this, though, it is clear from the beginning that Frowin Conrad was primarily a monk and only secondarily a missionary. In a letter of August 5, 1874, he wrote to Abbot Anselm: "My notions of monasticism have become much clearer since I have been here ... We must regain that simplicity which was the secret of the first Benedictines ... It is our task to exemplify Christian life in the light of the evangelical counsels and the precepts of our Rule. Our monasteries must not become comfortable boarding houses or college residences for professors."[5] Prior Frowin insisted that his foundation be a priory and not just a mission-house. He wanted to establish a novitiate immediately. The necessary pastoral work in the Conception parish and surrounding areas was to be subordinate to the full monastic life, the quest for personal holiness, and the solemn celebration of the liturgy. A good monastery, he felt, was a great blessing to the missions. He wanted his monks to have "a sincere devotion to profound learning, so that their cells never become a bore to them."[6] All this was to have its effect on the neighboring community of sisters at Clyde.

By November, 1873, Prior Frowin had already written to the sisters of Maria Rickenbach for help. In a letter to his abbot at Engelberg he states: "I have asked the sisters of Maria Rickenbach for help. I wish they could realize what their coming would mean for Conception. They would soon win the love of both Catholics and Protestants, and could lay the groundwork for convents at Conception and Maryville. If you approve the plan, and we urge you to do so, the sisters could come next spring."[7]

Fr. Adelhelm had also written to Mother Gertrude: "... We always remember Maria Rickenbach and hope for a Maria Rickenbach in America. That shall be one of our first enterprises in Missouri, to find a place for you!"[8] With letters like this traveling back to them from America, the sisters were caught up in missionary fervor along with the monks. The chapter vote to send some sisters to Conception was all but unanimous. Mother Gertrude herself dreamed of going but realized, after talking it over with Abbot Anselm, whom she consulted on everything of importance to the small community, that her foundation

11

was still too young to spare her. Not yet ten years old, Maria Rickenbach needed her guidance for some years to come. Finally, Mother
Gertrude chose five sisters to be the pioneers on American soil. These
five were: Sr. Anselma Felber, Sr. Agnes Dali, Sr. Augustine Kuendig,
Sr. Adela Eugster, and Sr. Beatrice Renggli. At thirty-five, Sr. Agnes
was the oldest. Sr. Anselma was thirty, and the rest were in their
twenties. But in those years, the community had more candidates
applying for entrance than it could accommodate. It was time to think
of the church in other lands.

The next months were spent busily packing what the sisters would
need. Prior Frowin had written in January, 1874, that they would
have to stay in Maryville for a while, but by April or May he hoped to
find a place for two of them at Conception. "But they must not expect
too much and I hope their zeal is greater than their expectations!"[9]
Characteristic of the prior's attention to detail is this advice in a letter
dated January 22, 1874: "The clothing they bring must be light for
summer, but very warm for winter. They should also bring forks and
knives, as well as sewing and embroidery needles. Here everything
costs so much and often the simplest things cannot be procured. . . .
Some material for embroidery and simple vestments will also be
useful, but most of the European school books should be left behind."[10]
The prior was also busy negotiating with Abbot Martin Marty for a
Benedictine sister from the Ferdinand community who could teach the
Rickenbach sisters English and help them adapt to their American
surroundings. Prior Frowin wanted the sisters to start a German
school at Conception for boys and girls, and an English school in
Maryville. Another problem was solved when Abbot Anselm was able
to find a guide and chaperon for the sisters in Mr. George Keel of
Benziger Brothers Publishing Company, who was leaving for the
United States in August. He agreed to take the sisters under his
protection and arranged to have their baggage picked up and shipped
with his own to New York.

After a last visit to the pilgrim chapel of Maria Rickenbach, a
farewell embrace to the sisters staying behind, the five pioneers set
out with Abbot Anselm's blessing and valediction still ringing in their
ears. He had told them they would need the strong heart of a missionary. They would lose heart at all the privations and dangers they
faced, if they were going to America for any other purpose than
dedicating themselves to the salvation of the children there for the
love of God. Their accomplishment of this aim in their new country
would depend on their fervent prayer, not long prayers at the expense
of their apostolate, but the spirit of prayer. The Benedictine Order had
never flourished more gloriously, said the Abbot, than when it dedicated itself to the missionary apostolate. Oddly, the Abbot who had
worked so long with Mother Gertrude to establish this community of
perpetual adoration of the Blessed Sacrament, hardly referred to this
at all in his farewell address. The one reference he made was: "Your

hours of adoration can scarcely have a more important intent than to ask God to bless the labors and missionary activities of the brothers and sisters of our Holy Order."[11]

NOTES

1. Interesting descriptions of this background to the Conception colony and of the Platte purchase can be found in Edward Malone, O.S.B., *A History of Conception: Colony, Abbey, and Schools* (Benedictine Studies, Interstate Printing Company, Omaha, Nebraska, 1971), pp 12–39; and Damian L. Cummins, O.S.B., *Catholics in the Early Platte Purchase and in Nodaway County* (privately printed, 1934), pp. 14–28.

2. In the work above, Edward Malone describes the early years of Frs. Frowin Conrad and Adelhelm Odermatt in Conception, pp. 49–60.

3. Joel Ripplinger, O.S.B., "Assimilating the Contemplative: I" *Benedictines* XXXVII-I (Spring-Summer, 1983–1984).

4. Ibid, p 42.

5. The excerpts from Prior Frowin Conrad's letters in this chapter are from a translation from the German by Sisbert Burkhardt, O.S.B., of letters to Abbot Anselm Villiger, preserved in the Conception Abbey archives.

6. Ibid, letter of Sept. 6, 1877.

7. Ibid, letter after Nov. 11, 1873.

8. From a bound volume of *Letters from Mother M. Anselma Felber and Others, 1873–1901*, developed from microfilm copies made by Edward Malone, O.S.B., 1963, translated by Sr. M. Dominica Bonnenberg, O.S.B., and edited by Sr. Kathleen Gorman, O.S.B., St. Louis, Missouri, 1977.

9. Letter to Abbot Anselm, Jan. 22, 1874.

10. Ibid.

11. From the German *Chronicles of Maria Rickenbach*, Vol. 4, translated by Sr. M. DeSales Markert, O.S.B., St. Louis, Missouri, 1974.

14

Chapter Three

The Engelberg Abbey carriage took the sisters to Lucerne. From there they traveled to Basel by train with their kindly chaperons, Mr. and Mrs. Keel. Having explored a few of the sights in this "see of Bishops," as Sr. Beatrice Renggli described it, they left their native Switzerland for a long, hot, overnight trip to Paris. According to Sr. Beatrice, "even nuns would be guilty of negligence if they had been in Paris without having seen the important and historic areas of that famous city."[1] So the five sisters were taken on a hasty tour of the more illustrious churches, along with the Louvre, the Tuileries, and the Arc de Triomphe, where they had a breath-taking view of the city. By 6:30 the evening of August 18, they were again on the train which would take them to the port city of Le Havre. After a day there, they boarded the transatlantic steamer, the ODER, which was on its third voyage to America. Sr. Beatrice, writing back to the community at Maria Rickenbach, describes the cabins as "little rooms six feet long, six feet wide, six feet high, with four beds, two bunks per room." She was amazed at the activity on deck: the frantic scurrying back and forth, "the chases, screams, and shouts."

They had been at sea only a few hours when everyone but Sr. Beatrice was overpowered by seasickness. "Mother Prioress took the lead and the others faithfully followed . . . Oh, how miserable does one feel in these hours! Yes, if the ship were to founder while one is in the clutches of this illness, one would not move a finger to save herself. Indifference depresses both soul and disposition." While her companions suffered, Sr. Beatrice inspected the ship. She writes an awed account of the first-class accommodations, but concludes with this acid comment: "The coffee is abominable. It is cold, insipid and in no way resembles Swiss coffee." Of the third class quarters she knew very little, only that they harbored, "from 500 to 600 persons. Those travelling third class furnish their own beds, food and laundry." On her tour of the ODER, Sr. Beatrice discovered that there were one hundred twenty employees on the ship who gave them "friendly, courteous and respectful service." Most of the passengers were Catholic, although there were some who were not, including an agnostic poet who accosted Sr. Beatrice at one point to argue about the infallibility of the Pope.

By the fourth day most of the passengers had recovered, but the dreary, foggy weather contributed to a feeling of abandonment and depression. Added to this was the sudden death of a man whose job was shoveling coal into the furnace. He was thrown overboard, to Sr. Beatrice's considerable distress, "without coffin, song or sound." Following this came a terrible storm at sea. "The waves rose like mountains and crashed on deck ... They forced themselves through the windows and inundated our beds ... Painful cold also accompanied the storm. Whatever we had, we put on ... but nothing protected us from the frost and cold. No such cold, freezing weather had we ever experienced at Maria Rickenbach. In my entire life I have never frozen like that ... The storm was uncanny with its howl ... We sat silently in our cabins and did not dare to retire." Toward two in the morning the storm at last abated, although sea sickness again reigned.

In calmer weather, Sr. Beatrice was able to study the sea creatures as her brother back in Switzerland had begged her to do. She told him: "Above all I enjoyed the dance maneuvers of the dolphins which accompanied the vessel. They are companionable even though they tease each other greatly. Their small black eyes look so friendly and trusting, and they display much confidence in people. It appears as if they love people and wish to capture their attention with affectionate leaps ... Among the birds, the most faithful escort is the three-toed sea gull, a dazzling white bird with black wings and feet, yellow bill and approximately the size of a duck." But it was the sunset over the calm sea that most entranced the Swiss sister. "Suddenly the azure blue disappeared and the water took on a light green shade. The sun sank, not gradually as at home. It disappeared suddenly and suddenly the reflection of its rays painted both eastern and western horizon. The great sea lay framed in gold and the silent flood mirrored a hundred times over the fleeting gold of the firmament." In this, Sr. Beatrice saw the "primitive, exquisite beauty" of her God.

On August 31, 1874, they sighted land. Sr. Beatrice was a little regretful. They landed at Hoboken on the right bank of the Hudson River and stepped for the first time on American soil at twelve noon. Immediately they were overwhelmed at the rush, haste, and confusion of this new land. Nothing was calm or restful. They were loaded bag and baggage into a wagon with a team to take them at breakneck speed to New York. That city reminded Sr. Beatrice of Paris, only she found it more striking and grandiose, despite the fact she thought Paris might be built to last longer. "Gala vehicles, chaises, omnibuses, horse-drawn street cars, carts drawn by dogs, run about in wild confusion, zig-zagging among each other, and above the heads of all the steam locomotives storm along with great pants, puffs and snorts. Tremendous confusion reigns in the streets so that one is unable to imagine anything worse. Wagons rattle, whips bang, firemen yell throughout the day." Used to the rustic quiet of Maria Rickenbach, high in the Alps, the sisters were understandably attacked by nostalgia and home-sickness. This was not alleviated at the Hotel Grutli, where there was Swiss food, Swiss dialect, but also "troublesome bugs and insects, perhaps also bedbugs."

On September 2, they boarded the train for St. Louis. Sr. Beatrice wrote: "We were fortunate in having the coach all to ourselves, because we were not to change coaches until we arrived in St. Louis. Our section is beautifully arranged. We use a small salon with sofa and two fountains. The sofa can readily be changed into a bed. We felt serene and very happy and the faster the locomotive travelled the happier we were because we were constantly drawing closer to Maryville." In Pennsylvania, Sr. Beatrice was attracted by "the American farm homes, most of which are in close contingency to large corn and maize fields. They are veritable huts in comparison to the giant structures of New York and Pittsburgh ... The most beautiful sights were the virgin forests usually following along the banks of rivers ... Forest culture as we have it at Maria Rickenbach has not yet reached here. Trees do not stand in orderly rows, nor in rank and file as in Europe."

On September 4, they arrived in St. Louis. Longing for some hot, cooked food after a diet of sandwiches, they hurried to a restaurant. "Because not a soul spoke German, we had to use all our ingenuity, a few words of English and point to the foods to obtain something warm. And then when it came to paying! What a scene was enacted! We spoke with our fingers, showed our money, but the people did not understand us and we failed to understand them. At last the proprietor wrote the bill on the wall. Now a light was turned on, our minds grasped the figure and we were able to satisfy the manager."

According to Sr. Beatrice, St. Louis was built on "terraces along the Mississippi River. The lower part of the city harbors a conglomeration of people engaged in robbery, gambling, cheating, as well as those who follow some trade. On a slight elevation are stately brick homes which dictatorially overshadow the suburbs that encircle the city. The farther one goes out in the country, the smaller the houses until they become mere wooden huts ... St. Louis has 300,000 inhabitants, of whom one third are Catholic. It contains many convents, educational institutes and churches, among them the large cathedral of St. Louis. The Jesuits are said to be a great blessing to the city and their ministry is very rewarding." All this information was offered by a kindly German who acted as the sisters' guide and interpreter until he put them on the train for St. Joseph at 9:30 that night.

After a brief and comfortable stay with some school sisters in St. Joseph, the five continued on to Maryville, arriving at 6 p.m. on September 5, 1874. "When we beheld it in the distance we prayed fervently: "O God, we praise you!" wrote Sr. Beatrice. "We felt we had recovered our hearts' contentment ... But what was this? Even here there was no one at the depot to meet us!" Fr. Adelhelm had forgotten the date of their rival. A German who happened to be at the station took them to the Catholic church where an astonished Fr. Adelhelm welcomed them. The sisters prayed before the Blessed Sacrament for a while, then tired and hungry, went over to the rectory where some ladies of the town hurriedly came and worked until midnight preparing supper and bed for the weary travelers.

At this time, Maryville, named after the wife of the first county clerk, was regarded as one of the best business centers in northwest Missouri. Sr. Beatrice's description in her letters back to Switzerland is lively as usual: "There are no high mountains here like those in Switzerland. We look out on waving hillsides as far as the eye reaches ... The land is open to all winds and therefore we now experience strong contrasts of painful cold and great heat in this early fall weather. Even though the winter has, of course, not yet arrived, still I have already frozen much more than I ever did on Mary's mountain in the middle of winter."

"Our little dwelling lies forsaken and alone about one hundred steps from the Catholic church, which is situated on an elevation about a quarter of an hour from the city of Maryville. It seems to be very dilapidated both interiorly and exteriorly and repairs are highly necessary, for during a rain not even the priest at the altar is safe from a downpour through a leaking roof ... The simplicity of the church is reflected in the simplicity of the services ... Picture to yourselves my role as sacristan and server, who ministers to the priest from a distance and also takes up the Sunday collection by means of a little basket fastened to a long pole."

A vivid word-picture of the townspeople follows: "If you were to meet them you would admire their friendliness, kindness and courtesy. They are ever ready with good advice and in charitable actions aid all in need, especially all newcomers. Their main virtues are vigor and self-sufficiency ... without due consideration these people rarely undertake anything. When heated, they do not jump into a cold bath! ... The people of Maryville esteem progress and wish to foster it, particularly in their school. They wish to educate and be educated for the present time. The English language and mathematics are their main concern ... An American without mathematical endowment is a handicapped American ... Americans neither spare costs nor time to educate their children properly. We came to America with the intention to found a German school in Maryville, but we had to give up this plan! We shall teach German, but merely as a foreign language."

18

It is obvious from letters of Prior Frowin that he would have preferred that only three sisters come in the beginning.[2] Then they could have been housed at Conception and he could have recalled Fr. Adelhelm to the monastery. But five sisters meant that all had to stay at the Maryville rectory with Fr. Adelhelm as guide and mentor, since Bishop Hogan absolutely refused to have the sisters under the supervision of a diocesan priest. The rectory of the Maryville parish was a flimsy wooden structure, housing the pastor on the first floor and the five sisters on the second, which was two rooms in an attic without windows or ventilation.

Fr. Adelhelm gave himself without reserve to the needs of his parish and far-flung missions. He expected the same of the sisters. Not only were they to conduct a school for the children of the area, they were to be his cooks, housekeepers, gardeners and stable-hands. They were the choir for the parish masses; they took up the collection; they cared for his horse. It was the sisters who fed the chickens, cooked both for themselves and the pastor, besides keeping the rickety church and rectory as clean as possible. None of this seemed to strike them as excessive. The propriety of the sisters sharing a house with a monk did, however, bother both Prior Frowin and Mother Anselma. It was not at all to her liking that the sisters be expected to make little articles for the parish raffle, and this on Sunday. The only one whose objections to other aspects of the life is recorded in Sr. Adela who announced stoutly at one point that she was no man's housekeeper and never would be.[3]

The sisters' major concern at this time was the school they were to open. One of the primary reasons they had come to America was the education of the children of German immigrants at Conception and Maryville. Many Catholic parents refused to send their children to public schools. At that era in Missouri the school system was nothing to boast about. Only in 1875, did the state constitution provide for the eventual establishment of free public schools. There was no college for teacher training until 1867 at the state university. The curriculum in those days was the three R's: reading, writing and arithmetic. After the pupils mastered the alphabet, they went on to study spelling and reading. "Figuring" was taught, along with exercises, by means of charts and diagrams on rough blackboards. After the first reader, the students got some instruction about plants and animals. Since the Americans wanted their children taught in English, it was obvious that the sisters could not open even the most rudimentary kind of school until they learned the language.

In October, the ever-helpful Abbot Martin Marty came with the Benedictine sister he had promised to Prior Frowin. Sr. Rose Chapelle, O.S.B., of the Ferdinand, Indiana community, was an experienced teacher, with one drawback. She understood German adequately, but could scarcely speak a word of it. Sr. Rose was to live with the five

19

sisters from Maria Rickenbach, giving them English lessons and preparing them to teach in English.

At this time, the Swiss sisters used the Exercises of St. Gertrude, divided into sections, as their choral prayer in German. Abbot Marty suggested that, like all the other sisters in America, they use the Latin "Little Office of the Blessed Virgin," explaining that the Exercises of St. Gertrude were a private devotion never meant to replace the office. They would not lose their status as sisters of Perpetual Adoration by adopting this Little Office, since it could become an integral part of their adoration.[4] When this reached Abbot Anselm in Switzerland, it appears to have alarmed him. He wrote back that since the sisters did not understand Latin, this could harm their spiritual life. The Maria Rickenbach sisters were Oblates of St. Benedict. Possibly he feared that Abbot Marty was assuming too much control of the fledgling community. In Abbot Anselm's mind the sisters chief work was to be perpetual adoration, not liturgical prayer. Prior Frowin pointed out in his reply that this would mean difficulties when the first American postulants arrived who would not understand German. The sisters could learn to understand Latin if properly taught. "The essence of their perpetual adoration remains unchanged because the Divine Office is adoration by its very nature."[5]

Meanwhile, the sisters were gradually settling into their new life. A letter from Mother Anselma to Abbot Anselm in September, 1874, says: "Each day we get more and more into conventual order, which I missed most, and now I hope our homesickness will also soon be overcome. The sisters are alright and cheerful: Srs. Agnes and Adela in the kitchen, Sr. Beatrice in the sacristy, Sr. Augustine at the organ and myself preferably in some corner or in silent adoration before the Blessed Sacrament. The people seem to be well-minded. They bring us many things, today a bed which we can use ... Fr. Adelhelm is teaching us English. It will be hard until I can speak English! Please pray that God may loose my tongue and make me hear right."[6] This plea was to be a refrain running through Mother Anselma's letters. Of all the sisters, it was the young superior who found the English language most difficult to master. Retiring by nature, she tended to take on herself any extra duties, leaving little time for study.

Another constant refrain is the goodness of the people, both in Maryville and Conception, to the sisters. From the first, they brought them food and other useful items. The Daybook has endless entries about flour, butter, potatoes, corn, meat, fruit, lard, firewood, tables, lamps, bedding: all gifts from the people. One September morning the sisters had to have soup for breakfast, since they were out of milk for their coffee; but just when they had nothing left, their "heavenly Father" would move some neighbor to come with milk, bread, apples, meat and other necessities. "People, especially the poor ones, are good to us ... The other day they brought us three big hams and some

20

pounds of butter . . . potatoes and cabbage we get from Conception and sauerkraut from Maryville."[7]

Nor were their spiritual needs neglected. From the first, the sisters prayed Lauds and Matins, along with meditation in the parish church at five a.m. At six there was Mass and the Little Hours. At noon they had the daily examen of conscience and the Angelus. Vespers were prayed at 2:30 p.m., followed by spiritual reading. There were some minutes of adoration at supper-time and after the evening recreation, they prayed the rosary and Compline. The Prior and Fr. Adelhelm between them managed to give the sisters a weekly conference. One thing none of the sisters appreciated was Prior Frowin's decision to allow them Holy Communion only three or four times a week. This followed the current American practice of the time, rather than their European custom of receiving daily. It was not until March of the following year that he yielded to their pleas and allowed them daily reception.

Sr. Rose Chapelle gave the Swiss sisters two hours of English instruction daily. Undaunted by the obstacles of language and un-skilled teachers, she also opened a small private school in the church building at Maryville for thirty-two children, only three of whom spoke German. The Rickenbach sisters helped by teaching sewing and embroidery. Sr. Beatrice, the only one who had some previous teach-ing experience, was studying diligently to obtain a one-year teaching certificate, qualifying her to teach in Missouri public or private schools. Mother Anselma began to pray fervently for American postu-lants who would be able to help them in the school situation. But where would they put them? As winter drew on, the winds blew across the plains in gusts. In stormy weather, the snow blew into the sisters' rooms. They were far too crowded in the rectory to accept even the thinnest applicant. Prior Frowin had drawn up plans for a small convent at Conception to house some of them and also to serve as a school. But it would not be finished until the following year; so far, the sisters had not even been to see Conception.

Their first Christmas in America was a peaceful one. So many good things were received as gifts that Mother Anselma was able to write to Switzerland that Srs. Augustine and Adela were becoming "like the full moon."[8] In February, 1875, Abbot Anselm Villiger wrote Mother Anselma a strong letter of encouragement. Like St. Timothy, she was to reproach, instruct, demand and entreat, stifling all self-will and stubbornness among the sisters. The five of them should exemplify the best of Maria Rickenbach. What concerned the community and the house should be talked about with her, their superior; what concerned their consciences should be talked about with the confessor.[9]

This was easier said than done. Letters to Abbot Anselm and Mother Gertrude from Mother Anselma, Prior Frowin, Fr. Adelhelm and Sr. Beatrice reveal considerable conflict at this time. The energetic Fr. Adelhelm, endowed with more enthusiasm than prudence, had a tendency to take over. Mother Anselma had no great gift for administration. Hers was not the forcefulness nor quick decision of Mother Gertrude. The sisters were young and the new spirit of America affected them like wine. Sr. Beatrice's liveliness could swiftly turn to restlessness and instability. Sr. Adela was not shy about domineering and interfering in matters that the rest felt did not concern her. Sr. Agnes talked too much to Fr. Adelhelm, serving up the day's gossip along with his meals. Sr. Augustine was often ill and very homesick, besides being overworked with organ practice, gardening and caring for the horse. Change was difficult for Mother Anselma. She longed for the peace of a little convent of their own, where her contemplative bent could be more satisfied, and for perpetual adoration which she felt America needed more than schools. Sometimes touchy and sensitive, she hesitated to take charge, with the result that Srs. Beatrice and Adela often went to Sr. Rose for advice with their problems.

Prior Frowin watched all this but determined not to interfere, feeling that things would reform themselves once the sisters had their own house and were more settled. He felt much mischief was done by the incessant writing to Abbot Anselm and Mother Gertrude in Switzerland. With conflicting accounts of what was going on, it was no wonder their advice was more confusing than helpful. Yet the prior did not think he should intervene since Abbot Anselm had retained ultimate authority over the sisters. Perhaps this was the basic mischief, as the abbot seems to have realized later when he handed this authority over to Prior Frowin.

By April, both Srs. Beatrice and Augustine could speak English fairly well. Since the previous fall the little community had prayed the rosary in English and now could have English table reading with their meals. It was not until August, however, and the contribution of $300.00 from the people of the area, that the construction could start on their convent at Conception. Mother Anselma had hoped that they could dispense with Sr. Rose's services by the summer, but now it seemed she might need to stay on, since the prior wanted a small school at Conception also, and this was too much for the five sisters to handle alone. Such private schools were a necessity for Catholic education at this time, as a letter of Prior Frowin indicates:

> The school tax is quite high and is spent only to aid the public schools. To get state aid for our future schools, the sisters would have to pass an examination and oblige themselves not to teach religion during the legal school hours: that is, between nine and twelve in the morning and one and four in the afternoon. Such schools might be established where only Catholics live in a district and the school superintendents are compliant. But nearly all the superintendents hate everything Catholic and would oppose the introduction of Catholic books into schools. For this reason even the Catholic press opposes such Catholic free schools. They main-

tain, and I agree with them, that we must have private schools where the state has nothing to say. On the other hand, private schools will mean a great hardship for our people: they will have to maintain their own schools, and at the same time be forced to pay the state school tax. In New York attempts were made in the legislature to obtain state aid for private schools, but instead a law was passed obliging all parents to send their children to public schools.[10]

In June, Mother Anselma fell sick for two weeks and was forced to stay in bed. Never strong, the pressures of her new life were telling on her. She writes of dreaming constantly of Maria Rickenbach and of feeling depressed and drained. Of concern, too, was the terrible grasshopper plague of that summer of 1875. Prior Frowin describes it to his Abbot:

> At noon on June 10th the grasshoppers came. As in a whirlwind of snowflakes they descended on field and prairie. Next morning our corn had disappeared and only isolated patches of green grass were left of the prairie. We had saved part of our potatoes because we drove the hoppers from the field with brooms. By Sunday they were gone and in the afternoon we held an outdoor procession to obtain God's protection. But on Monday new swarms appeared and kept coming until Wednesday. After that the farmers began to replant but on Saturday there was a new invasion. If now we are left alone, we still may save half a crop. The distress is much greater in parts of Kansas and Nebraska, where the grasshoppers ruined everything last fall and returned this spring to kill the last hope for a crop this year.[11]

Despite this, when someone attacked America, Mother Anselma was quick to defend her adopted country. In a letter of July, 1875, she wrote to Abbot Anselm: "America is a beautiful country, surpassing the dear Unterwalden. You should see the corn gardens, the plants of all kinds, and on the prairies the grazing cows and oxen, calves and sheep. You would then delightedly exclaim 'O beautiful country! Switzerland cannot compare with you!' Yes, Father, I am glad I am here and already understand a little English ... May God and the Blessed Mother save us from Europe!"

By November, their little house and school at Conception was well under construction. The decision was made to leave Srs. Agnes and Augustine at the Maryville school to help Sr. Rose do the teaching there, while Mother Anselma with Srs. Beatrice and Adela went to Conception. Some young women had been asking to enter and now at last there would be room to accept them as postulants. Mother Anselma began to dream of a novitiate and perpetual adoration. Up to then they had only been able to have a few hours of adoration in the Maryville church.

Would the people of the area be able to support two schools? Times were bad. While Mother Anselma worried about making vestments in the few hours she had to devote to her skilled needlework, as well as looking after Fr. Adelhelm who had "not one pair of good socks and no decent habit,"[12] the pastor himself had other worries. "Conditions are bad," he wrote to Mother Gertrude, "Is the party of some drunkards . . . to get the upper hand in town and are the priests and a large number of well-meaning people to be pulled into the mire? Or are the intentions of God to win?"[13]

On December 6th, such worries were far from Mother Anselma's mind. This was the day they were moving to the Conception convent. With Srs. Beatrice and Adela in a carriage belonging to the monks, she set out. The eighteen-mile drive took three hours over icy roads and swollen unbridged creeks. Their new convent, which was also to serve as a small school, had nine rooms. "We still have to improve much in our hearts until our Lord can find us fit to open a convent of perpetual adoration, which is more necessary than preaching or teaching to America," the prioress wrote to Mother Gertrude.[14] On December 10, the sisters were able to open their school to thirty-nine children, ages five to twenty. The teachers' monthly salary was to be $40. By the evening of December 6th, their beds and furniture were in place, the mattresses filled with fresh straw, the lamps with oil. All was neat and clean. Sr. Beatrice, with Sr. Adela's help, would teach school; Mother Anselma would look after the house, the kitchen and the guests. On December 8th, 1875, feast of the Immaculate Conception, the prioress wrote in the daily chronicle: "Now we belong totally to our heavenly Mother. O, pray for us and make us always understand better and live the spirit of our holy Order, the spirit of perpetual adoration. To you, O Mother, I recommend all my sisters and all who will enter our community. Please take care that none be admitted who has not been called by God!"[15]

NOTES

1. From an English translation of the original German by Sr. Agnes Voth, O.S.B., of *Von Rickenbach nach Maryville* (Stans: Casper von Matt, 1975), published in *American Benedictine Review*, 27:3, September, 1976, pp 248–68. There are microfilm copies of the original letters in the St. Louis archives of the Benedictine Sisters of Perpetual Adoration.

2. Letter to Abbot Anselm Villiger, O.S.B., October 13, 1874, translated by Sisbert Burkhardt, O.S.B.

3. Fr. Adelhelm related this remark in a letter to Mother Gertrude, dated August 17, 1876, in *Early Chronicled History of the Benedictine Sisters of Perpetual Adoration: Relationship between Maryville and Conception (Clyde), 1874–1893* (St. Louis, Missouri, 1982) p. 31.

4. Letter to Abbot Anselm, October 13, 1874.

5. Letter to Abbot Anselm, December 22, 1874.

6. Letter of Mother Anselma Felber, to Mother Gertrude Leupi of March, 1875 in *Letters from Mother Anselma Felber, O.S.B. and Others, 1873–1901,* a bound volume of such letters translated by Sr. Dominica Bonnenberg, O.S.B., from the original German, and edited by Sr. Kathleen Gorman, O.S.B., 1977. In the St. Louis archives of the Benedictine Sisters. No page numbers are given.

7. In *The Early Chronicled History of the Benedictine Sisters of Perpetual Adoration: Biographical Notes* (St. Louis, Missouri, 1984), p. 6. Translated and edited as above.

8. Ibid., letter of December 22, 1874.

9. Letter of February 18, 1875. Copied in the *Daybook*. These Daybooks, handwritten in German from 1874–1886, and then in English, are preserved in the St. Louis archives of the Benedictine Sisters. Translations are by Sr. Dominica Bonnenberg, O.S.B. A bound copy of the entries from 1874–1886 was made in 1976, p. 6.

10. Letter to Abbot Anselm, O.S.B., May 19, 1875.

11. Letter to Abbot Anselm, O.S.B., June 21, 1875.

12. From a letter to Mother Gertrude, dated mid-October, 1874 in *Early Chronicled Hisory: Relationship between Maryville and Conception*, p. 11.

13. Letter of Nov. 2, 1875, in *Letters from Mother Anselma and Others*.

14. Ibid., December 1, 1875.

15. *Daybook*, p. 19.

Chapter Four
1876 – 1882

1876 was America's centennial year. Its opening days brought three postulants to the new convent at Conception. Agnes Mayer and Angela Weber were German-born, but had lived in the area with their families for some time. Mary Schrader had come from Bastogne in Belgium as a child with her parents. Both Prior Frowin and Mother Anselma were constantly pleading with their Swiss motherhouses to send them good, Swiss-trained sisters and brothers. Mother Anselma understood that three more sisters were being sent to her from Maria Rickenbach that summer: "O Lord, let them be the right ones!"[1] The prior was more blunt about it. Having experienced Sr. Beatrice's and Sr. Adela's domineering ways, he asked for an experienced teacher or two and a good cook, but wanted no anarchists.

Along with postulants, the sisters had a steady stream of boarders, young girls who stayed with them while being prepared for their first communion. There were also poor children whose mothers were ill or in prison. Times were hard. Farmers had no ready cash. Mother Anselma wrote in a letter of October 5, 1876: "It happens that the richest farmer sometimes cannot pay the daily wages to his hired hands. Mr. Clever, our greatest benefactor, who possesses vast acres of land, had nothing left to pay a workman for one and a half day's labor. I had to come to his rescue."[2] Everywhere the barter system was in use. Farm wives traded butter and eggs for store goods. Farmers had trouble selling their stock, so that payment for school fees and books was quite often "a cow or fifteen ducks."

Yet the kindly people of Conception were concerned about the struggling little community of Swiss sisters. There are frequent entries in the Daybook such as "Mr. Gut brought a fine young pig."[3] Mrs. Clever sent over milk and eggs as often as she could spare some. Entries like that of March 25, 1876, are common: "Received six partridges, a chicken, sauerkraut, milk, bread and twelve goose eggs."[4] By 1878, the sisters were feeding poor railroad workers who were building a station at Conception. But sometimes they themselves had only black coffee and a piece of bread for breakfast. Firewood was often in short supply, which meant the sisters had to go looking for old logs and corncobs, until the brothers from Conception came to the rescue. Even with frost thick on the window, the sisters dared not keep more than one stove going at night for fear of exhausting their supply.

Writing back to Maria Rickenbach in reply to a question about how she liked America, Sr. Scholastica von Matt, one of the second group to arrive from Switzerland in the summer of 1876, said: "The rising and the setting sun, the starry sky at night are marvelous. But the dirt in the paths we have to take to get to church and the pigs searching for garbage: these are not attractive ... The sisters are thin and the humble appearance of their habits betrays that they have not much time for themselves ... It looks strange to me to see even grown-up people wearing a modern hat and shawl, walking without shoes and stockings."[5] With it all, however, the spiritual life was not allowed to suffer. The beloved customs of the motherhouse were carefully followed: nine Masses on Christmas day, the blessed wine of St. John on December 27, frequent conferences from Prior Frowin.

The prior was an overworked man. Superior, missionary to German Catholics over a wide area, financier, and builder, he nevertheless took seriously his duty as immediate superior to the Swiss sisters. In the practical realm, he saw to it that the brothers helped clear their land for an orchard and vineyard, dug their well, provided trees and vines. He paid the sisters for the vestments and altar linens they made for the monks. It was taken for granted that the sisters would do the washing and mending for them. Also taken for granted was the sisters approaching him as children to father. This was part of religious culture of the day. Superiors were fathers and mothers, expected to provide and care for their spiritual children. This kind of paternalism and maternalism are evident in the letters that streamed back and forth across the Atlantic. The path to virtue was considered to be slippery: great vigilance was needed on the part of superiors. Letters abound in signatures such as: "your little spiritual child" ... "your poorest spiritual son" ... "your most unworthy child," as do confidences entrusted to: "your loving, motherly heart" or "your Grace's fatherly heart."

Despite this, or because of it, Mother Anselma had a deep respect and trust in Prior Frowin. "There was a chance today to talk things over with Fr. Prior. God bless him for his fatherly love and care," is a typical entry in the Daybook.[6] She felt more at home with him and his insistence on being a monk first and a missionary second, than she did with Fr. Adelhelm, whose talkativeness and multiple enthusiasms she distrusted. Mother Anselma, however, could not agree with the prior's conviction that schools were important to their community here in Missouri and could be easily combined with perpetual adoration. She believed with all her heart that schools came second. There are numerous entries in the Daybook about the hours of adoration they were able to keep, at first in the Conception church, and then in their own little chapel in the convent. "The most reverend spiritual Father allowed us during winter-time to have four or five hours of adoration every night: thanks be to God, as perpetual adoration is our main task, the school is secondary."[7] With the community's first profession of novices in May, 1877, and another in October the same year, they had enough sisters so that in March, 1878, they received permission from the Abbot of Engelberg to have the long-desired adoration "for all time." In her letters Mother Anselma refers occasionally to enrolling benefactors in the League of Perpetual Adoration, an association of prayer modeled on one begun at Maria Rickenbach.

With the second group of sisters from Maria Rickenbach: Srs. Bernardine Wachter, Scholastica von Matt and Novice Anna Jann, there were four sisters, three novices, five candidates and a boarder in the Conception house that summer of 1876. Since Sr. Bernardine would be able to help Sr. Augustine teach in the Maryville school in the fall, Sr. Rose Chapelle could then return to her own community. Now Mother Anselma felt free to act more decisively. She did not approve of the sisters staying in the rectory and wished to change that situation, feeling that Fr. Adelhelm had too much influence on the sisters. She wrote to Abbot Anselm in Engelberg: "Our Lord will help us so that we can manage the school satisfactorily. It is His work! There are one hundred and eighteen children on the list for Maryville: thirty of these paid nothing; about twenty paid all the fees. About $200.00 in school fees were paid, not enough for the three sisters to live on. If the sisters did not live in the rectory and did not have to take care of it, then two sisters would be enough for the school and the house. Would you approve of my going in the fall with the two sisters to Maryville, to stay with them for a few days? To decide this by myself is very hard for me! I have learned now that it is infinitely easier to obey than to command."[8]

Mother Anselma's health was another concern. Her appetite was poor and a constant cough had developed. In a letter dated August 10, 1876, she says in passing: "I shall write to you another time provided God does not call me beforehand. Last year already the Fathers feared I was in the last stage of consumption. But I am still here and feel just as well as last year ... Though I would gladly go on working for our Lord for some years yet, I am also ready at any hour to die for him. I feel I have nothing left to give him but my poor life and he can dispose of this as he wishes. It may be that he will call me soon, my soul experiences a strange feeling that I have never had before."[9]

Affairs in both the community and the school pressed on the fragile superior. Conflicting accounts kept arriving from Maryville. Sr.

Bernardine was, according to Sr. Scholastica, "too severe and harsh."[10] Those two did not get along. It had become Sr. Bernardine's habit to go to Fr. Adelhelm with everything and to pay little attention to Mother Anselma. Fr. Adelhelm admired Sr. Bernardine and supported her with his usual verve. Prior Frowin was troubled. He felt Sr. Bernardine needed cautious guidance and above all, "an education in obedience."[11] Yet he respected her competence and feared that Mother Anselma was too suspicious. Then Fr. Ignatius Conrad, who was for a time assistant to Fr. Adelhelm in the Maryville parish, got involved in the situation. He supported Sr. Scholastica, who was feeling overworked and misunderstood. Everyone was writing to Engelberg and Maria Rickenbach with charges and counter-charges. Sr. Bernardine complained about Mother Anselma's timidity and inability to control Sr. Beatrice. Fr. Ignatius wanted to be a missionary and get away from Conception so then he would have more liberty and not be told how often, as he once expressed it, "to spray holy water left and right."[12] He felt that Prior Frowin was too inclined to imitate the Beuronese style rather than the Engelberg one.

His confidence in Prior Frowin shaken somewhat by all this, Abbot Anselm sent him a severe letter, warning him to hold to the Engelberg customs in all things. He wrote Mother Anselma in a similar vein, saying that he would make Fr. Adelhelm superior and confessor to the sisters. This brought a strong reaction from the usually gentle superior. In several letters she pleads with the Swiss abbot not to take Fr. Prior from them. They relied on his judgment and good sense. Fr. Adelhelm was indeed a good and generous person, but he was no manager, and his "overstrained and hasty procedures"[13] would not be good for the sisters. With the resilient humility typical of him, Prior Frowin accepted the Abbot's warning and agreed to conform in all things to the Engelberg style. Fr. Ignatius rethought his position and admitted he had been too critical. Abbot Anselm relented, probably feeling he had acted too hastily on a good deal of misinformation. In May, 1878, he appointed Prior Frowin as superior and visitator to both Swiss houses of Conception and Maryville.

Abbot Anselm hoped that Prior Frowin could make a visitation in both houses and try to reconcile the sisters to each other. He was too far away to understand the situation and needed, in the prior's rueful words, to take the letters from Missouri "with circumspection."[14] Sr. Bernardine wrote apologizing for her part in the discord, promising to do no more complaining or meddling in what did not concern her.[15] For his part, Fr. Adelhelm had written in January of that year to Mother Gertrude begging her to come to America to preside over both the sisters' houses, uniting them in benevolence — and educating as many English teachers as possible. By February he was telling his Swiss abbot about a former parishioner who had gone to Oregon and was now writing back about the beauty of the place, with its mountains and entire suitability for a community of monks.[16] Another letter of June 4, 1878, reveals some unusual introspection from the lively Adelhelm: "I must also confess that in some rare moments, I had the conviction that all the discord and dissension among the brothers and sisters in Conception, as well as in Maryville, was for the great part, though not all, my fault." This letter is signed, "your big good-for-nothing."[17]

Mother Anselma had evidently been aware of the possibility of Mother Gertrude being invited to America. In a letter to Abbot Anselm, dated August, 1877, she wrote: "Though I would be happy to have Rev. Mother here, I would not advise her to come. The climate would not do her good. Moreover, she does not understand English and everything here is so very different from Europe. Even the food might not agree with her." Apparently Mother Anselma guessed that Mother Gertrude's sympathies were with the Maryville sisters, which was understandable since she was in constant correspondence with Fr. Adelhelm. Prior Frowin was also doubtful. Writing a couple of years later to Abbot Anselm, he remarked: "I suppose Sr. Gertrude would have done better than Mother Anselma had she been here from the beginning . . . She is not looking forward to Sr. Gertrude's coming and there might be complications."[18] But Sr. Gertrude was determined to come. For three years she had been having serious difficulties with the chaplain at Maria Rickenbach. Abbot Anselm had conducted a visitation about the matter and found fault on both sides. He had tried to reconcile them, but in vain.[19] At the time for the election in September, 1879, Mother Gertrude steadfastly refused to accept. She had been prioress for nearly twenty-two years and was now fifty-five. Her former longing to be a missionary in America had revived. All she needed was Abbot Anselm's consent and an invitation from Prior Frowin in Missouri. Both hesitated. They could not approve two motherhouses so close to each other as Maryville and Conception. Prior Frowin was not willing to have Sr. Gertrude simply take over as superior from Mother Anselma. There matters stood.

Meanwhile there were other difficulties for Mother Anselma. The small house in Conception was overcrowded. Six postulants had received the monastic habit during 1878. On May 10, 1879, four more novices were professed. Building was a necessity, but there was no money. The sisters went out in twos collecting. Even taking on another school on Mr. Clever's property, called the "Wild Cat school," did not bring in that much. There were forty-one children enrolled in this school, aged five to nineteen years. The teacher received $35 a month, plus a horse to ride to her classes.

Another concern was the matter of the general chapter for all American Benedictine sisters for which Mother Anselma received an invitation from Sr. Teresa, O.S.B., prioress of St. Joseph's convent in St. Marys, Pennsylvania, on June 5, 1879. Sr. Teresa wrote: "The purpose of the General Chapter is to carry out the will of the Holy See by the adoption of a uniform constitution and the establishment of the 'Congregation' among all the communities . . . We expect to be assisted in our deliberations by Bishop Fink and Abbot Wimmer. The Chapter will begin August 4 and terminate on or about the 7th."[20] To Mother Anselma this sounded ominous. Would it mean giving up or curtailing perpetual adoration? Nothing must be allowed to do that! If a uniform constitution were to be adopted as a result of this chapter, what effect would this have on a struggling little community dedicated to perpetual adoration? After consulting Prior Frowin, she composed a careful reply:

> I must excuse our not being present at the General Chapter, for we are newcomers in this country; it is but a few years since we started a convent of our institute in America. We are sisters of perpetual adoration. The first and principal obligation of our institute is the cult of the most Blessed Sacrament. Without a moment's intermission by day or by night the members of our institute are, by turns, to adore this mystery of love. Besides this perpetual adoration, we are occupied in making and embroidering different kinds of vestments used for the divine service. We take charge of a school here in our settlement, where we also keep a boarding school for the education of female children of the poorer or common classes. We observe the Rule of St. Benedict, but we make only simple vows, renewed annually and pray the office of St. Gertrude, not daring to appear among the members of the Benedictine order.[21]

When they managed to get a small house for the sisters teaching in Maryville, Mother Anselma was happy as she felt this separation from the rectory would alleviate the friction that had existed. Then another blow fell. Sr. Augustine, the youngest of the pioneers who had come to America, became ill. She had been sickly most of the time, but now her condition was very serious. It was typhoid, which dragged on for some months. At first there seemed to be improvement but on October 27, 1879, early in the morning, Sr. Augustine died. She was twenty-eight years old and had been in America for five years.

The need for a new convent dominated Mother Anselma's concerns for the next few years. There was little money, but the sisters worked hard and long and prayed to St. Joseph. They set out in twos on begging tours, as had been done some decades before in Maria Rickenbach's need. Traveling through Indiana, Iowa, West Virginia, Colorado, and on to Wyoming was often discouraging work. The bishop of St. Louis at first refused to let them do any collecting in his diocese. Later he repented. When the sisters were denied permission to beg in one city, they simply set out for another to try again. In Cheyenne, a Jesuit pastor sent them packing, saying they were only dressed up as nuns. Little by little, they were able to send money back to Conception to help with construction once the site had been chosen. Besides this, Mother Anselma had to borrow money three times.

The question of a site for the new monastery was a problem. Mr. Clever had offered them plenty of land, but it was too far away to suit the good people of Conception. Moreover, it would be wiser to build close to the railway station for the supplies that would have to be hauled. There was another offer of land only two miles from the Conception monastery and a half-mile from the railway station, in the small town of Clyde, Missouri. In July, 1880, when the post office was established in this new town, which was the result of the construction of the Wabash Railroad, more than fifty of the townspeople met to choose a name. Two residents, Frank Bellows and John Wirth, had recently bought some Clydesdale horses from Canada. So the town solemnly took its name from this famous breed.

Prior Frowin estimated the cost of the sisters' monastery at about $10,000. He was somewhat optimistic, as it was to cost several thousand more. The monks were also building at this time, as was Fr. Adelhelm in Maryville, who was having a new convent built for the sisters who would teach there. It was definite now that Sr. Gertrude would be coming, along with four other sisters from Maria Rickenbach and some postulants. In the fall of 1880, Prior Frowin allowed the sisters to use the first floor of his new monastery to hold a fair to raise money for their monastery. By January, 1881, Mother Anselma had been able to put $1,445 in the bank. But their expenses kept mounting. The prior advised them to choose the Clyde site as it seemed more practical. The sisters' chapter voted to do this, turning down an invitation and pledges of money to build at Stanberry, Missouri. The railway workers whom the sisters fed also helped: a group of them collected $400 for the building fund and were invited to dinner with the sisters in gratitude. Mr. Keel of Benziger's remembered them and sent $700. On June 7, 1881, the foundations for their new monastery at Clyde were dug.

Now there was more begging for the sisters to do. Stones were desperately needed, so appeals were made to nearby farmers. Some responded at once; one or more of the sisters had to jump on horseback to go pleading with friends and neighbors to cart stones, lest the construction have to stop. On September 11, 1881, Abbot Frowin laid the cornerstone. He had been consecrated abbot of Conception Abbey on June 29th of that year. By December, 1881, the total cost of construction amounted to over $13,000. Mother Anselma wrote to Switzerland: "The days are so full of work that only a quiet night hour allows writing ... We have fifteen sisters, three novices. Six of the sisters are in schools ... Besides the three public schools we have our perpetual adoration, a little Institute (boarding school) and our own school ... sewing for the church and the Fathers' convent and their laundry. Thanks be to God our new convent is up to the roof... besides a basement and a ground floor, there will be two storeys."[22]

The Daybook entry for February 14, 1882, notes simply: "Expenses! Expenses!" They ordered a Gothic altar from a German-born artist for $300. A buggy cost $70 and a harness, $75. A bushel of corn at that time sold for $.60. The sisters were making hay to be used for the mattresses of the children who would be coming to the boarding school at the new monastery. They made their own candles and soap as well. Much as Mother Anselma disliked taking on new schools, she was forced to do so in order to get more money. But when Fr. Adelhelm wanted the sisters who taught to spend the summer vacation studying with "a Protestant lady," Mother Anselma refused. It would do them more good to study in the peace of their monastery.

The sisters who went out collecting money also recruited students for the boarding school. They obtained a good many from Colorado, so that by September, 1882, they had thirty-three lively children sharing their house, which brought them $400 in school fees. In one of her now less frequent letters to Maria Rickenbach, Mother Anselma notes that she would gladly have closed one of the public schools, but Abbot Frowin would not allow it. They were enlarging their boarding school under the patronage of St. Joseph and now had eighteen sisters and three postulants. "We have nine music courses. All here in America want to learn music . . . All day long someone is using the piano."[23] She went on to say that they had 150 children in their various schools, with twenty boarders. They had no more room.

By April, 1882, the sisters were often at Clyde working on their new land, planting trees and potatoes. April 18th was moving day. Their good friends, Mr. Gut and Mr. Henggeler, along with some others, moved the heavy furniture and beds. On the 19th the sisters had the first Mass in their new home, using a room set aside for a chapel. Their chaplain was Fr. Pius Conrad, brother to Abbot Frowin. By the 28th of the month, the sisters had a one-hundred pound bell hung in their tower. Besides his other duties, Fr. Pius also busied himself sowing oats for them in a large field. On May 3, Abbot Frowin, accompanied by all his monks solemnly consecrated the monastery and the little chapel. Then together they sat down to a festive dinner, enlivened by a "box of beer" presented to Mother Anselma in honor of her postponed nameday.

During these months Mother Anselma's health worsened; sometimes she had to take to her bed out of sheer weakness. Undoubtedly the strain over the situation at Maryville contributed to this. In July, 1880, Abbot Anselm had written from Engelberg that Sr. Gertrude would be coming to Missouri, the inference being that she would take charge of the Maryville convent. Abbot Frowin had written that same month: "You wrote that Mother Gertrude would not interfere with Conception . . . The convent of Conception should always remain the motherhouse of all convents of perpetual adoration that come into existence in this country."[24] By September he was writing that he would ask the bishop to allow the Maryville convent to be separated from the Conception one and to establish its own novitiate. Mother Anselma wrote rather wistfully to Maria Rickenbach: "It is a great relief for me that now Maryville and Conception are to be separated. With my best will I could not satisfy Maryville. Thanks be to God, all is over now and I trust in his help that all will turn out for the best ... Dear Reverend Mother (this was the new prioress in the Swiss convent, Mother Johanna Gretener, niece of Sr. Vincentia Gretener), do not quite forget us in favor of Maryville ... You know that we are completely under the direction of the new Right Reverend Abbot of Conception, and therefore seldom come in touch with Fr. Abbot of Engelberg. How perfectly God knows how to detach our hearts from all that is not himself!"[25]

Sr. Gertrude with her five companions arrived in Maryville on November 2nd, but did not come to Conception to see Mother Anselma and her sisters until November 11, 1880. The Daybook has a laconic entry for this date: "The meeting was not as joyful as we would have wished." On November 7th that year, Mother Gertrude opened a novitiate at the Maryville convent, formally separating the two houses founded from Maria Rickenbach. With her usual decisiveness, she began forging ahead. Within a month, she had an invitation from Bishop Marty to send some sisters to teach school at an Indian reservation, where the government would pay for house and salary. By December 11, 1880, Sr. Adela, one of the original group, asked to transfer to the Maryville house, as did a couple of the other sisters. This was very hard for Mother Anselma to accept. It did not help when one of Abbot Anselm's rare letters arrived February 11, 1881, with the news that Mother Gertrude was asking Maria Rickenbach to send her ten or fifteen more sisters.

In May, 1881 Mother Gertrude came to Conception, asking for two sisters to teach in Dakota. Mother Anselma declined, but Sr. Agnes, another of the pioneer group, decided to go to try out a missionary vocation. This was bad enough. Worse still, the enterprising Mother Gertrude wanted the Conception sisters to take over the Maryville convent with its considerable debt, so that she could move all her sisters to South Dakota. Abbot Frowin did not want Mother Gertrude to leave Maryville until the debt on the house Fr. Adelhelm had built for them was reduced. If it were not more than $1,000, the Abbot felt the Clyde sisters could take it over. He asked Abbot Anselm to see that good sisters were sent to Clyde as well as to Maryville. In fact, Maria Rickenbach did send four more postulants to Clyde in the next two years. Abbot Frowin felt the spirit of the Clyde monastery, which was now called St. Scholastica's, was good. Writing to Abbot Anselm on November 11, 1881, he said he was uncomfortable with the Maryville house and its debts:

We are embarrassed because of the sisters' convent. Prominent Catholics complain that at the collections, Fr. Adelhelm used to say, 'The sisters themselves will finance their convent. It will not be a burden for the parish.' He must have said that to keep the people from grumbling, as some did not like the sisters because of their many debts. He had also expected Mother Gertrude to bring more money from Europe than she actually did. So he told the parishioners that they had about an $8,000 debt because of the sisters' convent. He should never have said that. . . . If he had stayed until everything was in order, things might have straightened out.[26]

Characteristically, however, Fr. Adelhelm had not stayed. In June, 1881, he and Fr. Nicholas had set off to found a monastery in the west. By November, he was writing to Engelberg that they intended to settle in Gervais, Oregon, to take care of a parish there, about thirty-eight miles from Portland. The letter was a rhapsody about the beauty of Oregon, its similarity to Switzerland, the wonderful, fertile land where one could grow wheat, oats, potatoes, apples, and pears. He interested Mother Gertrude in this venture, so that by December, he was writing that Sr. Bernardine would be coming to Oregon as superior of a community of sisters. An account of the Idaho Benedictine sisters relates that a group of sisters from the abbey of Sarnen in Switzerland traveled across the Atlantic and on to Missouri, "where we arrived on Monday eve (October 22, 1882). Teams were ready to bring us to Maryville, a place several miles distant, where some sisters of Rickenbach were located. But, oh, the roads at that time! . . . We felt quite at home with the sisters and took a good rest, but it was no lasting abode. The next day we parted again to continue our journey. Two more members joined Rev. Fr. Adelhelm's mission-sisters: Rev. Mother Bernardine as superior and Sr. M. Benedicta as teacher of the Indians."[27]

The winter of 1883 was a cold one and Mother Anselma suffered greatly. She was forty years old on January 20 and had been professed for twenty-four years. By March, the weather had changed as "do happenings in human life" noted the Daybook on March 17th. In the last several years, the community chapter had met a number of times to admit novices to profession: so far they had all persevered. There was still a debt, but letters continued to come in from people asking to be enrolled in the sisters' Association of Perpetual Adoration. They could, therefore, turn down one request for another school in Colorado. Mother Anselma worried about the sisters having to walk to class, sometimes more than a mile and a half each way on frozen, icy paths, with sleet falling around them. Once, because of a blizzard, Brother Meinrad had to bring Sr. Beatrice back in a sleigh from the school where she taught. Mother Anselma herself was kept busy making vestments with the delicate embroidery that was her special skill. Because of the American girls who were joining them, she was glad that their adoration prayers could be translated into English and that now they prayed their office in that language.

On June 2, Abbot Frowin assembled all the sisters of St. Scholastica's for their first election of a prioress in their new monastery. Mother Anselma was immediately re-elected. Hardly a month later, a tornado destroyed their laundry building which meant a loss of $1,300, but Mother Anselma was just grateful that none of the sisters had been hurt. Early in August their Chaplain, Fr. Pius, became very ill with typhoid fever. Typhoid was a dreaded scourge at this time. Acute and highly infectious, it was transmitted by contaminated food or water and characterized by high fever, bronchitis and intestinal hemorrhaging. On the 13th of the month, Mother Anselma came down with it. A week later she was very ill, with two sisters nursing her day and night. In the early hours of August 26, 1883, the end came. After receiving the last sacraments, she died at 6:50 in the morning. Because of the heat, it was necessary to have the funeral the very next day. The Daybook says simply, "All seems empty and lonesome."

It was the end of an era for the little community, the end of a simple life lived in obscurity and faith. "Nothing is too much for Jesus," Mother Anselma had written to Maria Rickenbach and it was a fitting epitaph for her. She had come to America to found a monastic community with a focus on adoration of the Blessed Sacrament. This note of simplicity marked her always: "O please pray that our Lord may soon build a convent for us ... where we can bring up ignorant children and raise a small farm for our living in the way of the old desert fathers," she had said in one of her early letters.[28] Hers was not a broad vision but one that ran deep. Her convictions about prayer enabled her to withstand the dynamic and demanding Mother Gertrude. When Mother Anselma died, it was clear that the community she had founded would continue to place its priority where hers had always been, and that education or the missions would take second place to a life of prayer.

NOTES

1. *Daybook,* Feb. 7, 1876.

2. To Mother Gertrude Leupi, in *Letters from Mother M. Anselma and Others.*

3. *Daybook,* July 1, 1876.

4. *Daybook.*

5. To Abbot Anselm Villiger, O.S.B. in *Letters from Mother Anselma and Others,* July 17, 1876.

6. October 24, 1876.

7. November 27, 1876.

8. Letter of July 16, 1876, in *Letters from Mother M. Anselma and Others.*

9. Ibid., letter to Abbot Anselm.

10. Letter to Abbot Anselm Villiger, February 28, 1878, in *Early Chronicled History of the Benedictine Sisters of Perpetual Adoration: Relationship Between Maryville and Conception (Clyde): 1874–1893* p. 54.

11. Ibid., July 25, 1878, pp. 90–91.

12. In a letter to Abbot Anselm, September 13–17, 1876, in *Letters from Mother M. Anselma and Others.*

13. Ibid., letters of November 19th and 27th.

14. Letter of June 11, 1878, in *Early Chronicled History: Relationship Between Maryville and Conception,* p. 88.

15. Ibid., letter of June 3, 1878, p. 86.

16. Letter of February, 1878, in *Letters from Mother M. Anselma and Others.*

17. Ibid., letter to Abbot Anselm Villiger.

18. Letter of April 14, 1880, in *Early Chronicled History: Relationship Between Maryville and Conception,* p. 100.

19. *Sr. Gertrude Leupi,* p. 105.

20. This handwritten invitation is preserved in the archives of the Benedictine Sisters of Perpetual Adoration in St. Louis. Regina Baska, *The Benedictine Congregation of St. Scholastica* (Washington, D.C., 1935), pp. 126–128, gives interesting details of this proposed Chapter which had to be postponed because of an outbreak of smallpox at the chosen site.

21. A copy of this handwritten response, with pencilled corrections by Abbot Frowin, is preserved in the St. Louis archives.

22. December 18, 1881, in *Letters from Mother M. Anselma and Others.*

23. Ibid., February 5, 1882.

24. Letter of July 8, 1880, in *Early Chronicled History: Relationship Between Maryville and Conception,* p. 102.

25. Ibid., October 23, 1880, p. 104.

26. Ibid., in a letter to Abbot Anselm Villiger, November 11, 1881, pp. 121–22.

27. *Idaho Benedictines: St. Gertrude's Convent, Cottonwood, Idaho,* a synopsis of the history of this community by Sr. Ildephonse Nuxoll, O.S.B., 1976.

28. To Mother Gertrude, December 31, 1876, in *Letters from Mother M. Anselma and Others.*

Chapter Five
1883 – 1900

During Mother Anselma's illness, two of her community were in Colorado looking for students for their Academy at Clyde and also for donations to help pay off their debts. Srs. John Schrader and Gertrude Mayer only heard of their prioress' death when they stepped off the train in Maryville on August 30, 1883.

This was not the first time Sr. John had been out collecting. In 1881, with Sr. Scholastica von Matt, she met the legendary Vicar Apostolic of Colorado, Joseph Machebeuf. In 1860, Archbishop Lamy had sent him to Colorado to look after the miners in that new community. Soon he was a familiar sight in every boom town, establishing parishes, schools, hospitals. When Denver was made the see-city of Colorado in 1887, Joseph Machebeuf was its first bishop. By the time of his death two years later, there were 40,000 Catholics in his diocese and 102 churches.

Sr. Scholastica wrote a description of their interview with the Vicar, who was just back from a trip to Europe. "The Reverend Vicar received us kindly, gave us his blessing and had us sit down. Then we had such an interesting conversation we shall never forget it. Like children who ask their father about all he has experienced on his journey, we wanted to know whether he had been in Einsiedeln, Engelberg and Maria Rickenbach. He answered everything with great kindness and patience ... In Einsiedeln when he asked for priests, they told him to try St. Meinrad's in America. This he did ... and the prior told him that probably fathers from St. Meinrad and Conception could be sent ... Then His Grace inquired about everything concerning our institution and whether we would take over hospitals and orphanages in case we came to his diocese with the Conception fathers. We thought it might be permitted in such a case ... We cautiously asked if he would object if we tried to obtain members for our Eucharistic Association. We gave him Fr. Abbot's letter ... After having read it several times, the Vicar at last added to it: 'I hereby approve and confirm the above recommendation,' and signed it and put his seal on it ... The good Vicar gave us his holy blessing and personally showed us where to take the street car."[1]

On September 3, 1883, Abbot Frowin gathered the community of Clyde around him, read Chapter 64 of the Rule of Benedict to those who were eligible to vote and proceeded to hold an election for a prioress to succeed Mother Anselma. He had privately thought Mother Gertrude Leupi might be elected, which could have effected a reunion of the two houses in Clyde and Maryville. But on the first ballot the seventeen sister-electors chose Sr. John Schrader as their second prioress. Of the seventeen sisters, only two were in their thirties. Mother John was twenty-nine and had been professed seven years.

Abbot Frowin was impressed with the peace and calmness of the election.[2] He decided that it was for the best: Mother John has a "motherly" heart and spoke English very well, which was important. Having moved from Illinois to Missouri with her parents in a covered wagon, she had lived on a farm near Maryville. She was one of the first young women from the area to enter the new community, coming only six weeks after the Swiss sisters had settled in Conception. After her profession she had taught in the Wild Cat school, often riding there on a horse or mule. She was also a skilled seamstress and had helped Mother Anselma with vestment-making. When he heard of her election, Fr. Adelhelm wrote from Oregon in his usual merry style: "Can you imagine how I laughed when the old, ill-reputed Maryville (of whom someone asked, can anything good come from Maryville?), gave that land of promise, Clyde, their new Reverend Mother? ... I can still remember how about ten years ago, I used to encourage the little, vain Miss Mary Schrader until I had talked her into the convent."[3] Mother Gertrude had already expressed her opinion in a letter to Maria Rickenbach in 1881: "She (Sr. Gertrude Mayer) and Sr. John are the first who made profession in Conception and evidently they are also the best and most efficient ones there."[4]

It was a frightened young sister who accepted the election. Mother John spent the first weeks in tears before her practical good sense reasserted itself, and she felt able to cope with the problems facing her and her struggling community. One of these problems was her own health. Destined to be prioress for thirty-seven years, scarcely a week of those years went by without illness. Her lungs had already been a cause of concern: that was why she had often been sent on collecting tours to Colorado in the hope that the mountain air might benefit her. She suffered intensely from migraine headaches and often had to take to her bed with nausea and pain. Later, dropsy and diabetes would plague her.

It was Abbot Frowin's conviction that a monastic superior should remain in office as long as possible. Time and again through the years that followed, he records with satisfaction that Mother John was re-elected, often having to add, as he did in a letter of August 26, 1895: "In the afternoon there was an election of the Reverend Mother — as simple as possible in consideration of Mother John's condition. She was of course re-elected, but was so weak that I scarcely dared to have her reaffirmed in her office. But for years already we have been apprehensive for her life. So we shall now trust in the Lord for the future. Her loss would be a heavy blow."[5] The chronicles of the Clyde community tell of frequent trips to Minnesota, Colorado, to hospitals in Kansas City and St. Louis, all in the hope of helping her. But Mother John usually returned more tired than she set out, and went right back to an exhausting schedule of duties.

Poverty was also one of Mother John's problems. The community was poor, very poor. To one creditor alone they owed $2,000. Often enough they ran out of flour and fuel and could not afford to buy any. It was still common in 1889 to be offered a cow in return for six months schooling in their academy. That same year a workman's wages were $10 a month. The sisters could buy thirty bushels of apples for $.30 a bushel. Still, they spent days planting trees and hedges in order to have their own fruit. In 1885, 100 bushels of corn were sold for $.25 a bushel. The year before they had been able to buy eight turkeys for Christmas at $1.00 each. The sisters bought hay at $4 an acre.

Mother John spent the day sewing, either for the sisters or vestments, and then worked far into the night on her accounts, usually spending an hour of adoration at 4 a.m. Hers was a pioneer notion of economy. She hated waste of any kind: with the little the sisters managed to save, she was able to pay the annual interest on their loans promptly and to reduce the principal slowly, year after year. Later a local banker was to say of her with great admiration: "Mother John is the best business man in Nodaway County!"

The sisters had all the worries of other farmers in the area. The winters of the late 1880s and 1890s were piercingly cold. Often the sisters could not get out to teach in the schools. Grudgingly, another load of coal was ordered when they had hoped to get by with less. The summers were hot, sometimes the cisterns ran dry and the dreaded typhoid appeared. The spring rains meant mud and the buggy stuck so that the workmen had to get the sisters out. They planted a garden annually. On May 16, 1885, the Daybook notes: "Two thousand cabbage plants, fifty tomato plants." They went on outings and gathered wild grapes to make wine, as well as gooseberries. They went fishing in the small ponds thereabout. They churned butter, rendered lard and made molasses, as well as apple cider. They planted and picked potatoes and bought fifty-one bushels of them in 1888 for $.50 a bushel. It was common for the sisters to be called on to cut hay and shuck oats during the heat of July, as well as doing a full day's work in the house.

Poor themselves, the sisters did what they could for the poor around them. To the hungry men who came to their door in 1898, they served 389 meals. The sisters rarely refused to take poor girls into their orphanage, even though this meant more mouths to feed. One such girl lived with them from babyhood until she was fifteen and adopted by a local family. The Daybook speaks of a poor child whose mother did not want her, so the sisters kept her.

As more sisters were professed, the community was able to take on more sewing. Mother John's skill was a great help with the vestments. Fr. Lukas Etlin, a Conception monk, had been coming to Clyde to give drawing lessons since 1888. By 1895, he was drawing patterns for the sisters' embroidery. Soon they were able to put together a catalogue of their vestments, so that two by two, the sisters could go to Chicago, Kansas City, and St. Louis trying to sell them to interested priests.

The sisters were still traveling in Colorado and other western states collecting money and trying to recruit students for their academy. In June, 1885, Sr. Scholastica returned to her native Switzerland with the aim of raising a loan from the community of Ingenbohl at a low rate of interest. She spent a year in Europe. There are occasional notations in the Clyde Daybook as to her progress: "She does pretty well in collecting, but it is very hard for her as she is all alone."[6] In June, 1896, Abbot Frowin wrote worriedly to Abbot Anselm of Engelberg: "I myself was and am always against begging trips and allowed her to journey only because she gave Reverend Mother good hope that through the help of her people at home, she could easily get a loan at very low interest. Her long delay in Switzerland and southern Germany appeared to me rather useless and I would have preferred that, since she had decided to collect, she had tried England and the Rhineland. The new decrees of the Holy See will make things much more difficult for her. Let us hope that our Lord will help in another way!"[7] By September, Sr. Scholastica was back in Missouri with seven postulants and over $1,000. Even so, the Daybook notes with some pathos: "Money comes in very slow and very little of it."[8]

Sr. Scholastica's was not the first trip back to Switzerland by one of the Clyde community. Mother John herself, with Sr. Anselmina Jann, had made the journey in 1888. Sr. Anselmina's parents lived in Switzerland and were delighted to give hospitality to the sisters. It was hoped that the mountain air would be good for Mother John's lungs. Actually, she found Maria Rickenbach too high and the air too thin. She felt more comfortable in Stans. In a letter to Abbot Frowin, she wrote:

> We came here Saturday and were received with open arms by Rt. Rev. Abbot Anselm and all the dear sisters. They had made great preparations and had a great feast today. All seem to have a great joy that we came. The dear sisters are very anxious that we should enjoy the benefit of the journey. I find Switzerland very nice: the mountains are indeed different

from the Colorado mountains. Everything is so green and beautiful! The air, however, is fresh and very light. I fear I cannot stay here at first, but will try Engelberg for a week or so and then come here later. . .

We had a most beautiful journey: that is, beautiful weather with no storms on the ocean. We made the trip from Conception to Stans in a few hours less than twelve days. We travelled day and night and I can tell you we were all satisfied to rest! I think I have never been so tired!

We are rested now and feel well as usual. I am real nervous but think it is caused by the change and they *will* make me drink wine! I cannot stand it, but the Rt. Rev. Abbot and Rev. Mother cannot believe it and they all say I *must* drink it, so I will obey. The Rt. Rev. Abbot said he would write you that I would not eat or drink, but, dearest Father, I eat as much as I can! My appetite is poor, it is true, but I promise you I will do my best. . .

I like this place real well and the dear sisters are as nice as can be, but I miss my dear sisters in Clyde. I think from what I have seen and heard that we are stricter in America than here in Europe, but this may be only my imagination. . .

Most everyone I meet and speak with inquires about you, dear Father. Best regards from all, especially from Fr. Joseph at the pilgrim chapel. He, I think, has a touch of America-fever. . .[9]

Mother John and Sr. Anselmina returned in October, 1888, with fifteen postulants: "America-fever" was not confined to young men. Ten of these women remained to make profession in the Clyde community. Early in 1885, the novitiate had already been crowded. Besides this, there were fifty-three children in the academy. The original building had been erected at Clyde in 1882. With ceaseless scrimping and saving, Mother John managed to put $1,000 in the bank by 1885 to start a fund for the construction of a larger chapel and additional rooms for the academy. Abbot Frowin consecrated this addition in September, 1886, writing to Abbot Anselm: "When complete, the chapel with its three altars, will be so beautiful that with all my heart I would wish that the motherhouse in Rickenbach had one like this . . . The new wing with the chapel is very beautiful and will for a long time have enough room for the children."[10]

Unfortunately, the brick used for this addition was of soft clay. The cement pointing was not of sufficient consistency, so that the building rapidly deteriorated. By March of 1887, this new addition was already showing cracks. In 1889, it was necessary to brace the new chapel floor which was also beginning to sink. That same year the sisters put up a new laundry building. Five years later, a well was bored for better drinking water. Slowly, and with grim struggle for the means to do it, building went on as the community grew. In 1890, Fr. James Power visited Mother John at the Clyde convent. The founder of the original Conception colony was by now old and worn, though he was to live another nine years. Yet the same zeal burned in his Irish heart. There were that eighty acres of land he still owned near Conception. Would

Mother John undertake to staff and manage it, if he donated this land to the sisters for an industrial school where orphan girls could be educated and taught to support themselves? Out of her own love for the poor, Mother John, harassed as she was with debts and the struggle for growth in her community, could not refuse him.

In July, 1891, the industrial school, called "the orphanage" by the sisters, opened with six of the Clyde community stationed there, Sr. Placida Stephan being the local superior. Mother John herself worked mightily to make things ready. On top of all her other duties, she found time to sew carpet, cook and bake for the orphans. Later, whenever she could spare a minute, she liked to sew little dresses for them. On her frequent trips to Maryville, she would often stop to buy them hats and coats. Regularly Srs. Placida and Joseph Reardon could be seen at Christmas-time going from store to store begging for their orphans.

Troubles with the new chapel continued. One hot August night in 1891, a terrible storm blew up. Lightning struck. Fire seemed to surround the two terrified sisters who knelt before the Blessed Sacrament. It was four in the morning. An enormous hole was torn in the roof; a ball of fire bounced the length of the altar rail, scattered and smeared ash everywhere. Plaster fell around the sisters. To make matters worse, the chapel had been lovingly prepared for the first Mass of Fr. Lukas Etlin, the young monk who taught painting in the community. The chapel was patched up as best they could and by that November, the community-chapter had voted to repair it extensively, even though the insurance covered very little of the damage. They also decided to add new basement rooms at the same time.

Life for the young community was not all struggle and strain. The Daybooks record an easy flow of relationships between the sisters and the monks. If the Conception brothers made wine for the sisters, the latter reciprocated with molasses for the monks. Fr. Abbot would bring his junior monks down to visit the sisters and they could be sure of some home-made ice cream during their stay. There was a monthly visit of the Conception college students to see their sisters or relatives at the Clyde monastery. The sisters liked to go up in groups to see the new Abbey church; the senior sisters making a special pilgrimage there in 1898 in honor of the Swiss saint, Nicholas de Flue. Whenever a visiting prelate appeared at Conception, he was usually brought over to see the sisters. Fr. Ignatius Conrad, long stationed at the cathedral in St. Joseph, Missouri, was elected abbot of Subiaco in Arkansas; he had not forgotten the Clyde sisters and stopped in for a visit early in 1892. When Fr. Pius, another of Abbot Frowin's brothers and a former chaplain of the sisters, became prior at the Abbey, an operetta was put on for him by academy pupils. Fr. Anselm Ineichen was a frequent visitor, dropping in whenever he was in the area to see his sister, Sr. Georgia Ineichen, professed in 1890.

From the time of Mother Anselma, it had been the arrangement that the sisters did the washing and sewing for the monks. As far back as 1881, the Daybook noted with some satisfaction: "The brothers have accepted a candidate such as we have long wished for: he is an experienced tailor and can take care of the fathers' and brothers' trousers and cowls, old and new." The sisters wished him patience and perseverance. In 1890, they were still making shirts for their monastic brothers. It is also recorded that the prior was giving some of the sisters lessons in shorthand. A laconic entry in 1893 notes that the new typewriter was already broken.

Monks were not the sisters' only visitors. Their relatives were frequent guests. It was quite customary for aged parents to spend a week or two with the sisters. Nor was it uncommon for the sisters to spend time in the homes of elderly and ill parents.[11] As the number of students in the academy increased, so did the visitors, to the point where the Daybook once noted piously that many guests were a hindrance to prayer and recollection.

Clyde often offered hospitality to sisters of other communities. Sometimes they came to spend a week or so for their health. At other times, they were there to learn English before setting off again to begin their own communities. Among these were the Franciscan sisters from Switzerland, who later settled in Nevada, Missouri, with Sr. Scholastica accompanying them for the first months until they grew accustomed to American ways. It was to these sisters that the house in Maryville was eventually sold for a hospital in 1894. Another Benedictine sister came from France to stay with the Clyde sisters before going to Oklahoma in hopes of founding a house there. Not all such visitors were welcome, as one Daybook notation makes clear when it speaks of a sister who came from Chicago and ends that they hoped she would not stay long.

Besides relationships and hospitality, there was the joy of simple celebrations of feasts and holidays. On Mother John's nameday tableaux, songs and skits were presented, with the youngest orphan often called on to speak a piece. Once the boarders presented the prioress with a brand new sewing machine. Occasionally they had sleep-in days when the sisters rose as late as an unheard-of seven o'clock. It was traditional for the orphans to wear green ribbons on the feast of St. Patrick and to spend the 4th of July with the sisters. The younger members of the community enjoyed apple-picking or fishing, even when it rained, and Fr. Placidus had to bring them home in his wagon. The older sisters rejoiced in May, 1897, when they were able to make the ordination vestments for James Brady, grandson of the leader of the original Conception colony.

Then there were the community joys. As early as 1884, Fr. Abbot Anselm Villiger had written Mother John from Engelberg that, of all his American daughter-houses, Clyde was dearest to his heart.[12] He

45

sent them twenty-four of his conferences to prove this. On the first anniversary of Mother Anselma's death, word reached the sisters that they might make perpetual vows. Before this, their vows had been simple and annual. In July, 1884, Abbot Frowin had already written Abbot Anselm:

> I am of the same opinion as yourself in regard to perpetual vows for the sisters. Only I think it necessary for this country that no one be admitted who has not proved her fidelity for five years from her first profession . . . I would also agree with a vote of the Councillors in the event of not preferring a secret vote of the whole Chapter as is done in other convents . . . I agree with your other conditions and think in this way the good sisters may be admitted to their perpetual vows for which they have been asking for quite some time . . . We have to ask the bishop's consent here for perpetual vows, as all the sisters' convents are under the supremacy of the bishops . . . In the long run the papal approbation of the Statutes will become indispensable in order to be independent of the bishops. [13]

On the feast of St. Michael the Archangel, September 29, 1884, the Daybook notes happily: "This feast of St. Michael brought an unforgettable celebration. Our chapel was crowded with people who wanted to assist at the first perpetual vows of the twelve sisters and to share their happiness. God, give us the grace to remain faithful in what we have promised until you call us home!" These first twelve sisters were, besides Mother John: Srs. M. Beatrice Renggli, Scholastica von Matt, Gertrude Mayer, Anselmina Jann, Placida Stephan, Philomena Hoheisel, Mechtilde Hilgert, Columba Trainor, Walburga Hartnett, and Hildegard Voelkner. A more personal joy for Mother John was the profession of her own sister as Sr. Innocent in May, 1888. This was the second of her sisters to join her at Clyde, the first having been professed as Sr. M. Agatha in 1882. Both were destined to outlive their older sister by many years as each achieved seventy-one years of religious profession.

For the sisters it was a satisfaction, if not a joy, to begin wearing a black veil with a white lining, similar to that of other Benedictine sisters in America, instead of the Rickenbach veil, which was pulled back at the sides of the face. Having agreed to let the sisters wear this veil, Abbot Frowin was severely jolted when he saw the difference and wrote apologetically to Abbot Anselm: "If you would not want this change, I will try to retract it, though it may not be easy, as they say the sisters like it." [14]

The sisters were also happy when a telephone was installed in April, 1897. Although invented in 1876, this was the first telephone Clyde had known. It would help them to alert others to dangers like that of the tornado in June, 1893, which wrecked the barn and shook the convent till they thought it would wrench apart. Another real help was their first mimeograph machine ordered in October, 1898, to help with the letters for the Association of Perpetual Adoration.

Like St. Paul, Mother John was in journeyings often. Every week and sometimes more than that, she made a trip to nearby Maryville to buy supplies and then had the weary return trip on the evening freight train. Several times a year, she went as the community's buyer into St. Joseph or St. Louis to order large amounts of groceries. As a seamstress, Mother John dealt with agents of the McEvoy Company in New York as well as the Herder Company in St. Louis for laces, church goods, and habit material. The schools where her sisters taught also meant a good deal of traveling for her. In 1885, the community had accepted a school in Clear Creek, Missouri, and one in Boonville, Missouri, where Sr. Beatrice was stationed. Later in 1892, they sent sisters to teach in a small parish school in St. Joseph, Missouri.

Less happy were Mother John's trips with various sisters in search of better health for them and herself. It took more than the mountains of Colorado or the bracing air of Minnesota to obtain this. At Clyde, the sisters were overworked and the food was not always the most nourishing. Unsanitary sewage took its toll, as did raw milk from infected cows. Every winter influenza stalked the area, as did typhoid in the summer. Consumption and tuberculosis were dreaded and frequent visitors. Onion poultices were not effective against smallpox epidemics. Sr. Walburga Hartnett, who had made perpetual vows in August, 1884, died of consumption in June, 1885. Wasted with a long illness, she had nevertheless been able to laugh heartily at the rumor of her death in March. Several young sisters made their final vows on their deathbeds in the years 1889 and 1890. Of the fifteen sisters who died between 1883 and 1890, ten were in their twenties and five were in their thirties. The average life expectancy in America at this time was forty years. No wonder the chronicler could remark sadly after noting several deaths: "Life is really bitter. When will the happy hour of death come for us?"

If there was death, there was life in abundance. One evidence of this was the founding of the first daughter-house in 1887. In one way this was more a stepchild than a daughter-house, since neither Mother John nor Abbot Frowin really wanted it. Both were pressured into making it by the strong-willed Fr. John Eugene Weibel. Because of his increasing missionary activities in Arkansas, he wanted a community of sisters to teach in the territory's schools. After some Dominican sisters had withdrawn, he begged Mother John and Abbot Frowin to let him have some Benedictines. His bishop supported his request, as did a fellow-bishop, John Hogan of the new diocese of St. Joseph, Missouri. They wrung the consent out of Abbot Frowin, against his better judgment, since he knew that the Clyde sisters had all they could do with their own schools. As the Abbot wrote to Switzerland: "Toward the end of this month or the beginning of the next, Sr. Beatrice and Sr. Agnes with two other sisters will leave for Pocahontas, Arkansas, and at the urgent request of Rev. E. Weibel, a former professor at Maria Stein, found a new convent . . . I would sooner send others but we cannot. I did not want to have anything to do with it, but it was thrust upon us. The new foundation remains under Mother John until it can stand on its own feet."[15]

The sisters set out from Clyde on December 11, 1887, and found awaiting them a swampy, malaria-infested spot on which stood a two-room log cabin, with a one and a half storey addition on either side. Their purse contained all of 83 cents. From these unpromising beginnings much was to come and much of it related to the efforts of Mother Beatrice Renggli. High-spirited and intelligent, she now had a field of labor which gave full scope to her talents. In Fr. Weibel, stubborn, domineering and autocratic, she had met her match. A battle of wills between them ended some years later with Mother Beatrice being forced to resign as superior. She accepted this and went on to become a founder of missions and schools and an influential figure in her community until her death in 1942 at the age of ninety-four. With her was Sr. Agnes Dali, another of the pioneer group from Maria Rickenbach. Hers seems to have been a pilgrim vocation up to this time. She had gone from Conception to Mother Gertrude Leupi in Maryville. Mother Gertrude sent her with Sr. Bernardine Wachter to Oregon. Unsatisfied there, she had soon returned. Now she was in Arkansas, where she was to become the third prioress of the community and to die there much respected in 1915.

Abbot Frowin and Mother John wanted to do what they could for this little community, but their resources of personnel and money were severely limited. This left Sr. Beatrice to struggle on her own. Her tendency to independence stood her in good stead, but soon there was friction between herself and Mother John. Different sisters were dispatched from Clyde to Pocahontas and just as quickly returned. Finally, Fr. Weibel took matters into his own hands and had the community in Arkansas affiliated with the Olivetan Benedictines, thus effectively removing them from Mother John's jurisdiction, probably to her considerable relief.

During all this, the life of the spirit was never forgotten or neglected in the Clyde community. Retreats were given annually both in English and German, as well as weekly conferences on the spiritual life, the virtues, and the Benedictine Rule. Women from nearby towns often attended the retreats given for the academy girls. Sr. Gertrude Mayer, Mother John's profession companion, was novice director before becoming assistant to the prioress. Her novitiate instructions were preserved and faithfully copied by the novices. In faded ink and copper-plate handwriting, part of her explanation of the Rule of Benedict can still be read: "The second virtue of the first degree of humility is continual remembrance of the presence of God. The holy Rule says: 'Let her know that God is at all hours looking down upon her from heaven' . . . God is then omnipresent and we can nowhere withdraw from his presence. He beholds us for he is in us ... To preserve the presence of God when at prayer is a great grace, to remember this presence frequently out of prayer is a still greater grace; and to forget it but seldom is an altogether extraordinary grace. What is the consequence of this? ... A nun should ever keep the fear of God before her eyes and take heed lest she should ever forget it. How can we obtain this grace first at prayer? If we conscientiously follow the interior admonitions to acts of mortification and self-denial. How everywhere and continually? If we accumulate treasures of flaming prayers and ejaculations, making use of them everywhere either in the heart or with the mouth."[16]

That Sr. Gertrude or her sources could express themselves vividly is evident in this section copied by Sr. Alphonsa Sapp, who was professed in 1889. Explaining St. Benedict's fourth degree of humility, she wrote: "Remember it, my dears, during your life many hard things will befall you, injuries will meet you; you will not always be treated and judged without passion. In such cases God will pardon you a momentary surprise which does but prove to you that you are yet a pilgrim in the flesh. But I pray you, let that suffice: do not go further! Call then to mind the example of Jesus Christ, remind yourselves of the law of perfection of the fourth degree of humility. This unveils to you your whole future. If you have taken a fine footing on this degree, whatever may befall you will be explicable to you. If you do not reach this degree woe unto you! Every trifle will disconcert you; ambition will raise its serpentine head: the blood will boil in your veins three times quicker: your heart will beat and then what? Sad bursts of passion which even bitter tears cannot repair, expressions by which precious treasures are thrown into the sea ..."[17] However mixed the metaphors, the warning is clear.

Visitations were punctiliously carried out by Abbot Frowin and dealt with the essentials of monastic life: charity, obedience, prayer and silence. It was largely owing to the abbot that the sisters gave up the Exercises of St. Gertrude as their office, replacing it with the Little Office of the Blessed Virgin as the rest of the American Benedictine Sisters did at this time. Abbot Frowin urged them to do this and came down himself several times in January, 1888, to give them lessons in Latin. They prayed this office for the first time on February 1, and Mother John admitted that it went better than she expected. Fr. Gregory Huegle, later to be a well-known expert in Gregorian chant, was already coming to the monastery to instruct the academy pupils in music. When Fr. Lukas Etlin became chaplain in 1892, he was bothered by the way the sisters sang and wanted them to learn the chant. By December, 1892, he had Fr. Gregory practicing with the entire community and from then on the choral chant alone was used. The Visitation admonition for 1892 remarks: "The Divine Office, holy adoration and other spiritual exercises must take first place in your

49

daily obligations ... The praying is to be neither too fast nor too slow, not too high nor too deep."[18]

Through Abbot Frowin, the sisters were kept in touch with the mind of the Church. He was one of the seventy-two prelates attending the Third Plenary Council of Baltimore in 1884. By that time the church in the United States was growing at the rate of nearly two million every ten years, chiefly as a result of immigration. This Council was largely the work of Archbishop James Gibbons and had lasting influence on the building of Catholic schools, establishing diocesan organizations and the preliminary preparation for the Baltimore catechism.

Later in 1893, Abbot Frowin attended the first Congress of Benedictine Abbots called by Pope Leo XIII. The cornerstone of the new College of Sant' Anselmo was laid at this time. The abbots were asked to accept an abbot primate and organize this college. Abbot Frowin took advantage of being in Rome to bring the Statutes of the Clyde community to the authorities for approval. In September, he wrote to Engelberg: "The Statutes with Rome's decision have not yet come. It would be best if they (the sisters) were acknowledged as genuine Benedictines, which is what they themselves, of course, are waiting for."[19] The abbot was relieved when in November of this same year the new bishop of St. Joseph, Missouri, Maurice Burke, gave him full jurisdiction over the sisters. As far back as the fall of 1892, Abbot Frowin wanted the Clyde community to pray the full monastic office, but it was to be some years before this happened. It was his opinion that praying the monastic office would help to identify them more securely as Benedictines in the eyes of the Roman authorities.

Much of the devotional life of the sisters was expressed in the religious idiom of their day. They and their students were enrolled in the League of the Sacred Heart. May and June devotions were a part of life. When Fr. Lukas earnestly asked the sisters to pray for Mother John's health in 1893, he wanted them to offer nine communions and make a novena to our Lady of LaSalette. The poor souls were another favorite devotion. Deceased members of thousands of families were enrolled in the Association of Perpetual Adoration during these years. In October the rosary was honored.

At the heart of their lives, however, giving them meaning, identity and focus was devotion to Jesus in the Blessed Sacrament. The sisters' lives really centered around the tabernacle. Here they prayed by day and night. Here they brought their joys and their problems. Each step they were able to take to enhance this devotion is carefully recorded. In 1889, they could have two sisters instead of just one kneeling in adoration during the day. For the Forty Hours devotion the Blessed Sacrament was exposed, as it was on the three days before Ash Wednesday to make reparation for the excesses of that carnival time. During October there were extra Benedictions. Slowly, they were able to increase the times of exposition. From December, 1895, they were able to have four sisters kneeling before the Blessed Sacrament on Sundays and certain feasts, from High Mass in the morning until Vespers.

Because of this, the sisters felt it a crushing blow when their young chaplain decreed that less frequent communion would make them appreciate the sacrament more. Now the sisters of perpetual vows were allowed to receive only four times a week, the sisters of temporary vows and the novices only twice a week. Long before this Abbot Frowin had advocated less frequent reception. Whether this was due to the prevailing Jansenism of the period, or to the fear that familiarity was breeding some loss of reverence, is not clear. By April, 1894, Fr. Lukas had relented enough to allow Mother John, but only her, to receive communion daily. A pathetic note in the Daybook for October 31, 1894, remarks: "Monday, Tuesday and today no holy communion was received by the sisters. It is a fact to be put in the annals of this community, as this has never happened before in twenty years. It is so very sad and heart-rending. But we have deserved all. May God be appeased by this sacrifice."

The following year Fr. Lukas was sent back to Switzerland for his health. While there, he began to dream of a beautiful chapel worthy of the divine presence, a kind of shrine for the eucharistic Lord. The sisters' present chapel was anything but that. There were cracks in the walls, the plaster was peeling, with large patches falling off. A new chapel, grandiose in style, would marshal all their efforts. By 1898, the first alms for this chapel were on hand and by the following year, the sisters could engage a St. Louis architect. The dream was taking shape.

NOTES

1. Letter of August 7, 1881. In the Engleberg Abbey archives. A microfilm copy of Abbot Frowin's letters to Abbot Anselm is preserved in the Conception Abbey Archives.

2. In *Early Chronicled History: Relationship Between Maryville and Conception,* p. 131.

3. In *Letters from Mother M. Anselma and Others,* December 17, 1883.

4. Ibid., May, 1881.

5. Letter of August 26, 1895. Conception Abbey archives.

6. Daybook, October 19, 1895.

7. Letter of June 24, 1896. Conception Abbey archives.

8. Daybook, June 23, 1897.

9. Letter of June 24, 1888. Conception Abbey archives.

10. *Early Chronicled History: Relationship Between Maryville and Conception,* p. 140.

11. Daybook, September 2, 1898.

12. Ibid., November 7, 1883.

13. *Early Chronicled History: Relationship Between Maryville and Conception,* p. 136.

14. Ibid., p. 138. Letter of November 2, 1884.

15. *Early Chronicled History: Biographical Notes,* p. 166.

16. In the archives of the Benedictine Sisters of Perpetual Adoration, St. Louis.

17. Ibid.

18. From the Visitation admonitions in the archives of the Benedictine Sisters of Perpetual Adoration, St. Louis.

19. Letter of September 29, 1893. Conception Abbey archives.

Chapter Six
1900 – 1910

Fr. Lukas Etlin's influence on the Clyde community as it entered the 20th century was decisive in many areas. Chaplain, confessor, architect, editor, advisor to the sixty-seven sisters who then made up the community, he was everywhere and into everything. Some loved him, most respected him, but there were those sisters who found him autocratic and interfering.

Born in Sarnen, Switzerland in 1864, Alfred Etlin won a scholarship to the college of Engelberg Abbey in 1880, where he developed a marked interest in art and architecture. He had, in fact, something of a struggle to decide between the priesthood and a career in art. Then he heard Abbot Frowin Conrad speak to the student-body on monasticism in far-off America and his decision was made. With Caspar Lussi as companion, Alfred applied for admission to the novitiate at Conception, Missouri. By November 13, 1887, he had completed a year's novitiate and became Frater Lukas.

Fr. Lukas was ordained a priest on August 15, 1891. For a while he continued with the painting of frescoes on the walls of the Abbey church, "drawing and directing all day long," as a confrere put it. Then came the assignment that was to be his life-work: chaplain to the Benedictine Sisters at Clyde. At first he walked the two miles between the two monasteries for the daily Eucharist. However, when he lost his way one day during a blizzard and had to be rubbed with snow to restore his circulation, Mother John insisted that he stay at Clyde from then on.

A perfectionist with disdain for mediocrity, capable of sustained self-discipline and enormous drive, Fr. Lukas was now in his element with full scope for his talents. His love for the Eucharist complemented the community's focus on the Blessed Sacrament. Fr. Lukas was a man of many devotions: the Sacred Heart, the Passion, the Virgin Mary, the poor souls. When he spoke to the sisters about them in homilies and conferences or to the students in instructions, the emotional, vehement side of his nature was evident. Not in vain had he spent time in college dramatics. He could entertain the novices endlessly with tales about ghosts and apparitions.

Fr. Lukas also had a taste for formality and ritual. Many considered him a mystic. He was often found lost in prayer before the tabernacle or a painting of the Blessed Virgin. It was whispered that he took the discipline, and blood stains were certainly found in the room at the printing office where he worked and slept. The rosary was seldom out of his hand. His early years at Engelberg had given him an appreciation of the Gregorian chant. Long before the liturgical movement of the mid-20th century, he was urging the sisters to "pray the Mass." Coupled with this, however, was a hankering for private revelations, like those of Anna Catherine Emmerich, and a too-ready acceptance of apparitions and "privileged souls."

With a broader vision and experience than many of the sisters, who for the most part came from the small towns and farms of rural America, Fr. Lukas set about improving conditions for the growing community. Working with Mother John, he planned the new chapel. He supervised the work on a quadrangle of buildings to replace the older cramped and unsanitary quarters. It was his idea to publish a small magazine which encouraged devotion to the Blessed Sacrament and the poor souls. It was his designs that the sisters used for skilled embroidery on altar linens and vestments. With the farm, too, he was helpful. Sr. Patricia Kelly remembered him accompanying her father to buy stock for the community, insisting on only the best for the sisters.

Fr. Lukas was very much a man of his time. In his position it is easy to see why paternalism was a constant temptation for him although it was resisted by the more independent spirits in the community. Strong-willed himself, Fr. Lukas gave the impression that salvation was a matter of the will, that the harder you were on yourself and others, the holier you were. Many felt that he played favorites, while others smarted at the public humiliations he sometimes inflicted for mistakes in choir. Even Mother John had to put her foot down occasionally at his interventions in community affairs. There were those who resented his curtailment of the easy relationship between the monks and the sisters. The sisters laughed in secret when it was discovered that in his plans for the entire south wing, he had not allowed for any bathrooms on three floors. Monastic life might be compared to the angelic life, they said, but this was carrying things too far. Some of the sisters cried when suddenly he ordered all the bright geraniums near the printing office to be uprooted, lest the sisters grow too fond of them and be "unmortified" in this attachment.

With Fr. Lukas, Mother John made countless trips to St. Louis, to Council Bluffs and to Kansas City for the new chapel buying crushed rock and dressed stone, brick and lumber, hiring stone dressers and other laborers. Later the altar, the carvings and mosaics were ordered from Europe from the artisans of Munich and Innsbruck. Throughout the first years, carloads of rock arrived, one on the heels of another. So frequent were the brick and lumber shipments that Mother John decided to ask the railroad officials for reduced rates. When heavy rains fell in the fall of 1900, filling the newly-dug foundations with water, she worked with the sisters far into the nights dipping it out. When shipments of rock arrived muddied, the sisters labored in shifts around the clock washing the rock in large sieves made of extra-strong wire. Filling these half-full, they dashed them up and down, up and down in low water-tanks until their arms ached and their shoulders wrenched with the effort.

While the foundations were being dug, Fr. Lukas worked with the men. He worked a little too closely at one point when the quick swing of an axe left him with a toe injury he would feel for the rest of his life. Another time he fell sixteen feet from some scaffolding, rupturing blood vessels and injuring his ankle. He did take time to offer Mass and pray his breviary, but that was all. The rest of the day he was on the site with the men. By May 1901 Abbot Frowin was able to lay the cornerstone of the new chapel. Work continued after this with eleven laborers and four stone-dressers, who were paid $10.00 a week.

In August the pearly green granite pillars from Aberdeen, Scotland, had been set up. Already a steady stream of visitors came to marvel at the progress. By the summer of 1904 the sisters were able to move into the chapel, using the altar and other furnishings from the old one. In the spring of 1907 cases of mosaics arrived from Innsbruck, and by May the workmen, also from Austria, had set them up in all their glowing colors. Scenes from the life of the Virgin Mary decorated the clerestory walls, the crucifixion and the Last Supper, the sanctuary walls. In the apse a mosaic of Christ the high priest was one of the largest mosaics in the country at this time. Later, when the golden oak stalls lined the narrow nave, while the stained glass windows of the apostles diffused the sunlight, more than one visitor was to gasp in amazement. Who would have expected something that reminded them of the cathedral of Ravenna in the Missouri cornfields?

Early in 1908 the statues of six Benedictine saints arrived, seeming "almost ready to speak," as the Daybook noted. In 1909 Mother John paid the first thousand dollars on the new pipe organ. Fr. Gregory Huegle came to help install it and to give several sisters organ lessons. "May the Holy Spirit teach them so that they soon can play," was the cautious notation in the Daybook. The choir stalls were in place by January 1910. No wonder Abbot Frowin could write to Engelberg that the sisters had the most beautiful chapel in all the countryside.

The Blessed Sacrament was exposed on the high altar for the first time on Fr. Lukas' nameday in 1911 and by November 15th of that year all was ready for consecration. Abbot Frowin was the consecrator in a marathon ceremony which lasted from seven in the morning until noon. Most of the priests and fraters from Conception assisted in different capacities. The sisters sang under Fr. Gregory's careful direction. Bishop Maurice Burke of St. Joseph, Missouri solemnly exposed the Blessed Sacrament with Benediction after the pontifical high mass. While in Rome in 1909, the bishop had received from Pope Pius X permission for the sisters to have the Blessed Sacrament exposed daily from after mass until six in the evening, and all night on Thursdays, together with permission for Benediction twice daily at the time of exposition and reposition.

At the turn of the century the community was in debt. Building the chapel added considerably to this debt. They needed money. The Association of Perpetual Adoration was one source of funds. Begun in Mother Anselma's time, it continued in a modest way. The sisters checked the newspapers and obituary columns for names and addresses. To such people they sent a letter telling them about the Association of prayer. These letters were written by hand and run off on a mimeograph. They addressed the envelopes by hand as well. One such letter dated February 23, 1901 reads in part: "Your favor and $3.00 enclosed was received in due time and with many thanks. We are unable to repay you but our dear Lord himself will do so for us. He will repay your charity a hundredfold already in this life and still more in the world to come ... We also thank you heartily for the addresses you so kindly sent us and will be ever so grateful if at any time you can solicit a few members for us ... We are still lacking much of the money needed to pay for our new chapel."[1]

By 1902 the sisters were asking for donations in a small pamphlet of about sixteen pages which contained articles about the Blessed Sacrament and the poor souls. In April 1901 they purchased a small press just large enough to print two pages at a time. This was worked by a foot pedal. They also bought three hundred pounds of type, but could not afford to hire a printer to show them how to do the work. No sister knew how to set up even a line of type. One of the Conception monks came to the rescue: Fr. Jerome Veth had worked in a printshop during his college days. He came over daily to teach the sisters how to set type, how to make it secure, how to form a page. Since the community could not afford any more type, when they ran out of title type, the sisters, after printing two pages had to pick out the title type in order to print the next two, and so on. For many years the sisters did all the folding and addressing by hand, as they did not have the money to buy a folder or addressograph. Fr. Lukas would often lend a hand with this work. By August 1903 they could afford to buy another press that would print eight pages and a little gasoline engine to run it. They used this until 1917 when electricity was installed in the print shop and the rest of the monastery. Sr. Innocent Schrader, one of Mother John's sisters, was in charge of operations and was able to buy equipment piece by piece. The first devotional leaflet they printed was titled, "Offering to the Sacred Heart."

When the community bought the large Miehle press which could print a sheet of sixteen pages, the workmen who set it up also taught the sisters how to run it and to make up the forms. The folding they had to learn for themselves by ripping apart a catalogue whose pages had not been cut. Thus they discovered how the large sheet had to be folded and the type set so that each page followed in correct sequence. Mother John took Sr. Innocent to Techny, Illinois where the Society of the Divine Word had a printshop. They stayed two weeks, although Sr. Innocent later said that while the Fathers were good to them, they were mighty sparing in any useful information. All she learned was how to feed the large press. It was the Franciscans in Quincy, Illinois, who gave her real help and told her about the advantages of an addressograph.

In May 1905 the title *Tabernacle and Purgatory* was first used for their magazine. This was Fr. Lukas' choice as editor-in-chief. "These pages," he wrote, "should increase esteem for Holy Mass, encourage a frequent and worthy reception of holy communion and awaken and strengthen a lively faith in the real presence of our Lord in the Holy Eucharist ... Our readers shall frequently be reminded of the greatness and severity of the suffering of the poor souls and how they may be relieved by prayers." The magazine now had thirty-two pages and a subscription price of 50 cents a year. The first year there were four issues. In 1906 six issues were printed, and by 1908 the magazine came out every two months, one edition in English and another in German. It was 1920 when *Tabernacle and Purgatory* became a monthly at $1.00 per year.

At first, the printshop was housed in a frame building that had been used for guest accommodations. In 1907 a two-storey brick building was constructed. The printshop itself with its machines and paper-warehouse was on the first floor. The second floor was used for the correspondence and record-keeping connected with subscriptions and the Association of Perpetual Adoration. Another room became the book-bindery, since in 1906, Brother Conrad of Conception Abbey had started giving weekly instructions on bookbinding to several sisters.

From the beginning a spirit of camaraderie developed among the sister-printers. They worked together and when Fr. Lukas was not looking, they played as well. Sr. Innocent had an infectious gaiety which neither hard work, long hours or the troubles of a small printshop could extinguish. Together the sisters gathered around a small statue of the Infant Jesus of Prague for their devotions. Together they took time off either to help the sisters at the orphanage or go out to the woods for berrypicking. They were also involved in all that went on in the community as the printers' diary for 1907 reveals. "20 reams of paper came from Paper Mills. Tramp got into our furnace.

57

Rev. Fr. Lukas, P. Orendorf and Theodore arrested him, or meant to, but didn't succeed," says the notation for November 14 of that year. December 23 reads: "Had oceans of trouble, stitcher would not work. Stitched 4,000 pamphlets notwithstanding trouble." An entry for Sept. 29, 1911 has: "Setting addresses, cleaning machine, picking apples."

By 1912, the sisters were printing booklets as well as the magazine. Among their titles were: *Devotion to the Precious Blood, Communicate Frequently and Devoutly, The Magnificence of the Love of God,* and *Assist the Souls in Purgatory.* These booklets were in German as well as English. Together with numerous devotional leaflets, they helped to meet the needs of the Catholics of the time. Simply written, they appealed to the heart and the emotions rather than the mind, and were strong in the conviction that the troubles of this world were to be endured because of the consolation of the world to come.

Believing in what they were doing, conscious of a mission in what would later be called the "apostolate of the Catholic press," the sisters set out to solicit subscriptions for their magazine and members for the Association. As early as December 1900 two sisters were canvassing North Dakota for this purpose. The following year Srs. Bernard Willmann and Monica Schnitzer were in Milwaukee. Srs. Teresa Willier and Bonaventure Eikelmann won permission from Archbishop Quigley of Chicago to solicit in his archdiocese in 1905. In 1906 Srs. Bernard and Teresa returned from St. Louis with more subscribers. By now the subscription list of *Tabernacle and Purgatory* had reached 20,000.

Although she had delicate health, Sr. Gertrude Mayer traveled through Minnesota with Sr. Frowina Haehnlein in 1906, while the tiny, spirited Sr. Teresa went to Quincy, Illinois. Sr. Bonaventure and the indefatigable Sr. Bernard spent three months in Iowa in the fall of 1909 and were able to send home $3,000.00. It was in Iowa that Sr. Bernard had an accident that left her with a crushed arm when a runaway team of horses collided with the buggy she was driving. By July of the next year, despite the accident, she and another sister were in LaCrosse, Wisconsin, where the heat of the summer made their work very difficult, wrapped as they were in serge habits from neck to ankle. In 1913 Sr. Bernard took Sr. Cherubim Bremm with her to Michigan. The following year Sr. Anselma Joy traveled with Sr. Martina Born through Indiana. Away from their sisters and their monastery for months at a time, wilting in the summer heat, shivering in the winter cold, it is to be doubted that the sisters appreciated the notation in the Daybook on the return of Srs. Bernard and Teresa from a six-month collecting tour: "May God give them the grace to forget the world."

There were fringe benefits from such tours, besides the money collected. The sisters were becoming known in at least nine surrounding states and farther than that through their publications. It was in no small measure due to them that more and more postulants began applying to the Clyde community. Those years saw groups of seven, nine and eleven candidates being accepted.

Another, if smaller, source of income for the community was the vestment making. Mother John still supervised and sometimes worked at this herself. She sold a banner for $100.00 early in 1900. The following year, she was in St. Louis arranging for a display of the sisters' embroidered vestments and altar linens. An order of $300.00 worth from Washington in 1908 was very satisfying. More homely sewing, such as that for the orphans and mending for the monks continued. One notation remarks that someone tried to give them $3.00 for a shroud, "but we never charge for shrouds."

The schools, too, brought in a regular income. The academy at the monastery itself usually had between thirty and forty-five boarders and fifteen day students. Abbot Frowin used to come over to conduct the exams in catechism and Bible history. "He likes to question them himself," says the Daybook in 1906. Fr. Patrick Cummins, newly back from Rome with his degree in theology, came to instruct the teachers and Fr. Gregory continued to give music lessons. Sr. Maura Peak re-opened the Wild Cat school in September, 1913, while Sr. Pancratia (Agnes Josephine) Grosspitch was at Conception, Sr. Salome Eikelmann at the orphanage and another sister and novice at Clyde.[2] In 1911 Sr. Maura's silver jubilee of monastic profession was a real celebration. She had taught for eighteen years at the Wild Cat school, so that crowds of pupils, former pupils and parents attended the jubilee Mass in the new chapel of the Clyde monastery. Regularly each year the sisters went to Maryville to take the teachers' exams. By 1916 a lady was coming to give the sisters lessons in how to teach "physical culture, elocution and phonetics." In the late fall of 1917 the assistant superintendent of schools for the state came from Jefferson City, Missouri to inspect the academy as the sisters wanted accreditation for their school.

Another work that was to be important for the community was altar bread making. Early in 1910 Sr. Ursula Semon went to the Franciscan Sisters at Hartwell, Ohio to learn how to make these communion wafers. Many of the Clyde sisters had been in St. Margaret's Hospital in Kansas City which was run by these Franciscans. When they decided to give up making altar breads, they offered to assist the Clyde sisters in setting up a department to continue this work. Sr. Ursula learned about mixing the dough of flour and water, baking and cutting the breads and how to pack them in boxes. Back at Clyde, she set about the work. First a gasoline stove had to be ordered, along with a double cutter for large and small hosts, then a dampener. These were installed in the second storey of the building used for guests. The kindly Franciscan sisters transferred all their patrons to Clyde. Hansen of the Church Goods Company in Chicago asked the community at Clyde to furnish the breads he needed for weekly distribution. Hansen had learned of the Clyde altar breads through a Jesuit retreat-master who had used them while with the community. Clyde was to supply these altar breads for many years. By the end of 1915 more equipment and more sisters were needed as this work flourished and went on to become one of the community's main sources of income.

From its earliest days a small farm had supplied some food for the sisters, as an orchard supplied fruit. It was hard to find good workmen and the sisters were often called on to help with the hay or to butcher hogs. In the late summer, they were busy drying corn or putting up preserves like the thrifty housewives of the area. In the early winter of 1901 Mother John had to order a half a train carload of potatoes from Iowa. Later the workmen were occupied in hauling and packing ice. June of 1901 was very warm: hot winds were destroying everything in their path, while the leaves withered on the trees. In the fall Mother John was again on the road looking for good farmhands to hire, besides buying a carload of potatoes, cabbages and carrots for her growing community. In December they were able to sell "eight fat hogs" at 85 cents per hundredweight, and buy a load of flour at $1.85 per 100 pounds. Hay at this time was selling for $10.00 a ton and corn for 35 cents a bushel. By 1903 the sisters had to pay their workmen $20.00 a month. Mother John borrowed a thousand dollars from her brother to help meet some of the bills. "Everything is so dear!" lamented the Daybook.

In 1904 the sisters were able to sell the last of their property at Conception. Then in April 1905 the community Chapter decided to buy the Merrigan farm of some 120 acres so they could have a private road between the monastery and the orphanage. July that year brought in a good hay crop, which meant they had to enlarge their barn. The following year they were buying more pasture land, but they bewailed the loss of three work horses and two colts because the unfortunate animals had eaten poisonous weeds. In the fall of 1908 the sisters put up 500 lbs. of grapes, setting aside some for altar wine. Often the early spring brought worry about the orchard as a late and heavy frost sent the sisters hurrying to make smoke fires from two until four in the morning in an effort to save the apples.

Along with all this went an almost continuous building program. No wonder that Sr. Euphrasia Sanchez in her old age could remember Mother John being "in black despair" over all the bills. In 1901 and 1902 they had built a granary for "rye, millet and clover-seed," besides a new chicken house. It was in December 1901 that the community voted to build the new east wing of the proposed quadrangle designed by Fr. Lukas. The academy building was not in good condition, with the sisters overcrowded in this old structure which had been completed in 1882. Mother John made so many trips at this time for building needs that she managed to get a special pass from the railroad.

May and June of 1902 brought terrible rains to Missouri, washing out many roads; yet five cars of lumber for the new wing sat on the track. Undaunted, the sisters devised a plan. Each workman and his team of horses was given two wagons. When he got to the monastery with his load, he unhitched from the full wagon and rehitched to the empty one. Meanwhile the sisters did the unloading. They also set about washing the muddied bricks, besides pulling nails out of the lumber casings so part of the same wood could be used over and over again. On July 24, 1904 the last bricks of the new wing were set in place. There were no elevators, so the stronger sisters carried the heavier loads up the wide, long stairways to the new wing. Moving the kitchen range took longer and required the men. The range had to be carried a few hundred feet in the open to the main door to the kitchen. Clouds blew up suddenly baptizing both range and men with rain. This necessitated a change of menu for some one hundred hungry people. Moving the furniture did not take long as there was very little; chairs used at table doubled in bedrooms and workrooms.

In 1906 a new horse barn was completed, along with a narrow railway track running from the house to the coal-shed and the barns. By 1908 the sisters needed a new place for an infirmary, since there was much sickness in the community. Tuberculosis, as well as consumption were still dreaded scourges. The small frame building formerly used for guests and then for the workmen was enlarged and improved. A porch now ran along the south side for the benefit of those who had been advised to sleep outdoors in the summer. Some sisters needed more serious treatment in the Maryville hospital. One of these was Sr. Thecla Haas. When she lay dying of cancer, Mother John raced, literally, to her bedside. The roads were so bad that the prioress galloped on horseback to catch the train.

In 1903 the Clyde community numbered sixty-five sisters, five novices and five postulants. In the early 1900s large groups of candidates were entering. One pastor from Nebraska sent eight young women to the community. Eight Oblate sisters also belonged to the monastery. These Oblates were sisters whose emotional or mental stability was not considered sufficient for full participation in community life. Instead they followed a modified prayer schedule and did a great deal of manual work. The Oblates had their own director and made promises rather than vows.

By May 1907 Mother John had been prioress for twenty-four years. The following February she was re-elected for the ninth time. Abbot Frowin presided at the election as usual and was satisfied with the outcome. Writing to Engelberg Abbey some years later about another re-election, he said: "The abbess is the mother of her sisters, as the abbot is the father, and it does not become the children to displace

61

their mother."[3] It was not only the abbot who came regularly to the sisters' monastery. The other monks and students were frequent visitors. They were not alone. As the harassed portress remarked at one point: "We have a house full of guests. It seems as soon as one goes, another arrives!" Mother John's own mother, Mrs. Schrader, boarded with the sisters from 1901 until her death. Sr. John Berchmans Massing's father sold all his property and came to live at the monastery, working for the sisters. Sr. Ursula Semon's orphaned nephew made his home with them while going to school. When Sr. Dolorosa Mergen's brother was ordained in 1902, eighteen relatives came to stay at Clyde for the ordination. Fr. Lukas' sister from Germany came for a visit and remained for four years, helping with various works. A special visitor in July 1906 was Mother Beatrice Renggli. With her was Sr. Agnes Dali, who marveled that it had been thirty-two years since their arrival in America.

In the summers of 1905 and 1906 the community was host to groups of sisters who were there to study chant. As early as August 1903 Abbot Frowin had written to Engelberg: "About thirty sisters from other communities took part in the choral instructions Fr. Gregory gave at the sisters' convent here. At present he has such a course for the sisters at O'Fallon and another one next week in Cincinnati. These teaching sisters are supposed to introduce their children to Gregorian chant."[4] The sisters arrived from eight states, among them Dominicans, Franciscans, Sisters of Mercy, Precious Blood Sisters, Mother Seton's Sisters and, of course, the Benedictines. The *Motu Proprio* of Pope Pius X on sacred music was the inspiration for this course. "As the Church differs in its architecture from all other buildings; as the priest wears vestments peculiarly his own when celebrating the sacred mysteries; as the pulpit has a language of its own so also must Church music differ from everyday music," said Fr. Gregory, so "let the opera stay where it belongs; let concert pieces and marches, arias, solos, duos, etc., be relegated to their proper domain." He advocated attendance at the daily High Mass and Vespers of the Clyde sisters where the music was strictly Gregorian and "rendered in a manner that showed correct interpretation and classical taste."[5]

The first decade of the century brought three invitations for the Clyde community to found other houses. The first came from Fr. Alfred Mayer, a monk of St. John's Abbey in Collegeville, Minnesota and brother of Sr. Alfred Mayer. He asked the community to come with him to start a foundation in Canada. This was politely refused. A second invitation came from an older couple from Bavaria now living in California not far from Santa Rosa. The Schmidts had no children and offered to donate their 100 acre estate of fertile vineyards to the Clyde sisters. Fr. Lukas with Mother John's assistant, Sr. Gertrude Mayer and the sub-prioress, Sr. Cecilia Schildknecht, set off by train to inspect this offer. Fr. Lukas wrote back enthusiastically that it was a beautiful property situated on the Russian River with a secluded section ringed with California oaks that would be just right for the sisters. He told Abbot Frowin that the grapes were pressed and the barrels filled by steam. There were three large wine cellars, capable of holding between two and three hundred thousand gallons of the best red wine made in California. Besides this, there were thirty head of cattle, fifteen horses and half dozen milch cows. Unfortunately, the bishop of the diocese pulled the ground from beneath their feet, as Fr. Lukas expressed it, by refusing his consent to the transaction.

An invitation from a settlement of Swiss and German families in and around Frances, Washington, given through Abbot Frowin, could not be denied. Sr. Scholastica von Matt was sent out to explore the situation in 1907. She was delighted with what she saw and immediately started a catechism class to prepare the children of the parish for their first communion. In January 1908 Srs. Teresa Willier, Ignatia Williams and Antoinette Kreikemeier left Clyde to travel west via the Burlington and Northern Pacific lines. They, too, liked what they saw even though there was some trouble with the pastor. Despite this, they stayed on and others were sent to join them. However, Mother John decided she needed the sisters at home. Sr. Scholastica was heartbroken. In a letter to Abbot Frowin she had written: "In case one of your fathers should need some relaxation on account of health or a change of climate, just send him here, where there is a climate like that of Switzerland, with forests of fir and cedar trees all around. It is a good tonic for the nerves."[6] In another letter she pleaded: "Reverend Mother was looking for a place where sickly sisters might improve. When asked if this was a healthy climate, one of the oldest settlers replied: 'Yes! You have to beat people around here to death, otherwise, they won't die.' Many live to be in their nineties."[7] But Mother John influenced, Sr. Scholastica suspected, by Fr. Lukas was adamant. Always enterprising, Sr. Scholastica next wrote to the Apostolic Delegate. This scandalized the chronicler, who noted in the Daybook on September 26, 1908: "It really seems impossible for Sr. Scholastica to do as she is doing!" It was all in vain. The sisters were told to return to Clyde or be prepared to separate themselves from the motherhouse. By June of 1909, they were back in Missouri, the school in Washington having been taken over by the Benedictine sisters of Cottonwood, Idaho.

NOTES

1. In the archives of the Benedictine Sisters of Perpetual Adoration, St. Louis.

2. After Vatican II the sisters were free to return to their own names if they chose. When this occurred, the later name will be given in parentheses.

3. Letter of January 9, 1914 in the Conception Abbey archives.

4. Letter of August 24, 1903 in the Conception Abbey archives.

5. In the archives of the Benedictine Sisters of Perpetual Adoration, St. Louis.

6. Letter of December 26, 1907 in the Conception Abbey archives.
7. Letter of April 4, 1908 in Conception Abbey archives.

Chapter Seven
1910–1920

The 4th of July, 1910 found the entire Clyde community gathered in a shady grove of trees, enjoying ice cream and a keg of beer. It was a record hot day, which afterwards sent some of the workmen to the pond to cool off with a little fishing. They caught enough for supper for the whole group. Later in the year some of the workmen went rabbit hunting and supplied a meal for the sisters on a feast day. November 11 was Mother John's 56th birthday. She spent it at the old Clever farm with a number of the sisters and Fr. Lukas cleaning the barn and the yards. A highlight of 1910 was the visit of the first Abbot Primate of the Benedictine order, Hildebrand de Hemptinne, O.S.B. He arrived on November 22 and offered the community High Mass. Then he spoke to the assembled community "with many a kind word for us and allowed us to kiss his ring." The chronicler apparently felt they had had enough celebration, for her notation on Christmas day says only: "No guests, thank God!"

February 10, 1911 was the silver jubilee of profession of Srs. Teresa Willier, Ignatia Williams and Bernard Willman. The community owed a good deal to this trio of W's. Sr. Teresa had done years of soliciting for the magazine. Sr. Bernard had been constantly on the road also, and later was to enter on a second career of recruiting postulants in Germany after the first World War. At a time when it was frowned upon, Srs. Teresa and Ignatia managed to be very good friends and to remain so until the day they died.

June and July of 1911 brought another siege of record heat. On June 30, 1911 the Daybook remarks: "It is so hot the sisters are sleeping on the porch, the apples are baking on the trees and the grass is as dry as chips." It was 105 degrees in the shade that July 4th. This contributed discomfort to Mother John's poor health. In and out of bed most of July, she finally went to the doctor, who sent her to some mineral springs in Arkansas. "Poor Mother, if one part gets better, another part gets worse," noted the chronicler sympathetically. She also noted Sr. Scholastica's trouble with her teeth: "They do not fit."

Visitors were coming in increasing numbers to see the chapel. Three hundred students from the teachers' training school in Maryville arrived on July 13th in 1911. Of more interest to the community was the entrance of nine postulants that fall. More exciting for some was their first automobile ride with the parents of one of the sisters, who drove them to Conception Abbey for Vespers. It was 1916 before the sisters had a car of their own. Sr. Dolorosa Mergen's family made her a gift of one and Sr. Innocent was the first to learn how to drive. Mother John was undoubtedly glad of this for she had had a serious accident with the buggy in 1913. Coming home from the orphanage with Fr. Lukas, one of the wheels broke throwing Mother John and Fr. Lukas from the buggy. Mother John lay unconscious for some time. Fr. Lukas had a twisted leg and a sprained ankle. When she came to, Mother John with a bruised and bloody face, managed to walk to the house to get help. She broke her shoulder in this fall and Fr. Lukas was on crutches for some time. On August 8, 1916 the chronicler noted with awe that their car then registered 96 miles. They had had it since June. She also mentioned that relatives of Sr. Angela Bueche drove all the way from Phoenix, Arizona to Clyde in a Ford.

The years 1912 and 1913 continued to bring a good number of postulants to the community. According to the Daybook for October 5, 1912 a Mr. Brockman arrived from Europe with a postulant for them, but "lost her in New York." She subsequently turned up at her sister's home in Iowa. Learning from this, the community sent Sr. Teresa to meet the five postulants who were arriving in New York from Europe on October 10 of that same year. They now had twelve postulants. On January 18, 1913 six sisters made their final vows, eight professed their first vows and seven novices were invested with the monastic habit. After the ceremony a group of them went happily into Maryville to have their pictures taken. This, the chronicler noted cautiously, had been paid for by their relatives. Those years also brought deaths. Too many of the sisters were dying very young. Of the seven who died between the years 1912 and 1919, five were in their twenties. Sr. Leocadia Merscher was 26; her mother had stayed with her in the community's infirmary all during her final illness.

June 1913 brought some distinguished visitors to the community: Archbishop John Glennon of St. Louis, Bishop Thomas Lillis of Kansas City and their own Abbot Frowin Conrad. November 2nd that year was the abbot's 80th birthday. Three years later he walked two miles from the Abbey to Clyde, offered Mass for the sisters, had breakfast and walked back. Early in 1917 a young priest from Omaha came to look at the building going on at Clyde. He had started a home for derelict men in 1914, but was now convinced that these men had to be reached much earlier. This was Fr. Edward Flanagan, founder of Boys Town.

Because of the building programs and the needs of the academy, there was always coming and going at Clyde. Fr. Joachim came regularly to give violin lessons to Sr. Luca Bielman and Novice Edith Kraus. He also taught flute to Sr. Angela Bueche. Sr. Henrietta Kaiser went to the Sisters of Charity at Leavenworth, Kansas for painting lessons. Srs. Agatha Schrader and Humilitas Parzinger went to St. Louis to learn all they could about washers and boilers.

January 24, 1914 was an important day for the community. Eight novices made their first vows: among them was Sr. Carmelita Quinn who was destined to be the second prioress general of the Clyde congregation. Of the five postulants who were invested with the habit on that same day, Novice Edith Kraus was to be a much loved figure in the community, while the nursing career of Novice Therese Marie Kelly was to span six decades. By 1915 there were eighty-four sisters of perpetual vows in the community and forty with temporary vows. It was that September that the fringed cloth belt began to be worn by those in final vows, distinguishing them from those of temporary profession, who wore a leather belt.

The farm continued to flourish during these years. In June 1910 they were able to buy a "fine" horse for $200.00 and in September to purchase the old Clever farm to add to the Reardon farm bought in July. By October Mother John and Sr. Joseph Reardon, the farm manager, were out buying cattle. The next January they were able to purchase three head of Holstein for $450.00. By April of 1918 their herd had grown to the point where they were selling a carload of stock for $1300.00.

In June, 1911 peaches were selling for $1.65 a bushel. The sisters were busy planting potatoes and picking strawberries. In August they canned apples and corn. That fall their orchard yielded a thousand bushels of apples, which they sold at $1.00 a bushel, saving a bushel for Bishop Burke in St. Joseph, Missouri. According to the chronicler, they had seven hundred little chicks in May, 1912. It was the following year that St. Clementine Kaemmerling was put in charge of the chicken farm, after taking a course in poultry-keeping. A legendary figure in the community, Sr. Clementine was to relate in her older years that at this time she could shoot twenty-four sparrows in an hour with her trusty BB gun, and out of seven shots could get six rabbits. Her working day often lasted eighteen hours. Born in Wisconsin and a lover of the outdoors all her long life, nature had no secrets from her. She knew every bird in the region: where the loons nested and the night owls' favorite haunts. At 79 she was to lament: "It's just too bad I had to get old so quick!"

The sisters were busy setting out six hundred evergreens in the spring of 1913 as part of Fr. Lukas' plan of landscaping the grounds. In

November they planted seven hundred more seedlings. The following year it was catalpa trees they were setting out along the road leading to the chicken yard. The summer of 1915 brought rains so continuous that the men could not get the machines into the fields to cut the wheat, so that scythes had to be used. Two years later it was increasingly difficult to hire men at all, which meant the sisters had to help finish threshing 2,570 bushels of oats, 118 bushels of wheat and 9 bushels of rye. In February, 1918 Mother John was buying a carload of hay for $25.00 a ton.

The building program continued unabated all during this period. In August, 1911 even the orphans were called on to help the sisters move piles of bricks so the men could begin leveling the ground for the foundation of the new south wing. That September the vegetable caves were finished and soon filled with potatoes, as well as row on row of canned fruit and preserves. By December cars of brick and rock were arriving at Clyde again for the planned second wing of the quadrangle. The following May there were so many train carloads of materiel arriving that the railway company offered to put in a side track to Clyde, provided the monastery workmen would grade it. When the carpenters completed their work in August, 1913, the sisters moved in with paint and varnish. In the spring of 1914 the foundations were laid for the north wing of the quadrangle, called the "tower" building. In 1915 the sisters needed a new laundry at the orphanage. Then it was time for a new cow barn. New wells were also a necessity to relieve the chronic shortage of water. Anyone who has dealt with the maintenance of large facilities will appreciate the exasperated note of the chronicler early in January: "Plumbers here to fix the toilets. They are ALL leaking."

Much more serious than such leaks was the explosion on January 31, 1917. While the sisters were in chapel about 2 p.m., the gas plant exploded with terrific force. The brick plant itself was blown to pieces. All the windows on the north and east side of the monastery were shattered, the glass driven into doors and woodwork on the opposite side. In all, four hundred large windows were broken and many doors wrenched from their hinges. Neighbors came to help, but it was 10 p.m. before everything was boarded up in some makeshift way. To make matters worse, the weather turned extremely cold, the thermometer registering 23 degrees below zero that night and the next. Only candles and a few lanterns supplied light; pipes in different parts of the building began to freeze — and guests began to arrive for the profession ceremony on February 3rd. It was to take the carpenters a full month to repair all the doors, windows and roof.

Mother John and Fr. Lukas had not given up the search for a healthful climate in which the Clyde community might make a foundation. In November, 1912 they had gone to Santa Fe, New Mexico to look at some property they were offered. The warmer, dry air might just be what was needed for sisters threatened with consumption and tuberculosis. When this was not satisfactory, they looked at a farm in Coeur d'Alene in Idaho. Still not satisfied, Mother John and her companion went on to Spokane, Washington. Here they took time out for a forty-minute sleigh ride, according to Sr. Gertrude Mayer's letter home. By the time they returned to Clyde in February, 1914, Mother John and Fr. Lukas had decided to buy a property of some 496 acres near Chewelah, Washington. Lying one and a quarter miles from the town, the property had 200 acres in cultivation with the rest in timber, and a spring to furnish water.

That August Sr. Cecilia Schildknecht, the sub prioress of the Clyde community, led a group of five sisters to Chewelah to help them begin this foundation. They discovered little there: a frame building or two, no beds or tables. To get to church meant a walk of two miles; still they all fell in love with the place. When the recently appointed Bishop Schinner of Spokane came for a visit, he was very kind, perhaps influenced by a letter from Bishop Burke of St. Joseph which said in part: "I beg to congratulate you in getting such a good community into your new diocese. The Benedictine Sisters of Clyde are a splendid community of religious women and will be a great acquisition to any diocese ... They go, therefore, to you with my highest recommendation."[1] Bishop Schinner gave the sisters permission to keep the Blessed Sacrament in the house and to have a Benedictine chaplain as soon as Abbot Frowin could supply one. As early as that September, the sisters were busy in the orchard, and by January, 1915 they did have a chaplain from Conception Abbey, none other than Fr. Pius Conrad, who had been Clyde's first chaplain. Mother John borrowed money to buy more property in Chewelah and sent four more sisters in March, appointing Sr. Cecilia as local superior. In August, 1915 Fr. Lukas arrived to supervise some building. As usual, according to the chronicle, he could not resist intervening in community affairs, appointing Sr. Placida Stephan as superior, causing Mother John great concern.

Abbot Frowin came in September to dedicate the little chapel. This foundation was called "St. Mary of the Pines." The first to arrive seeking better health was Sr. Gertrude Mayer, Mother John's profession companion. Some livelier arrivals preceded her: a traincar of heifers, hogs and sheep shipped to Chewelah from Clyde. By 1916 the sisters were able to have exposition of the Blessed Sacrament each morning. Mother John visited them in the fall of 1917 and returned well satisfied, assured that the sisters there were happy and content. She sent them four additional sisters, so that by July, 1918 there were nineteen sisters at St. Mary of the Pines.

On Good Friday, April 6, 1917 the United States entered the first World War. This very soon began to affect all aspects of life at Clyde. It dimmed the celebration of Mother John's 40th anniversary of profession that May, as well as the first golden jubilee celebration the community had ever had: that of Sr. Scholastica von Matt, who was now the sub-prioress. Prices began to rise steeply. According to the chronicle for March 25, 1918: "Linen has been raised from $1.95 to $4.00 per yard. Serge for our habits from $1.65 to $3.64, sheeting from 17 cents to 55 cents a yd.... Flour is now $12.00 a barrel. The food inspector was here and we were obliged to give up some of our flour and sugar. We are only allowed to buy enough to last for sixty days and we have to use an equal quantity of corn, rice, etc. with the wheat flour." In October some "soldier-boys" home on leave visited at the monastery.

The added stress brought on a bad case of shingles for Mother John, besides her heart trouble and diabetes. Fr. Lukas' nerves gave way and he had to take time off to recuperate. Still there were joys: among them the profession of six novices, one of whom was Sr. Cornelia St. Cin, who was to endear herself to generations of the community. At this time the sisters were buying liberty bonds and donating to collections for the Red Cross. At the end of March, 1918 the government instituted daylight saving time. Mother John was again scouring the countryside for farm-workers. Since it was all but impossible to find any, the sisters were often called on to help make hay, sometimes working until nine at night. In July, 1918 one of the Abbey monks came to perform the distasteful duty of taking pictures of the twenty-six German-born sisters in the community who would have to register and be fingerprinted. Fear and dislike of Germans was very prevalent.

Everyone was too tired to celebrate the 4th of July that year, preferring to stay quietly in chapel and pray for peace. It was in mid-October that the sisters began hearing about something called "Spanish influenza." By then it was raging in many parts of the country, especially the camps, where hundreds were dying. In most cities the schools, churches and all public buildings were closed. Contagious and often fatal, the influenza crept closer and closer to Clyde. By October 26 all the sisters' schools except the academy were also closed. When peace was declared on November 11, 1918, worry about the flu almost obscured any celebration. By December 18 the flu was in the area. At Conception college twenty-five students were down with it. There had been several deaths. Conception Abbey was quarantined.

Along with the stress of war and flu, deeper than the daily ebb and flow of community life, ran the current of the spirit. There was a hunger for prayer and union with God in the sisters that nothing could quench. Overworked much of the time, exhausted by the sheer struggle for survival in the early years and by farm and building projects later, they never stopped seeking God in the ways that were open to them and in others they had to invent. Uneducated for the most part, subjected to the moralistic spirituality of the time, they still maintained a simplicity, spontaneity and a gentle cheerfulness that translated eucharist into life.

The annual retreats in English and German were faithfully attended, as were weekly confession and instructions on the Benedictine Rule. Exposition of the Blessed Sacrament on Sundays, feasts and first Fridays, processions with the Eucharist, were woven into their lives. If, in the unfortunate practice of those days, they prayed the rosary during Mass in the month of October, they also had days of prayer and silence for an end to "this cruel war." The sisters were enthusiastic promoters of the enthronement of the Sacred Heart in families through their magazine. They were caught up in the current burst of devotion to the Carmelite nun, Therese of Lisieux, praying to this "Little Flower" for better health for Fr. Lukas and to be spared the influenza. Deeper, though, and more pervasive than any of these was that Presence which drew them to the chapel. This had to be at night for many of the sisters, when the rosary could slip through calloused fingers, when tired minds and bodies could relax into an inarticulate response to a call they experienced though they could not define it.

NOTES

1. Letter of July 14, 1914 in the archives of the Benedictine Sisters, St. Louis.

Chapter Eight
1920 – 1930

It was February, 1920 when the influenza struck the Clyde community. Over ninety sisters were ill with it. Beds had to be set up in the novitiate and the study-rooms. Two trained nurses from St. Joseph, Missouri, were hired to help the sister-infirmarian. All classes were suspended and those of the students who were not themselves sick helped the sisters keep the hours of adoration. The only one to die of the epidemic was Sr. Marcella Foland at age twenty-four. It was the feast of St. Joseph in March before the last one was back on her feet, the rooms fumigated and class-work resumed.

Despite the flu, the general health of the community improved in this decade. Of the twenty sisters who died in these years, only five were in their twenties and thirties. On the other hand, only Sr. Scholastica lived into her seventies. Sanitary conditions slowly got better: the cattle were tested, the water supply was more plentiful. Tuberculosis remained a problem; Sr. Hiltrudis Homan died of it in 1924. As late as 1926 smallpox epidemics could rage in the area and at least ten sisters were down with it at one point. One dramatic event occurred in 1929 when Mother John's successor, Mother Dolorosa Mergen, needed a mastoid operation. She had suffered agonizing pain in her ear for a week before the doctor was called. He ordered her to the hospital immediately. Five foot drifts of snow on the roads meant that it was impossible to get a car even as far as the train depot. The big sled was gotten out, rigged with sideboards and a canvas top. Mother Dolorosa was carried on a stretcher to the sled and hauled to the depot to be placed in the train's mail-car. She was to spend two months in a Kansas City hospital, needing a second surgery after the first. With this, plus the inevitable accidents of falling from haylofts and being thrown from wagons, it was decided to send two sisters for nurses' training. Srs. Notburga Hermeler and Patricia Kelly went to St. Theresa's Hospital in Waukegan, Illinois, with Sr. Patricia being the first to win her R.N.

On Pentecost Sunday, May 1917, Pope Benedict XV promulgated the code of Canon Law. This code was to cause changes in the Clyde community. The code for religious frowned on more than two successive terms for superiors. Abbot Frowin and Fr. Lukas felt they must comply, but unfortunately did not take the time to prepare the sisters for all that it would mean. A hasty election was arranged for November 10, 1920. Feeling in the community ran high as it was hard to think of anyone but Mother John in office. She had been prioress for thirty-seven years. When the sisters assembled that November morning, they elected Sr. Dolorosa Mergen on the first ballot. She was forty-one years old at this time and had been professed for twenty-one years. For most of this period, she had been in charge of the correspondence connected with the Association of Perpetual Adoration, subscriptions to the magazine, orders for booklets, etc. She had been, as well, novice director and Mother John's assistant for the past five years.

As the sisters filed into the new prioress' office to kiss her ring in token of obedience, they could not have known then that Mother Dolorosa was to be one of the most beloved superiors in the community's history. Practical and cheerful, with sound common sense linked to trust in the goodness of most people, her staunch faith and deep spirit of prayer endeared her to generations at Clyde and the rest of the congregation. One of the first things she did was ask that Mother John might be allowed to retain the title of mother, as well as her convenient first-floor bedroom. More important, she involved Mother John in helping draft their first constitution.

The new code required religious communities to live by a definite constitution. This meant that the sisters' former Statutes would no longer suffice. Communities which did not proceed without undue delay to formulate a constitution according to the spirit of their founder or Rule were told to amalgamate with communities which did have a specific constitution. Such constitutions were to be sent to Rome for approval first on an experimental basis for five years and then for final approbation. The new code for religious also recommended congregations rather than isolated units.

Fearing that their devotion to the Blessed Sacrament might be compromised if they were forced to amalgamate with other Benedictine communities whose chief apostolate was teaching, the Clyde sisters voted in 1920 to write a constitution. When a Conception Abbey canonist's efforts did not satisfy them, they set about writing their own, electing a committee made up of Mothers Dolorosa and John with Srs. Angela Bueche, Aloysia Struck and some other senior sisters. Sr. Carmelita Quinn was their secretary. By October 1922 they were able to send their first version to the Abbot Primate for his suggestions. On returning them, he proposed that they omit the entire section on government. Clyde still had only one house, the fate of St. Mary of the Pines in Chewelah being uncertain as yet. Ordinarily

Rome required three houses before granting approval to a constitution. By April 1923 a revised version was ready. On his visit to Clyde in June of that year, the influential Cardinal Michael Faulhaber offered to present this to Rome. He had an audience with Pope Pius XI as well as Cardinal Laurenti of the Congregation for Religious. Cardinal Faulhaber supported the Clyde sisters' petition to be declared a Congregation of pontifical right. Great was the rejoicing when initial approbation of the constitution arrived on the feast of St. Scholastica, February 10, 1925.

The emphasis on perpetual adoration in this first constitution was unambiguous. "The sisters shall consider as their first and primary occupation the perpetual adoration which has been established for the purpose of rendering constant worship and adoration to the eucharistic God ... They shall regard the holy adoration, which is maintained day and night, as a most powerful means of self-sanctification and also as a most efficacious means of obtaining blessings for the whole Church and the individual faithful." According to this document both identity and ministry were found in the sisters' adoration of the Lord in the Blessed Sacrament. Each sister who did not have an assigned hour of adoration was expected to make one privately.

Another feature of this first constitution was a heightened emphasis on enclosure. It was firmly stated that because of their consecration to adoration, the sisters should "most willingly bring this sacrifice to God of never leaving the monastery to visit their parents or near relatives even in the case of serious illness and death." When Sr. Aloysia Struck did go to see her sister in the fall of 1922, the chronicle notes that this was an exception to the general rule with the hope that she would be able to influence the dying woman to return to the sacraments.

This emphasis also affected the schools in which the sisters taught. The constitution now required no work outside their own premises: "Consequently, they are not to teach in parochial or public schools; they shall not engage in hospital work or any other occupation which necessitates their absence from the monastery of perpetual adoration ... However, if the community is quite large and a proper place is provided, a juvenate may be conducted in connection with the monastery for the purpose of educating girls for the community. In this convent-school classes higher than the 10th grade are not to be taught." Since the fall of 1920 the sisters had not, in fact, taught at any school except their own academy at Clyde. The question of St. Mary of the Pines began to loom on the horizon.

Following the advice of the Abbot Primate, the first constitution omitted the government section which had been planned for it. In that appendix it had been stated that "as soon as a new convent has fifteen professed sisters, then the community receives its own prioress, with independent government of their affairs and management of their own property." This had worried the Primate, for as he wrote them, in post-war Italy the hills were full of small clutches of nuns living in virtual destitution because they refused to unite. The first constitution had planned a central novitiate at Clyde, but each house was to receive its own postulants, sending them to Clyde for the formal year of novitiate training. The prioress of a new foundation was appointed from Clyde for her first term. After this, the community would elect its prioress. All prioresses of foundations from Clyde would meet every five years in a kind of general chapter. In this constitution every sister of final profession had a vote on the admission of novices and postulants, on the founding of new monasteries and on any building which cost more than $12,000.00.

Helpful as such a constitution was, some of its effects were less happy. Among these was a kind of formalism which replaced the spontaneity of former days. Relationships between the sisters became suspect, watching of one another was subtly encouraged, which did little to foster trust. Even the unconscious humor of a statement like the following could not offset the moralizing spirituality it represented. "The sisters should strive most earnestly to show cheerfulness at recreation . . . Edifying conversation is always commendable, but on serious subjects it should not last too long." At his visitation of the community in August, 1922 the Abbot felt forced to tell the sisters: "Don't worry and talk nonsense about the constitution. Nobody makes a constitution to deprive you of your rights." Apparently the rights of the chaplain came up in this connection as the Abbot went on to say: "I know there is on the lips of many of you the question: what is really the position and rights of Fr. Lukas among us? Fr. Lukas as chaplain of this community has the duty of advising your superiors in everything temporal . . . and even of going over their heads in things spiritual, because he is a priest."[1]

Another significant change at this time was the sisters' use of the hard-won right of women to vote. In 1920 their bishop urged all the religious communities in his diocese to use this right. The banker from Maryville was called in to explain to the sisters at Clyde what the issues were. Although they still felt hesitant and uncertain, some seventy sisters exercised their citizenship at the polls that fall. They knew that the Ku Klux Klan was on the rise again and that it behooved them to do all they could to make sure that no klansman was elected. In November 1928 the presidential election was felt to be crucial, as the first Catholic candidate for the office was involved: Al Smith. Later the chronicler noted with resignation: "God will not let our prayers be in vain; He will know how to bring good out of evil." It is doubtful that Herbert Hoover would have appreciated these sentiments.

The early years of the 1920s could be called the era of beginnings and endings for the Clyde community. The beginnings were represented by Sr. Bernard Willmann's two Atlantic crossings to recruit postulants in Germany and Switzerland. Because of the terrible poverty in Europe after the first World War, there were many young women who did not have the necessary dowry to enter religious life there. Equipped with letters of introduction, Sr. Bernard set off. "She is surely brave to make this trip alone," says an awed note in the Daybook. A competent and determined woman, Sr. Bernard went from place to place in Germany, sending interesting accounts of her travels back to Clyde. On the way over their ship passed the place where the Titanic had sunk. In fact, one of sister's fellow passengers had been on the Titanic. She described jumping from the deck to a lifeboat below, while the Catholic priests stood to say the prayers of absolution until the end.

In Hamburg, Germany Sr. Bernard stayed with Mother Mary Ward's sisters and then went on to Berlin to register with the English consulate. In Paderborn the bishop himself took her to the diocesan newspaper office and prepared an article informing young women of her presence in the diocese. After a holiday in her former home, Baden, where the pastor announced at the Sunday High Mass that she was available to see any young ladies who were interested, Sr. Bernard went on to Rottenburgen to meet the well-known Bishop Kettler. Along the way she received gifts of beautiful hand-embroidered vestments, chalices and other items in gratitude for the financial help channeled to religious communities in Germany through the Clyde sisters. In Stuttgart after Christmas she registered at the American consulate and was told to inform them promptly if she encountered any difficulties in that part of Germany still occupied by French and American soldiers. Enroute Sr. Bernard visited the homes of some of the sisters' relatives, occasionally finding them so destitute that she bought food for them.

By March 1922 Sr. Bernard was at Herstelle where she found the community in such distress and hunger that twenty sisters had died in one week. She gave them money to buy provisions. In Switzerland she was able to spend two days with Fr. Lukas' sister. It was near Siegen on the train in a dark passageway that a man tried to grab her suitcase, but the undaunted Sr. Bernard held on calling for help, so that the thief ran off in a hurry. On August 25 she landed back in New York accompanied by twenty-three prospective postulants. They arrived at Clyde two days later at eleven o'clock at night, and together went to the chapel to sing a grateful "Grosser Gott."

Sr. Bernard's trip the following year was easier as she knew her way around and had already written to a number of possible candidates. One of these was the future Sr. Sophia Dietrich, who looked so pale and thin that Sr. Bernard hesitated to accept her. "Just take me; I'm healthy enough!" said the girl and was to prove this in the more than fifty years which ensued, during which she was one of the hardest working and merry-hearted members who ever blessed a community.

In this second round of European travel, Sr. Bernard was looking for workmen as well as postulants. Fr. Lukas wanted her to find carpenters, farm-hands, etc. In this, too, she was successful. The Clyde community was to owe much to the labors of men like Joseph Gemmeke, Paul, Carl and Justin Pappert, Karl Weiler, Henry Deters, Henry Lange and others. Of the thirty-five postulants Sr. Bernard brought to Clyde, seventeen were to make final vows with the community.

Along with beginnings there were endings in the early 1920s. In November 1920 the sisters received word of the death of Fr. Adelhelm Odermatt, founder of Mt. Angel Abbey in Oregon. On February 13, 1923 Mother John became seriously ill with pneumonia. She died the next day as simply as she had lived. For the community it was the end of an era, the end of a time of precarious struggle for existence during the pioneer days. Mother John had been a faithful steward, one St. Benedict could have heartily commended. She had known how to cooperate with Fr. Lukas, to keep the peace with great forbearance. She had seen Clyde grow from one building to what the newspaper called "almost a small town." As the paper went on to say, the sisters had "an academy, an orphanage, an extensive printing establishment and book-bindery, and ran the large farm on which the buildings are situated. Mother John had charge of all these places and made a wonderful success along business lines as well as religious lines."[2]

On March 24, 1923 Abbot Frowin Conrad died at the age of ninety. His passing meant the loss of one who had considerably influenced the community's beginning and growth. His balanced monastic guidance had helped both Mother Anselma and Mother John through very difficult times. The Clyde community would have thought this passage from one of his early letters to Engelberg, dated September 3, 1872, a suitable epitaph for him: "Every day I understand more clearly how much truth there is in the statement — and I have heard it made frequently — that America needs Benedictine monasteries more than others. Other orders accomplish great but mostly transitory things. The Benedictine order according to its very constitution is more adapted to create what is durable."

Two years later in January, 1925 Sr. Scholastica von Matt died. She had been in the second group of sisters to come to America from Maria Rickenbach and was seventy-five when she died. Lively to the end, even though she spent her last years in the infirmary, she had her first automobile ride when she was seventy-three and enjoyed it thoroughly.

One work begun at Clyde in 1920 was to have significance beyond the usual. Aware of the terrible conditions in Germany and Austria after the war, Fr. Lukas wrestled with the problem of how to help. What could be done from America to alleviate the appalling shortages of food and fuel, the bankrupt distress that prevailed everywhere? In one community a few sisters had literally starved to death, another was reported to have lost close to sixty sisters through malnutrition. During the war all religious communities in Germany and Austria had been expected to invest dowries and legacies in government bonds which were worthless now. After thought and prayer, Fr. Lukas wrote a series of articles in *Tabernacle and Purgatory,* which was now a monthly with 45,000 subscribers, many of them of German descent. These articles pleaded with readers to send offerings to the Clyde community, which would faithfully channel them through responsible sources in Germany and Austria to rescue the innocent and needy victims of war, especially religious and children.

The response was immediate and generous. The appeal went out in June. By September, the sisters were able to tell their readers that $12,000.00 had been sent abroad and that letters of gratitude were arriving from the bishops of Vienna, Linz, Munich and other places. Next, Fr. Lukas suggested that Clyde could transmit mass intentions to needy bishops. He devised an appeal for aid to impoverished seminarians in Germany and Austria. Would the readers adopt a student for a year, two years or his entire seminary training? Then they could say, "I have a priest in my family!" Within the next eight months ninety students had been substantially aided toward the priesthood. As this went on, Fr. Lukas received letters of thanks from both Popes Benedict XV and Pius XI.

Letters also came from readers in America: "I am enclosing $50.00 to be forwarded to Germany or Austria for a student in the priesthood ... I will send $50.00 each year for four years or whatever length of time it may be. I am twenty-one years old and while this takes nearly all I have, I know it will bring me more happiness to help one whom God has called to serve him at the holy altar than anything else on earth..." "Last week I sent you a donation for the poor sisters in Tyrol; today I have the pleasure of sending you $100.00 from a friend whom I have interested ... I do not feel that I am performing an act of charity in giving and asking others to give ... These sisters have the right to ask help to succour these orphans ... For them I have the most earnest regard. Such women make me glory in being a Catholic." From Minnesota came another letter: "I saw in *Tabernacle and Purgatory* that great want exists in Europe. I would like to help them but I am a poor man ... I work in a large factory and on Saturdays nearly all the employees quit at 12:30 ... I have asked the yard foreman to let me work in the yard after 12:30, and for the last six Saturdays I have had work and got $2.00 each time. I think I can get work on each of the next four Saturdays which will give me $8.00 more. So now I enclose $20.00 which please use for the poor in Europe as you think most pleasing to God."[3]

Through such appeals aid was funneled to the Jesuit seminaries: the Germanico in Rome and Canisianum in Innsbruck. The church of St.

Matthias in Trier was restored to the Benedictines who had been driven from it. The entire aid effort came to be known as the CARITAS work. By 1927 over two million dollars had been distributed in Germany, Austria, Italy and other places. Most of this money came from the small donations of ordinary people who responded with typical American generosity. Nearly 3,000 young men received help through CARITAS in their studies for the priesthood. Among these were Cardinal Stepinac, Cardinal Seper and Cardinal Wendel. After the Eucharistic Congress in Chicago in 1926 many grateful bishops, abbots and rectors found their way to Clyde to thank Fr. Lukas and the sisters. This work tapered off after the death of the former, but again after the second World War, the sisters were involved in helping the needy in Europe.

This CARITAS meant much extra work for the sisters who took care of the correspondence involved. In those years the sister printers were busy with orders for booklets, rosaries and devotional leaflets, especially at Christmas when an avalanche of mail reached them. By 1925 they were setting type for the new constitution. A new folder for small covers was a real help since it freed the sisters from hand-folding them. Later that same year Srs. Adelgundis Kaiser and Cornelia St. Cin, two experienced printers, made a visit to St. Meinrad's Abbey in Indiana to see the new type-setting machine, which visit resulted in the decision to invest in an intertype machine for the Clyde printing press.

With all this, it was a relief for Mother Dolorosa when the new bishop of St. Joseph, Bishop Gilfillan, after a visit to Clyde in 1923 decided in the early summer of the following year that he wanted a diocesan orphanage for boys and girls in St. Joseph itself. This meant that the sisters' orphanage could be closed, the building sold to the Franciscan sisters from Austria, who were doing the cooking for the Conception monks, and all the Clyde sisters recalled to their own monastery.

Before this, a fire had destroyed part of the laundry building at the orphanage in which all the community laundry was done. The new laundry on their own grounds at Clyde was not completed until the fall of 1922. This left the sisters with makeshift arrangements for the meantime, which Sr. Juliana Bresson described with some feeling. When she entered in 1920, the laundry was still being done at the orphanage. The sisters left right after Vespers to trudge across the fields to Conception where the orphanage was located. They slept in the attic of the orphanage on cots and rose about 2 a.m. to start the laundry. They went to the Abbey for morning Mass, came back to the orphanage for breakfast and continued the work until all was done. After the fire and before the new laundry building was ready, they worked out of the basement of the guest house at Clyde. All the equipment had burned, so the sisters had to put the clothes in boiling water to bleach them. After a double rinse, the clothes were thrown into old-fashioned wringers that had to be turned round and round. The sisters got up at two in the morning so that all the clothes: theirs, the students' and the monks' could be washed in this fashion. The real problem was getting the clothes dry. In summer they simply used the lawns between the infirmary and the chapel on the east side. Winter was more difficult. A little one-horse wagon was used at this time to bring milk from the dairy barn to the main house: this became the laundry wagon. Four or five baskets of wash could be piled into the wagon and then Sr. Hiltrudis Homan would drive it to the academy. There the baskets of wet clothes were carried to the attic up five flights of stairs. What could be hung to dry in the printery attic was taken there. At the blessing of the new laundry, Fr. Lukas named it "Hebron," because, according to the chronicler, "as the Blessed Virgin went with joy over the mountains to Hebron to visit Elizabeth, so the sisters should go with joy to their work here." After the attics in the printery and the academy, they probably did.

The laundry was not the only building underway during this decade. There was never a time when something was not going up. In April 1924 cars of crushed rock, sand and lumber were arriving for the annex that was to join the printing office to the guest house. That September scaffolding went up to finish the mosaics behind the high altar of the chapel. In April 1925 the men were digging the foundations for an addition to the north side of the infirmary. Then in the fall of 1926 they began the final wing of the quadrangle which would complete the Clyde monastery. The sisters held their breath and prayed fervently one May day in 1927 when the huge steel parts for the water-tank housed in the tower of the monastery were hoisted up. The next April it was necessary to choose a site for a chaplain's residence.

By 1930 the Kansas City architect, Mr. Joseph Shaughnessy, knew the route to Clyde by heart, he had made so many trips there for consultations on everything from rubber flooring to the chapel runway roofing. He gave his time, expertise and energy gratis to the sisters and was, literally, an answer to prayer. Sr. Laurentia Huppe, who was then in charge of building projects, had prayed to St. Joseph to obtain a good architect. Never one to hedge, she had specified that this architect's name should be Joseph. Just one week later Mr. Joseph Shaughnessy from Kansas City came to offer his services.

The farm was important at this time to the growing community, which in 1925 consisted of one hundred sixty-five sisters, fifteen novices and eight postulants, plus some seventy-four students at the academy. The community was proud that, after testing, their ninety-seven head of cattle were pronounced in good condition. Later the community bought milking machines and a separator to ease the workload. The sisters were still called on to help in different ways:

laying out the alfalfa in even layers in the loft of the dairy barn, picking potatoes in the five acres planted in 1922, or planting nut trees along with evergreens and willows. When the orchard was in full bloom, it was a favorite Sunday recreation to walk out to see the trees, going through the pine grove where the purple violets hid in the long grass. Thanks to the fine management of Sr. Josephine Gruenes, the farm had greatly improved by 1929. This was helped in no small way by the men Sr. Bernard Willman had brought to America some years before. Joseph Gemmeke, for example, became a master cattle breeder and a herd manager, whose superior ability caused the Clyde cattle to be praised throughout the state.

Their new constitution forbade the sisters to teach outside their own academy. The academy teachers continued to attend the Teachers' Association meetings in Maryville, as the community Chapter voted in 1928 that they should keep up their accreditation according to state law. Even Fr. Flanagan of Boys Town was regretfully refused when he came that year asking for teachers for his boys. In June, 1928 five sisters: Srs. Sennorina Zavadil, Rita Busby, Patricia Kelly, Pancratia (Agnes Josephine) Grosspitch and Elfleda Felten were in summer school at St. Louis University, boarding with the Precious Blood sisters. In the fall of 1929 a teacher from Maryville State College was hired to teach the sisters a course in psychology. The following summer arrangements were made to have two teachers give courses in adolescent psychology and the principles of teaching.

CHEWELAH

In 1920 there were nineteen sisters at the Clyde foundation of St. Mary of the Pines in Chewelah, Washington. They worked hard, lived simply and loved the life. Four of them taught at the parish school, experiencing considerable difficulty, according to their chronicle, with the pastor. He seemed to want to dominate, leaving the sisters uncertain of who was in charge. The community also looked after an extensive farm, raising pigs and selling them, along with wheat. They bought Holstein cattle, cared for apple and pear trees and had a good-sized chicken farm.

Mother John had already warned the Chewelah sisters that when the new constitution was approved, it would probably mean the end of teaching in parochial schools and that they should devote themselves more fully to perpetual adoration. In another letter in 1920, she asked each one to keep a half-hour of adoration daily. When Srs. Placida Stephan and Alphonsa Sapp got back to Chewelah from a visit to Clyde in 1920, they brought word that there was some thought of closing St. Mary of the Pines. The sisters began a novena to avert this. They heard a rumor that Fr. Lukas had offered their place to a

European community, feeling the sisters were too involved in farm work.

The sisters carried on after Mother Dolorosa's election, reassured by her letter which promised that the Chewelah monastery would not be closed. They had eighty children in their little school, although difficulties with the pastor continued. Still confusing letters from Clyde continued to arrive throughout 1921, saying at one time St. Mary's would be given up, at another it would not. Toward the end of that November, Mother Dolorosa arrived to see the place. She asked if the sisters would prefer to give up Chewelah and return to Clyde, or stay there and become independent. On her return to Missouri, she wrote back to say that nothing could be decided until they had their new constitution. However, she had no teacher to replace Sr. Frowina Heinlein when she got sick. Then Abbot Philip Ruggle of Conception Abbey arrived to conduct a kind of visitation. He seems to have felt that the Clyde community would have done better to make a foundation closer to home.

This somewhat schizoid state of affairs continued into 1925. By then Fr. Lukas and Mother Dolorosa were interested in a foundation in Mundelein, near Chicago. Chewelah's superior received a letter from Mother Dolorosa asking if the sisters wished to disband Chewelah and return to Clyde or stay there and be an independent foundation. Sr. Cecilia Schildknecht wrote back that they did not feel they knew God's will for them with any certainty. Another letter came from Mother Dolorosa on November 14 to say that the Clyde Chapter had voted to close St. Mary of the Pines and call the sisters home. The Chewelah sisters promptly went to Bishop Schinner to ask if they should appeal this decision to Rome. This they did, sending with their letter a short history of the foundation, a detailed description of the property and a financial statement. The note in the Chewelah chronicle ends: "May God's will be done."

On January 29, 1927 the blow fell. Rome had replied and Mother Dolorosa wrote that St. Mary of the Pines would be closed. It took nearly two years to complete this closing. This meant that Sr. Placida Stephan could celebrate her golden jubilee in Chewelah, she being the second sister of the Clyde community to celebrate such a jubilee. By mid-March of 1928 the last of the sisters arrived back at Clyde. This obedience cost them dear, for as one sister wrote, they would have walked back to Chewelah, so much did they love St. Mary of the Pines. Ironically, in the consolidation that followed on the second Vatican Council the foundation for which Chewelah had been given up was itself the first to be closed.

✻   ✻   ✻   ✻

At Clyde, community life went in its orderly way. In the fall of 1921 it was decided to have all the European-born sisters become naturalized American citizens, so that thirteen sisters went into Maryville to secure their papers. In the fall of 1922 Mother Dolorosa went with Fr. Lukas to see Archbishop Harty of Omaha, who had requested a foundation in his diocese. By the fall of 1925 Bishop Chartrand of Indianapolis was also asking them to come and look at some property which he thought might be suitable for a community of perpetual adoration. With these possibilities for new monasteries, Mother Dolorosa was glad to receive the first vows of four sisters professed on February 19, 1922, among them her own sister, Sr. Hildelita Mergen. That August ten postulants were invested with the monastic habit and seven novices professed first vows. All these were from Germany and Switzerland.

Clothing was on the agenda at community meetings in the winter months of 1925. Mr. Daleiden made their coif machines, but he was getting older. What would they do when the last machine wore out? Their new constitution stated that they wore black veils. This meant that the stiff white lining had to be removed from them and the veils redesigned. Fr. Lukas had designed an emblem to identify the sisters as adorers of the Blessed Sacrament.

December 6, 1925 was the golden jubilee of the community at Clyde. Abbot Philip Ruggle came to celebrate with them, witnessing a play entitled "The Ten Virgins," put on for this occasion by the sisters. This soon became staple of entertainment provided for distinguished visitors. Since Abbot Philip usually accompanied these, he must have known it by heart before long.

New Year's Day, 1926 was a solemn one for the sisters of final profession. After the High Mass Fr. Lukas spoke to them briefly, then wearing their new black veils, they went two by two to the communion rail to receive the new emblem from him. Six at a time, they entered the sanctuary to kneel on the top step of the predella and renew their vows, consecrating themselves anew to adoration of the Blessed Sacrament. Then each one took a copy of the constitution from the altar-step. "It seemed as though our Lord himself gave each this precious book," says the chronicle.

The altar bread department was a scene of great activity in June 1926, making the communion hosts for the Eucharistic Congress to be held in Chicago. The Clyde sisters furnished over one million breads for this event. In return, the secretary for the Congress promised to distribute ten thousand booklets composed by Fr. Lukas specifically for the Congress. After this event Cardinal Faulhaber paid the sisters a second visit. He was received with all the ceremony dear to the heart of Fr. Lukas. The assembled community met him at the front gate where a welcome address was read. Then all marched processionally through the yard to the chapel where Benediction was given. In the evening the sisters gathered to enjoy recreation with His Eminence. Sr. Carmelita read an address, expressing the sisters' gratitude for three special favors he had obtained for them: the speedy approval of their constitution, the privilege of nocturnal exposition of the Blessed Sacrament and the treasured faculty for Fr. Lukas to bless rosaries with the Holy Land indulgence. This last was understood to mean that each bead of the rosary had the same indulgence one could gain by a trip to the Holy Land. Before his death Fr. Lukas had blessed hundreds of such rosaries.

On November 2, 1926 Mother Dolorosa was elected for a second term of six years with one hundred twenty-six sisters voting. In June, 1927 Sr. Angela Bueche, who had been assistant prioress for eleven years, celebrated her silver jubilee along with Srs. Laurentia Huppe, Coletta Rast, and Petronilla Boehmer. By February 1928 there were two hundred in the community, including postulants. On the following March the great tower bells could ring out jubilantly for such occasions. Blessed solemnly by Abbot Philip, each bell bore a name, from the largest to the smallest: in honor of the Eucharist, the Annunciation, St. Luke and St. Scholastica.

On Christmas day in 1928, the gift packages for the sisters were piled on tables in the community room. After all had been opened, each sister was allowed to take a good handful of candy, while the rest was turned in to be shared with the entire community. For a special occasion each received a banana as a treat. According to the chronicler, "bananas are expensive." The telephone bill for one month that year ran to $15.55. Fr. Stephen Schappler came over from the abbey to make new arrangements for the students' laundry; from now on they would be charged according to the number of pieces sent, instead of the flat rate of $2.50 a month they had been paying. In July 1929 Mother Dolorosa gave a short financial report to the community. She told the sisters that so far they had been able to meet their bills and pay off some $40,000.00 on their loan. However, "this should not make us extravagant, but rather urge us to keep our vow of holy poverty more strictly and be more grateful to God."

The fall of 1929 found the sisters involved in helping Conception Abbey celebrate the 1400th anniversary of the founding of the Benedictine order. An excursion train ran on the Wabash and Great Western lines since so many visitors were expected. The Clyde community loaned the monks chairs, rugs and then roasted five hundred pounds of beef for the festive meal. On their way back from the celebration, Archbishops Glennon of St. Louis and Rummel of New Orleans, Bishop Gilfillan of St. Joseph and the Lieutenant Governor of Missouri dropped in for a visit with the sisters.

As the community edged toward a cautious prosperity in the last years of this decade, the nation slid into the worst economic depression in history. The rapid evolution of U.S. industry and competition had spurred mass production. This required mass consumption. Advertising began advocating buying rather than saving. Installment buying

85

developed. The earlier American habit of thrift and financial stability began to erode. The amazingly rapid growth of the automobile, motion picture and radio industries set standards not only for what was produced, but also for culture. Women started working outside the home in greater numbers. The divorce rate increased and so did the gap between generations. Prohibition led to a huge, illegal liquor traffic with bootleggers like Al Capone reaping the profits.

The wonderfully prosperous world of the 1920s came to a sudden halt. There had been warnings of enormous changes in the economy. On September 7, 1929 a reaction started which culminated on October 24 — known afterwards as "Black Thursday" — when almost thirteen million shares of stock were sold. Prices dropped as never before in history. This crash on the stock market began a slump that was to last for years. Factories closed, the number of unemployed rose to staggering proportions, mortgages were foreclosed, banks failed, dividends were not paid, prices kept falling, the buying power of the nation was all but paralyzed.

The sisters at Clyde began to realize how bad times were when more and more poor men appeared at their back door asking for a meal and clothes. To do what they could, the sisters fed them and watched for sales of clothing in Maryville. By the spring of 1930, four to six men a day were being fed. On April 8, 1930 the Farmers' Trust Bank in Maryville closed its doors. The bank's president assured Mother Dolorosa that all would be paid back, but he could not tell her when. The chronicle notes: "It seems as if in the history of our country there have never been such hard and depressing times as at present."

MUNDELEIN

It was at this very time that Clyde was making a foundation at Mundelein near Chicago. In 1922 Sr. Benedicta Forschner's brother had sent a sizeable check for a new foundation. Through Bishop Gilfillan, Fr. Lukas asked Cardinal George Mundelein of Chicago if he would be interested in having a community devoted to perpetual adoration located on the extensive grounds of St. Mary of the Lake seminary. The Cardinal's reply is dated October 24, 1925:

> Reverend and dear Mother Dolorosa,
>
> I received in due time your letter of September 28 which was enclosed with the letter of Bishop Gilfillan of October 1. You can rest assured the message conveyed by them received long and serious consideration. I laid the matter before the faculty of the seminary and asked their counsel . . . In the beginning I may not have been too friendly to your request, but gradually a change has come and I think I now see the finger of God in your petition. To understand my viewpoint it is necessary to look at it in this way: the indications are that Chicago will be the greatest city in the

world. It is growing so fast, the facilities for transportation, the food and fuel sources are so near at hand; everybody thinks so and indeed it looks so. The only spiritual influence in such a Babylon can come from the church and that influence will be potent or indifferent, just as we make it. That means that if our priesthood is great, both as to quantity, but more so as to quality, only then will we exert the right influence in the Chicago of the future.

That explains why I have made the main undertaking of my life the building up of the priesthood. Into this seminary I have poured every resource of thought, money and effort. We are giving the students there advantages such as no student for the priesthood ever received before. We are giving them every bodily comfort and every intellectual advantage, as well as every spiritual help we can think of. All we ask in return is absolute obedience, blind, unquestioning submission to the rule. And we are getting it! For the religious in charge of the spiritual life admit that not even in their novitiate is there better discipline than in our seminary. All this is told you so that you may understand that we have done all in our power to produce the result desired. Like Paul and Apollo, I have planted and watered, and now we need God's help and that help can come through prayer.

That is why your offer seems to fit in, to dovetail, so to say, with our whole plan. I have heard of your Rev. Chaplain before, so I am not surprised that this inspiration would come to him when he visited this abode of the Master, where we are preparing the newest disciples. Such a foundation will not only be a place of prayer for the future priesthood, it would be a place of inspiration for the future priests. If it is established nearby, it is my intention to have the young student-priests who are to be ordained in the beginning of their final year, take their turns week by week to say the morning Mass for the Sisters before the Blessed Sacrament and give Benediction, and I am sure they will consider it a privilege. As to the confessor, that was the reason of the delay. You would naturally like a Jesuit as confessor to the sisters. The Jesuits are not allowed to act as ordinary confessor to sisters, but I have suggested that the provincial make an exception in this case, considering your community as part of the parish.

I see no difficulty, therefore in granting you the permission to establish a foundation of perpetual adoration near the seminary at Mundelein, Illinois. I am glad to hear you assure me that the community will be self-supporting. For more reasons than one is this gratifying, but principally because too often mendicancy becomes the chief occupation of a community when they rely on it for support. In looking for the site or location, I would advise the matter to be undertaken soon and with utmost care as there has been a boom in all this section and hence a decided raise in prices.

In conclusion I can only add the hope that this may be for your sisters a new encouragement in their work and that they will begin even now the task they have asked for themselves, to pray for the clergy of this vast

archdiocese and its head. With my sentiments of deepest appreciation of
your offer, I send my good wishes and my blessing for yourself and your
sisters.

Sincerely yours in XTO
George, Cardinal Mundelein
Archbishop of Chicago[4]

This letter, as typical of the man as of the spirit of the American
church of that era, spurred Fr. Lukas and Mother Dolorosa to great
activity. They visited the Cardinal in April 1926, then engaged the
same architect who had designed the seminary to draw up plans for
their monastery. Through the generosity of the Forschners they already had ten acres of land bought from the Cardinal.

In April 1928, Mother Dolorosa with Sr. Carmelita Quinn made the
first of their innumerable trips from Clyde to Mundelein. Mrs. Forschner met them at the train, and on one trip took them into Chicago to
find a restaurant. Leaving them for a few minutes to park the car, she
found them on her return standing outside a small, dark-looking
place, confronted by a very nervous man who was jumping up and
down, exclaiming: "Jim Maloney! Jim Maloney!" Correctly interpret-
ing this, Mrs. Forschner quickly shepherded the confused sisters in
another direction, away from the speakeasy they had selected for
lunch, and the poor man who was trying to warn them that the place
was for "gentlemen only." Another time, according to an oft-told tale
of Sr. Carmelita, the sisters were carrying a bottle of elderberry wine
for "medicinal purposes." That night they dropped and broke the
bottle in their compartment, which spread a heady scent throughout
the carriage. The sisters spent a good part of the night trying to mop
up and disguise the odor, since it was the era of prohibition.

On May 28, 1928 nineteen sisters left for Mundelein, having first
made a retreat together and promised fidelity to the motherhouse and
the Clyde prioress. Parting was an ordeal with tears of farewell. By
June 19 more sisters had arrived to make thirty-three in all who
would form the permanent community. Sr. Irene Prugger has left a
description of the first days in the new monastery. "What a sight met
their eyes upon entering the convent! Not a chair in the building, nor
any other piece of furniture. The floors had been sanded cross-grain
and were like rough sandpaper. The walls were bespattered with
tobacco spittle, while all the windows were blotched with dried paint
and sand.

"After dinner at the seminary the sisters were taken to the Franciscan convent on the seminary grounds and assigned rooms as they were
to remain there for the next eight days. During the day the sisters
worked at preparing the new convent-home. They arose early for
meditation and holy Mass in the Franciscan convent chapel and were
given breakfast there. The Franciscan sisters prepared a box lunch
which was taken along to work. In the evening, these same sisters had

a hot dinner waiting for the sisters. Some returned to the new convent to work until late at night. It was impossible to do much about cleaning the walls. There was not time enough to have them painted and it was also too expensive. Nothing could be done about the rough floors except for the room used for the chapel, which the sander corrected and which the sisters then oiled and waxed. After complaining to the contractor, all the floors were sanded, but this took months and the sisters expended great energy in oiling and waxing to rectify the contractor's first error.

"After a few days the truck arrived from Clyde with bedding and the sisters' personal belongings ... By June 6 the house was in readiness to welcome twenty-two more sisters so that it was no longer necessary to impose on the charity of the Franciscan sisters ... There was much rain all summer and little springs gushed up through the cracks in the basement floor ... The winter was severe and as the sisters were told to save fuel, the night adorers often suffered greatly. Thirty-three members were assigned to residence, and adoration was kept with two sisters at each half-hour during the day and three at night every hour. There were four adorers on Sundays and feasts so at times a few sisters had five periods of adoration in twenty-four hours."

Corpus Christi, June 7, 1928 was the formal opening of the new foundation. Cardinal Mundelein officiated, offering Mass in the little chapel and blessing every room in the house from the basement to the third floor. All the sisters were in tears when Mother Dolorosa, who had been with them from the beginning, had to leave on June 13th. They promised her to do their utmost to maintain the right spirit in this new monastery. From the opening day they had many visitors, foremost among them the ever-generous Forschners, who donated a Buick sedan and later a Ford truck. Mrs. Forschner could always be called on to drive the sisters or meet them at the train station. When the seminarians came back to St. Mary of the Lake in the fall, four hundred in number that September, they became steady visitors and by the 26th of the month, the first of the newly ordained priests was offering Mass for the sisters. This was to continue for the next fifty years. Never did the sisters forget their serious obligation to pray for these young priests. Ordination cards, brown and curling with age, were often found in the prayerbooks of older sisters who had been stationed in the Mundelein monastery.

Very often in those days Carl or Paul Pappert with Joseph Gemmeke would drive a truck from Clyde to Mundelein, laden with barrels of apples, potatoes, sauerkraut, squash, pumpkins, furniture, dishes, etc. So many trips did the sisters make back and forth that both the Rock Island and the Great Western gave them half-fare passes on their trains. The men helped the sisters install the heavier equipment for the altar bread department so that by December the sisters were busy baking, cutting and sorting hosts to fill the Hansen orders.

Cardinal Mundelein visited them on December 8 to ask if they were comfortable, how they liked their chaplains, how they kept adoration at night. He was also eager to know when they were going to build a permanent chapel and spoke movingly to them of their great mission to pray for his priests.

In February 1929 the community was busy with another project: "bandaging the fruit trees on account of the destroying work of the rabbits." In May the Forschners presented Mother Dolorosa with the deeds for more land, bringing their property at Mundelein to twenty acres. Even though the country was in the midst of the depression, a few substantial checks came in toward the permanent chapel. After an appeal in *Tabernacle and Purgatory* in 1930, there was a steady flow of small donations for this purpose. Grateful to God for his goodness to them, the sisters at Mundelein tried to live exactly as they had at Clyde. No deviations from that norm were allowed. As much as possible, the schedule was the same, the customs were uniform and Sr. Benedicta Forschner, the first prioress, adhered with all her heart to whatever Mother Dolorosa suggested. To be able to turn the sod for the new chapel in June 1930 was reward enough.

✳   ✳   ✳   ✳

In this era the spiritual life of the Clyde congregation was similar to that of most religious in that it was in many ways characterized by perfectionism and formalism. The outcome of the reform of church law was a kind of juridicism that was to afflict religious orders for decades. A truly theological understanding of monastic life had to wait until the second Vatican Council. The biblical and patristic grounding had been lost. Religious observance was a measurable thing; behavior rather than the inner yearning of the heart was the criterion. A rigid adherence to outward observance engendered an atmosphere of serenity that could be deceptive, together with a feeling of moral certitude that would have verged on arrogance had it been consciously examined.

At this time the sisters at Clyde and Mundelein were still praying the Little Office of the Blessed Virgin. The real heart of their life was their commitment to adoration of the Lord in the Blessed Sacrament. Here they found a warmth and identity that the somewhat truncated monasticism they knew did not provide. Back in 1919 Fr. Lukas had composed an adoration manual full of devout selections from various sources. On September 29, 1920 the sisters had been granted permission for nocturnal exposition of the Blessed Sacrament. Now every hour of the day and night at Clyde and Mundelein they knelt in adoration and reparation. It was impressed upon them that they must atone in their hours of prayer for the many who neglected the Blessed Sacrament. It was not unusual then for the entire community to rise at

90

two or three in the morning to be sure of having daily Mass at times when Fr. Lukas was leaving early on some business trip. Pope Pius XI's declaration of August 1, 1926 as a day of special prayer for an end to the persecution raging in Mexico led them to more hours of adoration, as did the celebration of the new feast of Christ the King later that year. Now they knelt in the sanctuary before the high altar, rather than in the side chapel as formerly. Now, too, the sisters wore the full black choir cloak or cuculla, with its rows of pleats and hanging sleeves when they went to their adoration. Benediction twice daily was a solemn service.

A note in the chronicle for Holy Saturday, April 19, 1930 reveals more of the liturgical state of affairs in those days than the chronicler realized: "During services this year we did not pray the stations privately, but were permitted to follow the prayers with the priest, and this took the place of meditation. The prayers were very beautiful, in particular those for the blessing of the Easter candle, which Rev. Father sang. The sisters all appreciated this change very much . . . The new monstrance was used for the first time for Benediction this evening. It is beautiful beyond words to express, but the luna is quite a bit smaller than our other one, which was a great disappointment to us, as we all appreciate seeing the large sacred Host."

Extremely work-oriented, with little time for or understanding of lectio, unable to reflect theologically on their own lived experience, cut off by their semi-cloister from the best currents in culture, the sisters lived this sentimental, privatized spirituality with its intense focus on Jesus as their immolated spouse in the Eucharist, with a love and genuine faith that were a saving grace. Through their Lord they did try to reach out to people everywhere in a prayer that released them from the bonds of externalism.

The one who best typified this spirituality was Fr. Lukas. According to the record of the chronicles, he was into every aspect of the sisters' lives. His were the plans that guided their buildings, their publications, their contact with the world outside Clyde. It would have been difficult for any sister in 1927 to imagine life without him. Yet, with terrible suddenness, that is what happened late that year. On December 16, 1927 Fr. Lukas and the community's faithful chauffeur, Mr. Enis, left for St. Joseph to pick up some ornamental lamps for the altar. On their return trip a car drove out from a side road at full speed and crashed into their car. Fr. Lukas was thrown out, struck his head, and was killed instantly. The chronicler could hardly believe it: "My God! My God! What a terrible shock to the community! What a heavy cross, but we bow to thy adorable will — Thou knowest what is best."

About 11 p.m. that night Fr. Lukas' body was brought back. All that night the sisters took turns watching and praying beside the coffin. Sixty sisters went to the Abbey for the solemn requiem on December 19. After all was over, Fr. Lukas was laid to rest in the Clyde cemetery. He had often said that since he had lived and worked among the sisters, he wanted to rest among them when he died. Telegrams and letters of condolence poured in for weeks after. The sisters faithfully visited his grave to pray. They kept his room above the printing office exactly as he had left it. Writing to the sisters at Mundelein in December the following year, Mother Dolorosa said that as the first anniversary of his death approached, she felt a cold chill down her spine just remembering.

This was again the end of an era for the Clyde community. They owed much to Fr. Lukas: they would long remember him. But never again would any man, chaplain, confessor or bishop, hold a like influence in their lives. Priests were always treated with respect, bishops with all due reverence: their opinions asked, their wishes consulted. But when it came to the governance of their lives, the sisters took charge. They wrote their own constitution, they planned all subsequent buildings, they decided when and how to arrange their prayer. Perhaps Fr. Lukas had taught them more than he or they realized.

NOTES

1. In the archives of the Benedictine Sisters of Perpetual Adoration, St. Louis.

2. *The Maryville Forum*, February 14, 1923.

3. These letters are preserved in the archives of the Benedictine Sisters of Perpetual Adoration, St. Louis.

4. Ibid.

Chapter Nine
1930 – 1940

In 1930 the United States was still in the throes of the depression. Those banks which remained open were paying only one half of one percent interest. On April 20, 1930 the chronicler at Clyde noted: "Appalling distress everywhere. Some have been out of work for two and three years. In one day we sometimes have twenty to thirty poor men at our door asking for food." By March 1933 twelve states had declared a bank holiday, Missouri among them. People were frantic as land value and real estate fell to almost nothing.

When President Franklin D. Roosevelt was inaugurated on March 4, 1933, all but four states had closed their banks. The sisters prayed at their adoration periods all that day for the new president. His inaugural address on March 6th instilled fresh confidence as he spoke of the necessity to take immediate action on the financial crisis and on getting the unemployed back to work. There was a gold deficit and none was being paid out lest there be hoarding. By March 14 that year banks in two hundred and fifty large cities had reopened with the Maryville bank opening its doors on March 15. When the president ordered the U.S. off the gold standard, Srs. Carmelita Quinn and Eulalia Wagner hurried to Kansas City to send immediate payment to Germany and Austria for the monstrance just shipped, fearing inflation. On June 23, 1933 the chronicle noted that there were more than twelve million people out of work in the country.

By 1934 things were slowly improving, although there was still much want and misery. The sisters realized this when they heard that over one thousand meals had been served the poor who came to their door that year. Because of the depression only the most necessary building was done at Clyde. Instead, the workmen spent time cleaning out the pine woods east of the small pond. In 1931 a grotto of Our Lady of Lourdes was put up near the front entrance. In the hall outside the chapel, floor to ceiling bookcases were erected. A bad fire in the dairy barn near the end of 1933 made it imperative to build a new one. In

June the huge water-tank with its 75,000 gallon capacity was ready, but it was 1935 before drinking water fountains were installed in the monastery. Before this the sisters had to use the hand pumps outside the house.

It was July 1935 when the community began to plan for a new infirmary in what had been the academy section of the monastery. On December 9, 1936 the chronicler wrote: "The renovation of the academy building into an infirmary is expensive but needed, as the old infirmary is much too small and leaks when it rains. We have so many sick that it is expedient to try to make things sanitary and convenient for the nurses, so they don't break down. The painting of all the interior walls is needed because they are so dirty after years as an academy. Srs. Cyrilla Weilert and Angelica Diffendal will decorate the chapel for the sick. We have no mortgage on any of our buildings or property." Her notations about constant trips to Maryville, St. Joseph, Kansas City or to the Mayo clinic in Rochester, Minnesota bear out the necessity of the new infirmary. On January 18, 1937 the last of the sick, some of them on stretchers, were moved to this new section. By the following April, twenty sisters were being served in the dining room of the infirmary, while eleven trays were carried to patients in their rooms. In 1938 the old infirmary was remodeled into a canning center and was to serve that purpose for the next thirty years.

The depression also affected the Clyde farm. Grain prices were very low: oats sold for less than 30 cents a bushel, wheat for not much more. "The poor farmers can hardly harvest the grain for that," wrote the chronicler, adding: "In Kansas and Nebraska grasshoppers are eating up the crops and in the Dakotas extremely hot weather has burned everything up." This was in July, 1931. In the fall of the same year a railway car full of potatoes could sell for 60 cents a bushel; butter was 20 to 25 cents a pound. A secondhand truck in good condition with a five-ton capacity, sold for $65.00.

The weather, too, was a disaster. June 1931 was so hot that the workmen got up at two in the morning to plow corn. Water was so low in the wells that people were hauling it in temperatures of 105 degrees. By June, 1934 there was a general drought in the central states. Cattle had to be slaughtered for lack of feed. As they watched the scorching sun dry up the corn, the sisters prayed for rain, while the grass on the lawns grew browner than in winter. It was the worst drought in living memory. Finally it eased, but the sisters then learned of terrible flooding in the east. On March 22, 1936 the chronicler reported: "Hundreds of thousands of people are being left homeless. Property damage amounts to millions of dollars. It is said that in some Pittsburgh streets the water reached eighteen feet." Later she noted disastrous floods in the Ohio Valley and parts of Kentucky.

The summer of 1937 was kinder with fields and gardens yielding a good crop of strawberries, peaches, beans, tomatoes and apples. At the

94

time Joseph Gemmeke was working steadily to build up the dairy herd. "Because of Joseph's skill and interest, we now have one of the finest records of the Holstein Association in this state," was the proud comment on April 10, 1939.

The printing presses rolled busily as well. A new stitching machine was a great help. It was the constant appeals in *Tabernacle and Purgatory* that brought in a small but continuous flow of donations to help keep on with the construction of the permanent chapel for the Mundelein community. When the Clyde chapter voted to make a second foundation, one of their reasons was the possibility of "a good field for printing in Spanish" in the southwest. The sisters redoubled their efforts before Christmas of 1937, printing hundreds of Christmas cards to be sold for the benefit of the new monastery. Another reason for this hard work was Abbot Philip's advice that no more building be done until they had paid off some of their debts. Printery records for 1938 show booklets coming off the press in a steady stream. Their titles are almost a catalogue of popular Catholic devotions at the time: All for Thee, O Heart of Jesus, The Infant of Prague, Mary's Seven Sorrows, Devotion to St. Joseph. Besides the monthly magazine and the booklets, the sisters printed thousands of devotional leaflets and holy pictures each year.

Near the adoration chapel was another chapel which housed the collection of relics of the saints. This was completed in 1931 and would in time hold hundreds of such relics, including the body of little St. Beatrice, a girl-martyr of the late second century. The next year, thanks to a generous check from Mrs. Forschner, a statue of St. Benedict was placed in a niche in the front reception hall. This was just in time for the celebration of the community's fiftieth anniversary of the move from Conception to Clyde. Eighteen sisters had made that move, and four of them were still living: Srs. Aloysia Struck, Placida Stephan, Mechtilde Hilgert and Agatha Schrader. When Sr. Agatha celebrated her golden jubilee of profession that May, 1932, the honored guest was Mother Beatrice Renggli, sole survivor of the five sisters who had come from Switzerland in 1874.

In the fall of 1932 Mother Dolorosa was in Kansas to look at some property offered for a foundation near Kansas City. The community needed a third house to form a congregation of their own. That November 21, 1932 Mother Dolorosa was again elected prioress. Since she had already been in office for twelve years, the sisters had to postulate Rome to have her again. One of the first things Mother Dolorosa did after her election was confirmed was to set up a committee to work on a new constitution for a congregational form of government. Then the search for possible sites for a new foundation continued through most of 1933 and 1934. Mother Dolorosa traveled through Colorado and Iowa to look, but in those hard times local bishops were

not eager to have a new religious group in dioceses already overbur-
dened financially.

As work on the new constitution proceeded at the Clyde monastery,
the sisters reached the decision to close their academy, the last of their
schools. They were over-busy as it was, with the farm, the printing,
and the fact that forty sisters had gone to be members of the Mundelein monastery. To keep their prayer life alive, something had to go. In
June 1934 the academy was closed. A letter of Mother Dolorosa's,
dated September 8, 1932, indicates some of the pressure: "We are real
Marthas these days, yet we do not forget to take Mary's place at our
Lord's feet when the time comes. Silo filling, canning bushels and
bushels of tomatoes; out by the cave are loads of potatoes to be sorted
over and carried into the cave; many visitors coming to be shown
around and visit the sisters; the children coming in already for school
which opens next Tuesday: all these are on the go and some more too!"

On Christmas day, 1933 after the dairy barn fire, Mother Dolorosa
wrote in the same vein: "Greetings through our Infant Savior. With
our solemn Christmas services, we also have to have insurance, fire
and barn troubles on our minds this year. But it is all for Him who does
all things well. He knows how much we would like to rest quietly at
His feet these days. Tomorrow the insurance men are to be here again
— I hope for the last time. Then early the next morning we are to start
out on a hard trip to look at some barns and silos. Only a few days ago
we heard of a new way of building barns and silos which is fireproof.
We feel it is our duty to look into this before we build . . . We are going
to South Bend and Wisconsin."

Often enough these letters of Mother Dolorosa were written on
trains or in depots on scraps of paper as she came and went on her
incessant travels. One such scrap preserves some rueful lines she
wrote in 1934 to the prioress at the Mundelein monastery: "Thank
you, dear Mother M. Thiadildis (Edith Marie) for your prompt obedience (in sending two sisters back to the Clyde monastery). I give and I
take, but no doubt you will all agree that I am far better at taking than
in giving! It should be the other way, shouldn't it? . . . We never know
what is ahead of us. Never before did our printers have such a rush
before Christmas."

After the academy closed several reunions of former students were
held. A number of these enrolled as Benedictine Oblates. This was an
association of those who felt that the Benedictine spirit could be
helpful to them in their own lives and who affiliated themselves with a
particular monastery. By 1938 there were more than ninety such
Oblates among the former St. Joseph Academy women. The academy
had been one source of vocations to the community. Now that it was
closed, some sisters expressed a concern about attracting new members. In October 1933 there were eight postulants, one of whom had
walked two miles to the monastery at midnight when she found no one

at the depot to meet her train. In 1934 eight novices professed first monastic vows. In March 1935 the community received twelve postulants from as far away as New York state and Newfoundland. Yet in 1937 and 1938 the chronicle notes plaintively: "We need new members so badly!"

The matter of a new foundation from the Clyde motherhouse continued to be urgent. On January 15, 1935 Mother Dolorosa left for Pittsburgh, asking the sisters to pray for good success as they needed a new foundation in order to have their constitution approved. Unfortunately, Bishop Boyle did not feel the time was opportune for a foundation in his city. In May the Clyde Chapter was considering an offer from Archbishop Murray of St. Paul. He was so interested in having the Clyde Benedictines in his diocese that he had gone to Mundelein to meet Mother Dolorosa. The bishop's consultors, however, were not so enthusiastic. Financial conditions, they thought, prevented any new foundations at that time. Then came an offer from Bishop Daniel Gercke of Tucson, Arizona, which was to be the site of the third foundation. Even with this, investigation of other possibilities continued. Archbishop Cantwell of Los Angeles invited them to inspect his see. Early in November 1936 Mother Dolorosa learned that Fr. Charles Buddy of St. Joseph, Missouri had been appointed first bishop of San Diego, California. Long a friend of the Clyde community, the new bishop immediately and persistently invited the sisters to come to his diocese, saying "Nothing would please me more than to have a sanctuary of perpetual adoration in this rim of Christendom." Bishop Buddy repeated this plea when he visited Clyde early in 1937, and again in 1939.

Meanwhile monastic life went on at the motherhouse. In 1936 meals were served to 200 persons daily from the huge Clyde kitchen, where routinely sisters, workmen, guests and the poor were cared for. The winter of 1936 was a cold one. When Sr. Loyola Churan fell and dislocated her shoulder that February, the doctor had to be brought to the house on a sled. For the golden jubilee of Srs. Teresa Willier, Ignatia Williams and Bernard Willmann, instead of the large number of guests expected, only two monks from Conception Abbey were able to ski through the drifts to celebrate with them.

In September 1937 Abbot Philip Ruggle, now retired, accompanied Conception's new Abbot, Stephen Schappler, O.S.B., to Rome, taking with him the finished version of the constitution the sisters had worked on. In gratitude for this help in obtaining final approval, the Clyde community boarded six students of the Conception Seminary free of charge. After each sister had received a copy of the approved constitution on July 11, 1938, Abbot Stephen began a series of explanations of them, timed to end just before the first General Chapter of the new Clyde congregation. Used to being a community of just one monastery and then of two, the sisters now had to try to understand what a "generalate" form of government would mean for them. They knew that Rome wanted religious to band together for greater unity and strength, and that a single house would have a hard time winning approval. But was the congregational form of government really monastic? Traditionally had not Benedictine monasteries cherished their autonomy? It was a question that would continue to surface for years to come.

At 9 a.m. on November 21, 1938 the sixteen delegates from the Clyde, Mundelein and Tucson monasteries assembled to elect their first prioress general. By 9:45 Mother Dolorosa Mergen had been chosen, subject to postulation. When she was confirmed, Abbot Stephen solemnly conducted her to her choir stall in the chapel before entering the sanctuary to intone the Te Deum. On November 24th the delegates elected four sisters to act as councilors: Srs. Angela Bueche, Aurelia Rudholzner, Rita Busby, and DeSales Markert. The rest of the Chapter was spent setting up the finances of the three houses. Subsequently, Sr. Adelgundis Kaiser was appointed prioress of the Clyde monastery, while Sr. Thiadildis (Edith Marie) Kraus and Sr. Carmelita Quinn were re-appointed to the Mundelein and Tucson communities.

It had been in 1931 that the sisters decided to pray a more complete monastic office, ordering Latin breviaries and psalteriums from Belgium. That October the printers set about making a small Compline book with an English translation. By the Lent of 1932 the sisters were practicing to be able to sing the Easter antiphons and hymns. Each sister now had a breviary and a psalter. It was quite common at the time for priests and sisters in neighboring parishes and schools to bring their students to hear the Clyde sisters singing the chant. Paraliturgy also had its place in their lives such as the procession to the pine woods on July 4th that year to stand around the little grotto singing "To Jesus Heart all Burning" in reparation for excesses on the national holiday. By September 15, 1933 everything but Matins and Lauds was prayed from the monastic breviary. A one-nocturn Matins was added in the summer of 1939, but it was Holy Week of 1944 before the complete Matins of ferial days was chanted. Slowly then the formative influence of the daily Hours began to shape the sisters' lives in a process that was as gradual as it was inevitable.

The last five years of the 1930s brought ominous warnings of persecution and war. In October 1935 the sisters heard more and more about the violence being done to Catholics in both Russia and Mexico. Workmen returning from visits home to Germany brought reports of threatening political and religious conditions there. On November 3, 1935 news of the war between Italy and Ethiopia came to Clyde. By the summer of 1936, Mother Dolorosa was asking the sisters to pray fervently because of the uprising in Spain, where religious were being driven from their monasteries or martyred while churches were being destroyed. In the fall of 1937 China and Japan were at war. A visit from Abbot Stephen early in 1938 confirmed first-hand that there was a very real persecution of the church going on in Germany. As conditions became more and more critical, Pope Pius XI broadcast a radio appeal for peace. But in October 1938 when the representatives of Germany, Italy, France and England met in Munich, they yielded to Germany the territory she was demanding in Czechoslovakia. That November the sisters were saddened to hear that their friend Cardinal Faulhaber's residence in Munich had been attacked by Nazi youth gangs.

On March 2, 1939 Abbot Stephen phoned the sisters to tell them that Cardinal Eugenio Pacelli had been elected to succeed Pius XI. At this time radios were not allowed in the Clyde congregation, so it was from newspapers that the sisters learned the new pontiff would be called Pope Pius XII, that he had toured the United States in 1936 and could speak eight languages. The Pope appealed to Catholics all over the world to pray for peace during Our Lady's month of May. Yet within four months World War II had broken out. By the fall many Americans were worried about Roosevelt's desire to change the Neutrality Act so that arms could be sold to England and France. That year the Prince of Peace came to a world at war.

TUCSON

On June 28, 1935 Mother Dolorosa received an invitation from Bishop Daniel Gercke to found a community in his diocese, which at that time included both Tucson and Phoenix, Arizona. The bishop hoped that a community with a dedication to adoration of the Lord in the Blessed Sacrament would be a means of reparation for the persecution rampant in neighboring Mexico. In fact the completed chapel of the new foundation was to be dedicated to Christ the King in memory of the last cry of the martyred Fr. Pro. Needing a third monastery for the Congregation, Mother Dolorosa was very ready to consider this, especially since the dry climate of the southwest might help a number of sisters who suffered from tuberculosis. On July 11 that year she and Sr. Carmelita set out for Tucson; their tickets, clergy-rate, cost them $12.75 each from Kansas City to Tucson. Accompanied by the bishop, they scoured the city for possible sites, including an attractive location in Phoenix. The bishop, however, really wanted them in his see-city of Tucson, which had the advantage of being less humid than Phoenix with its extensive irrigation.

Finally they came to the Steinfeld home at 300 North Main Street in Tucson. Considered a fine example of Spanish-Moorish architecture, the house and furnishings, with two and a half acres of land, had a price of only $26,500.00. The two sisters agreed this was what they were looking for and proceeded to convince the Chapter at Clyde. The sisters there were at first surprised. Tucson was a dry desert spot more than a thousand miles from Clyde. How would the sisters support themselves? Convinced, finally, by the enthusiasm of both Mother Dolorosa and Sr. Carmelita, they voted to begin their second foundation there.

In mid-August, 1935, Sr. Carmelita with Srs. Ursula Semon and Euphrasia Sanchez left for Tucson. While overseeing the renovation of the Steinfeld house, they stayed with the sisters at St. Mary's Hospital. These kindly women gave them a hot breakfast daily, sent them over to Main Street in their car and had a meal waiting for them on their return. By August 19 the house had been fumigated, thoroughly sprinkled with holy water and a procession with a statue of the Infant of Prague had traversed its length and breadth to invoke protection and aid. The sisters sold the furnishings that were too elaborate for their use, after Mrs. Steinfeld removed some of the precious crystal and china, while her son took all the cases of rare wine.

On September 20th the sisters were able to move from the hospital to the house and had bought half a dozen cots for those who would arrive the next month from Clyde. There was not enough room inside for all to have a bedroom, so six sisters had to sleep on the second floor porch over the inside patio for the duration of their stay at 300 North Main Street. In October a railway car full of furniture and other items for the new community arrived from the motherhouse, along with four of Clyde's workmen to unload it and lend a hand in all that had to be done to turn a mansion into a temporary monastery. Henry Lange, Clyde's master carpenter, had been there before this, making pews for the small chapel.

Toward the end of October, more sisters arrived with the chaplain, Fr. Willibrord Becker of Conception Abbey. Mother Dolorosa herself came on October 27 with the fourteen sisters assigned to this foundation. On November 7 the formal opening of the chapel took place with a Mass celebrated by Bishop Gercke and Abbot Philip. Among the forty-two guests who were served dinner that day was Mrs. Albert Steinfeld. On future visits to Tucson, she continued to show interest in the Benedictines who had bought her home, often sending them flowers or baskets of fruit.

Mother Dolorosa appointed Sr. Carmelita as the first prioress. For most of their time at the Steinfeld house, one or more of the sisters were bed-patients. Several were recuperating from tuberculosis or were sent there to help their lungs. One northwest room became a kind of isolation unit for this disease. Other sisters in the Tucson community suffered from crippling arthritis. This meant constant visits from doctors, all made without charge, to the community. Nurses, too, came frequently to check or give injections. This kind of charity was to continue for many years, leaving the sisters with a debt they could try to repay only with prayer.

Immediately after the chapel dedication, the sisters set about earning an income with altar bread making. The first hosts were baked on December 12 that year. By the following February orders were increasing and by April 1937 more than ninety-three parishes were using the sisters' altar breads. For additional income, the community began doing some sewing: a little embroidery, mending altar cloths, monogramming and communion veils.

The fact that this fledgling monastery was in the heart of the city, unlike Clyde and Mundelein in their rural areas, made it more accessible to people. And from the very beginning people came. Business men, professional people, Mexican and English, they came to the chapel, "where one may find peace" as one out-of-town visitor expressed it. A Mexican grandmother brought her grandson, begging the sisters to teach him his catechism and prepare him for first communion. Within three years at least a dozen such children had been instructed. These were the result of Mexican-American marriages: the mothers knew only Spanish, the fathers were too busy earning a living to teach their children, so they came to the sisters.

Their first Christmas in Tucson was a happy experience for the sisters. All day long the doorbell rang as people came with gifts of turkey, crates of fresh fruit, flowers and wine. They ate a treat of ice cream on Christmas day sitting on the patio porch; they had never done this at Clyde! Different, too, was the sheer abundance of fruit and flowers. At that time eighteen dozen carnations could be shipped from Los Angeles for their Corpus Christi processions for $5.00. Friends were always bringing bouquets of flowers from their gardens. When the sisters canned fruit, it was no longer apples, but peaches, grapefruit and figs. A Phoenix fruit orchard once sent them 12,000 large, fresh grapefruit in one shipment.

In April 1936 Mother Dolorosa, with Sr. Carmelita, approached the bishop about starting nocturnal adoration one night a week for Catholic men who would want to keep vigil before the Blessed Sacrament. The bishop was interested, but not sure there would be enough such men. He was to be proved wrong. By May Mr. Albert Dyke and Mr. Urietta arrived, ready to begin. They promised to see that there were sufficient volunteers. In July it was already evident that these "Knights of the Blessed Sacrament" were in earnest. They kept faithful vigil, hour after hour, even in the wilting heat of the Tucson summer in a small chapel that was not air-conditioned. That December a group of Spanish-speaking women met to begin a weekly hour of adoration. The following April it was the turn of the English-speaking women. At a special enrollment ceremony one hundred and thirty of these women pledged to keep an hour of adoration weekly. Many of them who belonged to the Catholic Daughters of America gave up their weekly socials during Lent to assist at evening Benediction in the chapel.

The sisters were eager to spread their apostolate of the Eucharist still farther. With Bishop Gercke's permission, a letter was written to the Grand Knight of the Tucson Knights of Columbus, Andrew Grondona, asking if their council might undertake to sponsor all-night adoration each Friday. By June 1938 fifty of the Knights had signed up to participate. Now there were Spanish and English women "Sentinels of the Blessed Sacrament," as well as Spanish "Knights of the Blessed Sacrament" and the English "Eucharistic Guard." For many years, these groups continued faithfully to keep their hours of adoration, fathers in some cases passing on the duty to their sons. Often enough, Mexican priests would drop into the chapel, then leave again in disguise to slip back across the border. Devotion to the Blessed Sacrament had a special appeal at that time in the still largely mission territory that was Arizona. Three hundred people showed up for the sisters' Corpus Christi celebration in June 1938.

Bishop Gercke was delighted with this and continued to take a paternal interest in the young community. He always came for the feast of St. Benedict to offer Eucharist for the sisters, often returning in the afternoon to speak to them and give Benediction. He still retained the custom of reciting the rosary each evening with his own household. It made him happy to celebrate Mass in the little chapel for Sr. Placida Stephan's diamond jubilee on October 5, 1937. Not many jubilarians enjoyed health like Sr. Placida's. She saw a doctor for the first time in her life when she fell ill with flu in 1938 and was then seventy-five years old. It was the first diamond jubilee in the congregation. The bishop also approved when the sisters agreed to sing some chant numbers from their chapel in a radio broadcast for the benefit of the famous old San Xavier del Bac mission. When he urged the sisters to vote, the bishop himself came over to inform them about those running for office. A typical prelate of his time, he would probably have approved of the note the chronicler entered for November 3, 1936: "We mingle but little with the world. It is a sacrifice for us to think about politics, when our only aim is to love God better."

Within the community, monastic life went its accustomed way. The sisters were amazed with the rest of Tucson when it snowed twice in January, 1937. They were glad to change into lighter habits each June as their serge was uncomfortably warm in the Tucson heat. When Mother Dolorosa arrived on her frequent visits, they thoroughly enjoyed visits to the beautiful Sabino Canyon. They were sorry to see their chaplain, Fr. Willibrord, recalled to Conception Abbey, but ready to welcome Fr. Michael Baumgartner in his place. Their chronicle relates of him that one St. Patrick's Day in 1939, when the bishop's decree allowed Catholics to eat meat even though it was a Friday, the indignant Fr. Michael "did not touch food all day in reparation."

This newest foundation paid careful attention to the regulations from their Clyde motherhouse. How detailed these could be is apparent from a chronicle entry related to Sr. Irmengard Eberhard's silver jubilee of monastic profession on August 26, 1936: "A silver jubilarian may have twenty-five printed holy cards, half colored or fancy and half cheaper. The sisters who ask to do so may give the jubilarian a holy card. One Mass is said for her, near or on the date of her jubilee. On the day at dinner a white napkin is spread under her plate. She is given two pieces of cake, one for dinner, the other for afternoon lunch, and two kinds of fruit, such as oranges and bananas."

Far more serious was the number of poor men coming to the monastery door for meals. In 1936 there were sometimes as many as ten a day. This worried the Border Patrol police who warned the sisters to stop, as they felt this was drawing such transients to the neighborhood. Yet the sisters were still feeding them and giving them clothing in 1939, aware that these poor people were often half frozen, not realizing how cold the desert nights could be in sunny Tucson.

At the end of the congregation's first General Chapter, Sr. Carmelita Quinn was appointed to her second term as the Tucson community's prioress. Earlier in 1937 she had already begun to look around Tucson for a possible site for a permanent monastery. Busy as he was, Dr. Mahoney who did so much for the sisters, found time to take Sr. Carmelita around the city in his car. The most promising location appeared to be a new addition to Speedway Place. On November 22, 1938 Sr. Carmelita signed an agreement to purchase several lots there and by March had selected Mr. Roy Place, designer of many of the University of Arizona buildings in Tucson, as the architect. The monastery was to be in the Spanish renaissance style with a red tile roof, patios and arches.

In August 1939 Mother Dolorosa arrived to go over the plans for the new monastery on which Sr. Carmelita had already spent hours of labor. On September 3 war was declared in Europe. Mother Dolorosa was worried: the Clyde motherhouse already carried a large debt for the Mundelein building. Perhaps they should wait. Obediently, Sr. Carmelita rolled up the plans. The contractor, the architect and the bishop, however, urged that they go ahead. Materials would be cheaper now than they were likely to be later because of the war. Considering this, the sisters decided to go ahead, but to scale down the plans, leaving unfinished a large assembly room beneath the chapel, as well as the interior of the second floor's middle wing. On November 7, 1939 Bishop Gercke was delighted to break ground for the permanent monastery, amid what a newspaper called "a representative group of Tucson's church, professional and business circles."

MUNDELEIN

The major preoccupation in the Mundelein community in the early 1930s was the construction of their permanent chapel. Mother Dolorosa was making almost weekly trips in these days to oversee developments. November 1931 brought the mosaic stations of the cross from Innsbruck, Austria. The following June two large statues of the Virgin Mary and St. Joseph arrived. By July 1932 the chapel was nearing completion. The choir stalls were on hand in September, so that October 2nd could be set as the day of dedication, though it was to be some years before the stained glass windows were installed or the great mosaic in the apse completed. Two of the Clyde community's artists: Srs. Cyrilla Weilert and Angelica Diffendal had done the large paintings of the seven sorrows of the Blessed Virgin in the auxiliary chapel. The much-commented on granite pillars had come from New York, where they had been originally intended for a bank that failed.

The Mundelein chronicle contains a glowing account of the dedication: "At 6 a.m. Bishop Gilfillan began with the consecration of the high altar. At the same time Bishop Sheil consecrated the altar in the Mater Dolorosa chapel ... At 11 a.m. His Eminence and the clergy with their attendants began the blessing of the new church. After that, pontifical High Mass was celebrated by His Excellency, Bishop Hoban of Rockford ... After Mass, Cardinal Mundelein delivered a very impressive sermon, then followed the procession of the Blessed Sacrament outdoors ... Every available place in pews and stalls was filled and a great many had to remain outdoors ... His Eminence and the clergy were served dinner in the refectory, about one hundred in all ... There were four traffic policemen on duty to keep the cars in order ... At 5 p.m. Reverend Fr. Abbot conducted Pontifical Vespers and the chapel was again crowded."

Thirty-seven sisters renewed their perpetual vows as an act of devotion on the first day of the new year in 1932. Their ordered monastic life went on its quiet way that year. Abbot Philip of Conception made a formal visitation of the community and found little to correct. Some years later the sisters were reading at table from a booklet called "Points of Observance," a collection of customs and exhortations. The Mundelein spirit could well be summed up in one of its aphorisms: "If we apply ourselves well to their observance, it can soon be said of us that we are perfect religious."

After the dust storms of the early years of the decade which left floors and choir stalls filmed in grey, the sisters experienced different trouble in 1936 when, according to the chronicle, they had to empty 150 buckets of water from their flooded basement. Their garden was beginning to produce, which meant that most of August was spent canning beans, spinach, corn and tomatoes. By September 1937 the sisters were able to can plums from their own trees, while their bees produced fifty pounds of honey. They decided, though, to give up keeping chickens, especially after their dog killed half the hens. Their apple orchard netted them thirty-five bushels of winter apples in 1938 and forty bushels of early ones.

The community's main source of income continued to be the altar breads. By the end of this decade they were sending out millions of them to various parishes. They had also begun to make surplices, linens and stoles for the seminary which was appropriate to their devotion to the priests of the archdiocese. These were flourishing days for Chicago's seminary. In the fall of 1931 coaches full of seminarians had returned to St. Mary of the Lake on the North Shore line and that May, a class of fifty-six newly-ordained was graduated. Four hundred clergy of the diocese were present for the priests' retreat at the seminary in 1933. When Sr. Salome Eikelmann of the Mundelein community died in 1939, over one hundred seminarians assisted at her wake.

When Sr. Benedicta Forschner died in 1934, Sr. Thiadildis (Edith Marie) Kraus was appointed second prioress of the community and reappointed twice in 1936 and 1938. A sodality attached to the community, known as "Marian Pages," sent its first postulant to the Clyde motherhouse in the person of Josephine Wojtanek, later to be known as Sr. M. James. In January, 1939 the community had its first full eight-day retreat. In September the chronicler could note smugly: "Today we began to pray ferial Matins; we can now read the psalms in Latin with only one rehearsal." On November 2, Poor Souls' Day, the sisters tried "to empty out purgatory" by making as many visits to the chapel as they could manage.

The tranquil routine was shattered on September 1st when their confessor brought the news that Germany had invaded Poland. Ironically, just the November of the year before, "Armistice Day" on November 11th had been proclaimed a legal holiday. Even more immediately shocking to the community was the sudden death of Cardinal Mundelein on October 2nd. Twelve of the sisters attended a private requiem for him at the seminary.

Chapter Ten
1940–1950

The tranquillity of the Missouri countryside that spring of 1940 made it hard to believe that the Nazis had marched into Holland and Belgium, having already subdued Norway and Denmark. While the sisters at Clyde were busy setting out cabbage plants and opening the canning season with strawberries, asparagus, spinach and rhubarb, they heard that Germany had invaded France and the invincible Maginot Line was crumbling before the invaders.

In late June, 1940, there was a reunion of some one hundred sixty former St. Joseph Academy girls and then a picnic for girls from St. Mary's orphanage. This was followed by a pilgrimage of more than one hundred Knights of Columbus to see the chapels. At the end of the month the community was notified that all aliens must register and be fingerprinted. Ten German-born sisters had to submit to this process.

That July the harvest was a good one after so many years of drought. In September the vines were loaded with grapes. Another cause for rejoicing was the raising of the Conception Abbey church to the rank of a minor basilica, the fifth church in the United States to be so honored. All rejoicing was dimmed when the sisters heard of the bombing of English and German cities. "Something more terrible than can be imagined," was the chronicler's notation for September 13, 1940.

October brought the first draft registration ever held in a United States at peace, when an act of Congress required all men between the ages of twenty-one and thirty-five to register. By November the sisters were praying for the presidential elections, offering hours of adoration for world peace. Though the community approved of Franklin Roosevelt's unprecedented third term, there was an increasing tension for the German-born sisters. Shielded by their semi-enclosure and the lack of radios and newspapers, it was inevitable nonetheless that they become aware of the loathing in which most of the world held the Nazis. All mail from Europe was now censored.

The early months of 1941 brought few changes. Prayers for peace were re-doubled. In June the sisters ordered next winter's supply of coal, lest the trains be even more involved with troop transport. They contributed what they could to the drive for old aluminum as there was a great shortage of the metal needed for the national defense program. August, according to the chronicle, was "unbearably hot," and once again, the water shortage at Clyde became acute. Even the Sabbath rest at this time was not very restful, to judge by the Sunday schedule. The sisters rose at 4:45 a.m. for morning prayer and meditation. This was followed by Prime and sung Terce, after which High Mass was sung, then Benediction and Sext. The chaplain gave a conference at 9:30 a.m. In the afternoon there was singing practice, followed by Vespers. Then Matins and Lauds of the next day were anticipated, as was then quite common.

December 7, 1941 began quite placidly. It was the vigil of the feast of the Immaculate Conception. During the noon recreation, the sisters went to the Lourdes grotto to sing a hymn in honor of Mary. Only after this did the shocking news of the Japanese attack on Pearl Harbor reach them. At 3:10 p.m. on December 8 President Roosevelt formally signed a declaration of war. That Christmas was not a merry one. No mail or packages could be sent to or received from Germany. Many of the sisters' relatives were being called up for service. On December 28 Japan invaded the Philippines. By the end of the month, Sr. Josephine Gruenes, the farm manager, went to the registration board in Maryville to see if some of the Clyde workmen could be exempted from military service. Two had already volunteered and left; two had been drafted and two more were rated 1-A. Since the government was eager for the increase of dairy products, there was some hope of deferment.

Early in 1942 all the remaining workmen at Clyde volunteered for civil-defense duty as fire-fighters or ambulance-drivers in case of air raids. The sisters were doing knitting and sewing for the Red Cross. On January 2 it was reported that Japanese forces were pouring into Manila; ironically, the Philippines were to have become independent in 1945.

In March there was a pleasant break from war concerns in the arrival of the Von Trapp family. They had escaped from Austria three years before and were establishing a growing reputation as folksingers. The family knew about the Clyde sisters because of the help given Austria through the CARITAS program after the first World War. Their chaplain, Fr. Wasner, was acquainted with many of the students who had received scholarships for the priesthood through Clyde. It was a comfort for the German-speaking sisters to hear the old familiar songs again. When the Von Trapps made a second visit in the fall of that year, the four-year old Johannes was with them. These visits were to be a tradition for several years to come, long before the movie "Sound of Music" made the Von Trapps famous. Another small blessing in March was a check from the government as payment on the soil conservation program which the Department of Agriculture sponsored for the farmers of the nation.

That June the sisters in the correspondence department were kept busy answering over five hundred letters daily which poured in in response to the Novena to the Sacred Heart, an annual opportunity to send petitions for prayer to the community. That same month the chronicler noted that the Congregation now had twenty-two sisters who had lived to celebrate their golden jubilee of monastic profession. The canning rooms were busy that July, but there was time for a few outings to the woods to pick blackberries. The work grew steadily heavier on the farm as more workmen left for service. It was the sisters who had to shock acres of oats, do the milking, fire the furnaces. They were proud, despite the hard work, when the Clyde Hill Farm received the Holstein-Friesan certificate, the Association's highest award.

By October 1942 nearly all the workmen were gone. As a precaution the younger sisters held a fire-drill. It was real labor: pulling the wagon with unwieldy coils of hose around the buildings, attaching the hoses to the fire hydrants and then straining to make the stream of water reach to the high roofs. Rationing was another difficulty: now they had to register for gas and get certificates of necessity to operate the farm trucks. The war news in October was increasingly grim. German armies were deep into Russia; Stalingrad was all but a ruin. There was heavy fighting in North Africa, with U.S. troops rushing to meet the Germans in Libya. On December 14 there was a practice blackout across America for twenty minutes.

The sisters learned about the war's progress from newspaper clippings read once a week during the noon meal, so they were often confused about reports from the battlefields. Had the Russian troops recaptured St. Petersburg and were the Japanese really withdrawing from Guadalcanal? Closer to home, it was clear that rationing was going to be with them for some time. It was by now a full-time job for one sister to keep up with all the regulations, applications and instructions. Coffee was rationed, so were shoes. The sale of canned goods was cut in half to three or four cans a month per person. By April, meat, cheese and butter were also rationed. To add to the sisters' troubles, a tremendous electrical storm knocked out all their power lines, so that for nearly a week all the water for cooking, dishwashing and lavatories had to be pumped by hand and carried to different parts of the buildings. At night they used coal oil lamps.

That June when heavy rains began to destroy the crops, the sisters were praying for good weather. It was the wettest month in thirty-three years, as July was to be the hottest in nearly fifty years. Despite the poor weather, there was a good crop of tomatoes. Sr. Josephine had to ask the sisters' help to husk corn, the novitiate made a picnic out of it, gathering two hundred and fifty bushels. July brought alarming news for Catholics: Rome was being heavily bombed. Both the Allied and Axis powers were watching every move Pope Pius XII made. On September 8, 1943 the sisters heard that Italy had surrendered to the Allies, but later German armies took Rome. Would the Nazis hold the Pope hostage? By October the Allies were on the march toward Rome, with Monte Cassino, cradle of the Benedictine Order, lying directly in their path. What would be its fate? By now the grim reality of war came home to the sisters as more and more relatives were reported missing or wounded in action. U.S. military chaplains were asking the Clyde press to send German literature for the German prisoners of war held in camps in the U.S.

In Lent, 1944 the sisters were dispensed from fasting for the duration of the war. Like Benedictines everywhere, they grieved at the bombing of Monte Cassino. A welcome relief in all this worry was the arrival of Fr. Mateo to give them a series of conferences. Known as "the apostle of the Sacred Heart," he had carried this crusade throughout Europe, the far East and North America, visiting thousands of religious communities with his message. The sisters' publication, *Tabernacle and Purgatory,* enthusiastically supported his work. Thought to have the gift of reading hearts and revered in his own lifetime as a saint, Fr. Mateo had enormous impact on the community. Each conference lasted at least two hours, filled with anecdotes and personal reminiscences of great sinners and miraculous cures. His words were taken down to be preserved and copies run off for each sister. The conferences ended with an "enthronement" ceremony before a painting of the Sacred Heart, amid a dazzle of flowers, ferns and vigil lights. With his ringing words of encouragement to "give all for love," as they knelt before the "throne of the King" during their adoration, the sisters were assured that they were the chosen few who were to make reparation for all the neglect experienced by the Heart of Jesus.

At the end of May the war news was more then ever urgent. Allied troops were said to be only sixteen miles from Rome. On June 6th the community heard of the invasion of France, with four thousand Allied ships on the Normandy coast, along with eleven thousand planes. To the Catholic world's great relief, Rome was found to be all but intact with few religious monuments destroyed. On the Pacific front, the sisters were told that U.S. forces had completed the conquest of Saipan in one of the most costly campaigns of the war. On July 22 Roosevelt was nominated for a fourth term, campaigning against Thomas E. Dewey, governor of New York, with a senator from Missouri, Harry S Truman, as his running mate.

That fall the sisters contributed to the Red Cross and War Fund campaigns, as they thanked God for a generous harvest. During recreations they liked to walk to the caves to see the large pumpkins, squash and Chinese cabbages waiting to be canned. There was no lack of work for the printers, either. In 1944 an average of one thousand booklets were sent out daily. There were occasional suggestions that these devotional booklets needed to be updated, but others affirmed them as holding to the old, solid spirituality and "not giving in to the worldly spirit."

On November 16, 1944 the first delegates to the second general Chapter of the Clyde congregation arrived. There were now two hundred and sixty-three in the Congregation, including novices and postulants. There were four monasteries, each of them self-support-ing. The delegates listened to the advantages of this central form of government as these were set out for them. They also heard of the monumental work accomplished by Srs. Sennorina Zavodil, James Wojtanek and others in translating the entire monastic office into English, then binding this in book-form so that each sister might have her personal copy. The Chapter proceeded to set up some further delineation of the duties of the Prioress General and the local prior-esses. They agreed to ask permission of Rome for a loan of two million dollars for the proposed monastery in Kansas City, Missouri, the similar loan for the Tucson building having been paid off.

On November 21 the delegates again postulated Mother Dolorosa for their prioress general. Now sixty-five years old, she had been prioress for twenty-four years. The election of her council followed and then the appointment of the prioresses for each monastery. This exercise somewhat resembled musical chairs, since Mothers Thiadildis (Edith Marie), De Pazzi and Carmelita merely moved around the congregation. Sr. Blandina Cummins was appointed to the Mundelein community.

The war dragged on through the early months of 1945. With the rest of the country, the sisters were shocked at the sudden death of President Roosevelt on April 12. Mother Dolorosa in a letter dated April 15 described the three-minute silence observed in his memory in the Kansas City train depot. "At three minutes to three loudspeakers announced a three-minute silence to be kept in memory of Franklin Delano Roosevelt. Promptly at three o'clock the announcement came: 'All rise and stand with bowed heads in silence for three minutes in memory of our nation's great leader.' Instantly everyone rose, traffic halted, men removed their hats and all stood in perfect silence, while all activities ceased. At the end of the three minutes the loudspeaker said, 'Amen' and activities were resumed."

By May the end of the war was in sight. Mussolini had been hung by the heels in a Milan square. Hitler was dead in a Berlin bunker. It was five years and eight months since the second world war had begun. On May 7th peace was declared, Germany having surrendered uncondi-tionally the night before at General Eisenhower's headquarters. Pres-ident Truman proclaimed victory in Europe Day on May 8. That June the International Peace Charter was being drawn up in San Francisco.

This, as the Clyde chronicler understood it, "does not ensure peace, but provides a means of adjusting disputes by discussion and arbitration rather than war." She also noted that on June 20 when General Eisenhower passed through Kansas City on his way home to Abilene, Kansas, all stores and offices closed until 4 p.m. to pay him homage.

In the summer and fall of 1945 the Clyde community lost two sisters who had been influential in its growth. The first was Sr. Dorothy Keyes, a teacher for twenty-seven years, she had then gone on to write and edit booklets for the Clyde press. A woman of integrity, simplicity, humor and deep faith, she was noted for her devotion to St. Joseph. Many had seen her stop by his statue in the hall on her way to her room to shake hands with him or blow him a kiss. Three months later, Sr. Bernard Willmann died. One of the congregation's early stalwarts, she was a competent, forceful and faithful woman. Her early years were spent in arduous collecting tours for the community and it was she who made two trips alone to Europe to recruit both postulants and workmen.

Late July that year was very hot. "Good corn weather," noted the chronicler philosophically when the temperature reached 100 degrees. Far more terrible was the heat released by the bomb dropped on Hiroshima on August 6, 1945. "This is a new kind of bomb," wrote the chronicler, "called 'atomic.' It is so destructive that a single bomb dropped on Monday nearly wiped out the entire city of three hundred and forty-three thousand people." On August 9 the sisters learned that the U.S. had also used the atomic bomb on the city of Nagasaki. "It is terrifying to think of the loss of lives and injuries resulting from the use of this atomic bomb, but it is a last desperate effort to end this bloody war," reads the notation for this day.

On August 14 Japan accepted the Allied peace terms. The Clyde and Abbey tower bells rang out joyfully. August 19 was declared a national day of prayer with President and Mrs. Truman leading the nation in prayers of thanksgiving. On a less spiritual plane, the Office of Price Administration announced an immediate end to the rationing of gas, fuel oil, canned fruit and vegetables. Meat fat, butter, sugar, shoes and tires were still rationed. The bells rang out again on September 15 to celebrate Mother Dolorosa's silver jubilee as prioress. Abbot Philip sang the High Mass as incense almost hid the gold vases and lace altar-cloth from view. In 1939 Mother Dolorosa had written in a diary she kept sporadically: "One year today since a still greater responsibility was asked of me, a very hard year — but all for Him!" She was more used to the burden now, but could still pray: "Dear Jesus, let me always do justice to each sister." Mother Dolorosa never lost the simplicity that had marked her as a very young sister. Part of a letter she wrote when traveling on May 15, 1945 is typical: "It is 7:30 p.m. My prayers are finished, supper is over. I have said night prayer and examined my conscience."

112

As 1946 began, the council at Clyde came to a decision. For the first time, they would send pictures of the novices and postulants to a diocesan vocation publication in hopes that with the war over, vocations might increase. Another first was the purchase of war surplus materials. As a returned veteran, their carpenter, Henry Lange, had access to information about what was available. He had already obtained for the community two truckloads of heavy cabinets for $1.00 a load; oak tables, chairs and typewriter desks for $50.00 and a fireproof safe for $25.00.

By the end of February, 1946 President Truman was calling for reduced food consumption in the U.S. to help meet the acute needs abroad. Earnest appeals were made in *Tabernacle and Purgatory* for the starving victims of war in Europe. By May 8 a coal strike was seriously slowing down trains and steel mills. Toward the end of that month, lightning struck the Clyde dairy barn, setting fire to the upper floor and sending flames towering into the sky. Abbot Stephen sent monks and seminarians from the Abbey to help. With baled straw continuing to smolder for days after, the decision to buy fire-fighting equipment from the War Assets, along with a jeep for use on the farm, was easy to make.

More building was done in August, when the men began clearing the ground and excavating the foundations of a central heating plant. The community was going to switch to gas instead of coal for cooking and baking. It was at this time that some interesting visitors were welcomed to the Clyde motherhouse. The first was a monk who had spent ten years in Japan. He urged the community to begin a foundation in Tokyo, convinced that the Japanese would respond eagerly to the monastic thrust of the congregation. Mother Dolorosa briskly informed him that she had received many such requests for foundations but had scarcely enough sisters for their present monasteries. In mid-November Dom Mauro arrived. He was the librarian from Monte Cassino, who was soliciting funds to begin restoration of the ancient abbey. He showed slides of the ruins, claiming that thirty-thousand volumes had been lost in the bombing. Now just a few monks were living there in a shelter built by the Italian government. The Allied supreme command had sent soldiers to clean away the debris. The final visitor of the season was the former Empress Zita of Austria. Long an exile, she, too, was soliciting aid for the poor in Austria.

That November one of the first movies ever shown in the Clyde monastery was seen by all who chose to come. "The Bells of St. Mary's" starred Bing Crosby and Ingrid Bergman. The chronicler's comment was cautious: "It was a very good picture, more recreational than devotional, though the title would seem to indicate more of a devotional picture." Devotion was better satisfied when the community was able to obtain a relic of the first American citizen saint, Frances Cabrini, who had been canonized in August, 1946.

In 1947 the sisters were finally able to chant the entire monastic office, adding the two nocturnes of Matins for Sundays and feasts. In Holy Week that year they experienced the Tenebrae service for the first time. The schedule of the Hours was also altered with Matins now prayed in the evening and Lauds in the morning. A much appreciated change was the decision that meditation could be done privately, rather than in common. Another change was to have long-enduring consequences in the congregation: the appointment of Sr. Hildelita Mergen as novice director. A woman of intense inner life, a strong spirit of self-sacrifice, great loyalty to her vocation and the ability to inspire love, she was to influence the sisters in formation as few others had done.

The lingering effects of the war were still evident in some food prices. More serious was a spreading fear of communism which led to some drastic measures, such as the loyalty investigation conducted on all applying for government jobs. The sisters were more immediately worried about the heat wave and lack of rain at the end of the summer which meant both cattle and crops were suffering. They also worried about the lack of vocations. At this time American religious communities were being forced to give up hospitals and schools for lack of members, although seminaries and some monasteries of men were crowded in these post-war years. Another issue — which none of the sisters recognized at this time — appeared in a group of blacks who made a trip from some distance to the Clyde chapel in September, despite the fact they had been told that no white restaurant en route would serve them a meal.

In April 1948 the Apostolic Delegate, Amleto Cicognani, dropped in for a visit, having officiated at the installation of Bishop Bergan in Omaha. He was delighted with the Clyde chapel, which he called one of the most beautiful in America, and the sisters were charmed by his simplicity and refusal of any formality. In June, 1948 their attention turned to the Holy Land as they prayed that the conflict between the Jews and Arabs might end soon. On May 14, 1948 the state of Israel, the first Hebrew nation in two thousand years, had been erected by the Jewish declaration of independence. Now war had erupted.

Another distinguished visitor arrived in the person of the new Abbot Primate of the Benedictine Order. When he came in December that year, he was welcomed with liturgical correctness and pomp. Making his first tour of American monasteries to acquaint himself with conditions in this country, Abbot Bernard Kaelin was much struck with the efficiency of operations in the Clyde press and correspondence department. Before leaving, the Abbot remarked candidly that he would like to see the Benedictine college of Sant' Anselmo built up and developed, rather than Monte Cassino rebuilt on a grand scale. He could see no practical purpose in rebuilding the latter exactly as it had been: an immense structure with walls eight feet thick in some places.

The first retreat of 1949 was given by a monk of St. John's Abbey, Collegeville, Minnesota. Fr. Paschal Botz was to be connected with the Clyde congregation for many years. It was he who suggested to Mother Dolorosa that it was time some of the sisters received a more theological education. Another significant figure in the congregation's life came as chaplain to the community in June. This was Anselm Coppersmith, O.S.B. of Conception Abbey. One of the first things he did was begin a series of instructions on the Rule of Benedict. As a charter member of the American Liturgical Conference, he was able to lead the sisters toward a deeper understanding of the monastic office as well as the eucharistic liturgy.

In June a multitude of friends and relatives came to Clyde to help the community celebrate Mother Dolorosa's golden jubilee of monastic profession. She had particularly asked that nothing more be done for her than for any other sister. This was not very realistic. Telegrams of congratulations poured in from the Abbot Primate in Rome, from Cardinal Faulhaber in Munich, from the sisters of Maria Rickenbach. From the Vatican came a signed photo and personal letter from Pius XII. This had its own story: when the Pope was presented with the usual inscribed photo, he set it aside and told his secretary, Monsignor Giovanni Montini, what he wanted said. Then he signed the message himself.

That fall three hundred bushels of apples were picked from the laden trees in one day in the orchard. Later, early the following year, Sr. John Berchmans Massing lay dying in the infirmary. It was she who had seen to moving the orchard and trimming the three hundred and sixty apple trees. She let it be known that she had not expected God to take her quite so seriously when she had prayed for one really good crop before she died. But it was probably the postulants who were happiest at the end of the year. Up until then they had worn a kind of cap to cover their hair that resembled nothing so much as a black shower-cap. Now this was changed to a neat, short black veil with a narrow white band.

In this decade of constant building and expansion, a strong emphasis on work and saving predominated. There was little time for contemplative leisure in the sisters' busy lives. Constant appeals for the sacrifices of self for the love of God and the good of "souls" induced a feeling of fervor and piety. The hours of adoration were considered the heart of the sisters' day. Invited to one diocese after another, the sisters went not so much as a monastic community, but to open another shrine of perpetual adoration. Only in the succeeding decades was the monastic emphasis to prevail.

The European model of monasticism was still predominant in American Benedictine communities at this time, although moderated by lived experience as regards cloister. The sisters did not work outside their own premises and never went home, even at the death of a parent. Most of what they needed was provided in the monastery. Their status as semi-cloistered religious did allow them to go out to see doctors and to hospitals, as well as for necessary shopping. Intense scheduling of common activities and devotions tended to produce a sense of security within a comprehensive structure that touched every facet of daily life.

Regularity was all important as was a kind of formalism both in ritual and life-style. The sisters were allowed to write to family and relatives only four times a year. Mail was not received during Advent or Lent and all mail was opened by the prioress or her delegate. Twenty minutes was allowed for the daily rosary and twenty minutes for meditation. The library was kept locked except for a few hours on Sundays and feasts. Time was permitted in the late 1940s for private Scripture study, but lights out occurred at 9 pm. Except for one or two cars at the motherhouse, the sisters did not drive. For the city monasteries this meant hours on the phone, trying to arrange transportation.

KANSAS CITY

The major thrust of the congregation in this decade was the founding of another monastery in Kansas City, Missouri. Friends in that city had been urging such a foundation for years. Now that the war touched families everywhere in America, they felt it even more imperative that there be a chapel of perpetual adoration where people could come to pray for peace. Mother Dolorosa was with the Tucson community in May 1943 when she heard from her attorney in Kansas City, Mr. Hugh Downey, that Bishop O'Hara was interested in speaking to her about such a foundation.

Back in Clyde, Mother Dolorosa talked over this possibility with Abbot Stephen of Conception. He felt it would be easier to build now than later when the war ended, adding that the bishop might intend to offer the use of the diocesan seminary which might be closing. Abbot Stephen suggested renting a house before building, so they would have time to discover the best place in the city for a chapel and monastery.

On Pentecost Sunday that June Bishop O'Hara came to Clyde to propose his idea to Mother Dolorosa and her council. He wanted to begin immediately. "I never believe in waiting," he said, according to the notes taken of this meeting by one of the councilors. "I don't think we should wait. Certainly there was never more need of prayer! Our prayer has been too much concerned with individual needs and not enough about the needs of society. If there is peace in labor, if employers and employees can work together, then hatred dies down. We must catechize, instruct — even on street corners! For we are a missionary church! We MUST do this. Justice, charity, peace — these are the things to pray for. If corporations and other agencies crush the less fortunate, there is going to be a reaction. This is what we need YOU to intercede for!" As the interview continued, Mother Dolorosa shared some of her anxieties with the bishop. The shortage of sisters was the chief concern; they had so many aged and ill sisters, there was so much to do at Clyde with their large farm. The bishop wanted to know if they would need so much acreage in Kansas City. To his mind an acre was quite a bit. Did they really need a garden? Yes, insisted Mother Dolorosa, for privacy and fresh air for the sisters. Before leaving the bishop promised to see his consultors soon. "Kansas City," he told Mother Dolorosa, "is not a Catholic city. We have about 50,000 Catholics, but they are very loyal. We can count on a turnout of about fifteen thousand for any public event. We have fine schools: ten Catholic high schools, some very large, with over two thousand five hundred students."

The next step was for Mother Dolorosa to consult the sisters. In a letter she asked them to let her know what they thought of a possible foundation in Kansas City, reminding them that they had all too few sisters, and that it was war time with a scarcity of material and labor. As the letters came back, it was apparent that the majority of the sisters favored the idea. Such a shrine would attract many people, especially to pray for peace and an end to this dreadful war. It would be close enough to the Clyde house, so that some of Clyde's activities could be transferred there. Some felt there were too many sisters at Clyde; they wanted to see more and smaller communities. Would there be more peace in the house if there were fewer sisters? There was too little contact with people outside the community at Clyde: the chapel was too small for guests. Sr. Imelda Felten wrote from the Mundelein monastery: "The Mundelein chapel was erected during the depression; the Tucson chapel was begun in the face of war, so if God wants it, the Kansas City chapel can be started in the midst of war."

On June 19, 1943 Bishop O'Hara formally invited the community to his diocese. Before accepting this invitation, Mother Dolorosa was careful to check some points with him. Would the pastors favor the participation of the laity in the sisters' eucharistic devotions? Could inter-parish associations be formed for keeping holy hours and night hours of adoration? Would the bishop impose particular devotions on the sisters, as Bishop Buddy had recently done in San Diego, when he insisted that all the religious in his diocese institute the novena to the Sorrowful Mother? Reassured on these points, Mother Dolorosa took Sr. Carmelita with her to Kansas City to begin the search for a temporary location.

Tactfully refusing the bishop's offer of his own residence, as well as the diocesan seminary, the two looked at some twenty-five possible sites. By August they had chosen a property on Rockhill Road, north of the Nelson Art Gallery. Their search had involved "crawling under fences" to look thoroughly at what was offered, as Sr. Carmelita wrote. By October they had gone over the renovations needed to transform the house on Rockhill Road into a temporary monastery with the contractor, Mr. Ernie Dunn. He told them he was willing to donate four acres of a site near Hogan High School at the intersection of the Paseo and Meyer Boulevard when they were ready to choose a permanent place. With some changes in the heating and electrical lay-out of the Rockhill Road house, an altar bread department could be set up there, so that the sisters had a means of support.

By the end of October the renovations had begun to the point where when the bishop dropped in he could hardly make himself heard above the noise of hammering, sawing and drilling. The sisters were hard at work, scrubbing old flooring, planting a hedge for some privacy. "Gee, but you gals know how to work," remarked one of the workmen admiringly to Sr. Georgia Nacke. Another time when she was outside, a man who would not divulge his name gave her an envelope containing $5,000. Other gifts also came their way. One Saturday, Mr. Downey and his wife arrived by streetcar, he carrying a baked ham, she a chocolate cake. The sisters at Lillis high school sent over a cooked dinner. During all this time, the seven sisters working there were taking the streetcar each morning at 5:15 a.m. to get to daily Mass. By November 11 they were able to have the first Mass in their own chapel. Various diocesan priests were their chaplains at first, offering Mass at what one called the "unearthly hour" of 5:45 a.m.

With the date of the opening set for December 5, the sisters worked until midnight, washing the walls, staining and revarnishing woodwork. Friends of the community also helped. On Saturdays the men painted and hung wallpaper, while women friends sewed drapes. Altar bread equipment arrived from Clyde; from Mundelein and Tucson came sheets of breads, which the sisters in the Kansas City house cut with an old foot-treadle machine and packed for shipment.

On December 5 everything was ready for Bishop O'Hara to celebrate the opening Mass. Even though it was raining, a large crowd gathered for the occasion. Almost at once the sisters began keeping hours of adoration from 6 a.m. until 8:30 p.m. Before returning to Clyde, Mother Dolorosa asked the small community always to welcome the people who came to the chapel. This little chapel was thronged on Christmas day and for a midnight holy hour on New Year's eve. Some Knights of Columbus pledged to keep adoration each First Friday night.

At the beginning of 1944 there were sixteen sisters in the Rockhill Road community. Some worked in the altar bread department, but others were still busy painting, washing and cleaning. When they did the laundry they had no place to hang the wet clothes except on the third floor on the shower rods and in the bathrooms in the basement bakery and boiler rooms. The community room was so cold due to faulty heating, that they took to wearing their woolen mantles there. By February this house was already a stopping off place for sisters from Clyde on their way to the Tucson monastery. It was to remain a stopping-off place for the duration of its existence.

In the early winter months the Knights of Columbus kept a monthly holy hour with as many as fifteen men present for some of these hours. On Holy Thursday, the sisters could count over one hundred people stopping in to pray on their way home from work. The community itself continued to grow with twenty sisters stationed there in May. Sr. Carmelita, with the help of Mrs. Virginia Madigan, a neighbor, was busy organizing a group of lay Oblates and was soon able to see sixty-four invested as novices. There was a special holy hour for peace in the chapel when the Allied invasion of Europe was launched and close to a thousand of Kansas City's Catholics took part in the sisters' Corpus Christi celebration that year. The number of parish holy hours kept increasing. The sisters worked hard and long in their cramped quarters. There was little chance to get outside except for Sunday suppers in the summer months.

As the war dragged on into 1945 the sisters learned from newspaper reports that over eight million lives had been lost in battle. So they had all the more reason to thank God when VE day was declared. That May they began negotiations with Mr. Dunn for the property he had promised. This had a commanding position on a high knoll. Early in June the zoning board allowed the community to acquire the new site to build a "three-story structure of native stone, of Romanesque architecture." That August tractors commenced clearing the ground. Srs. Carmelita and Incarnata Hartmann were spending hours on the plans, deciding on an E-shaped building, like the one in Tucson.

From October 1 to 14 the Kansas City diocese was host to a meeting of the directors of the Confraternity of Christian Doctrine, whose episcopal chairman was Bishop O'Hara. He asked the sisters to pray especially for the success of this work so dear to his heart. Even as a diocesan priest, this far-sighted prelate had promoted education in rural districts. While still in Oregon, he had established a rural-life bureau and organized the first Catholic religious vocation school. As bishop, he advanced the Confraternity of Christian Doctrine and catechetical reform. It was he who headed a commission of bishops to prepare a revised version of the Baltimore Catechism, which had not been changed since 1884. Bishop O'Hara also organized a commission of theologians and exegetes to begin a revised English translation of the Scriptures. This led to the formation of the Catholic Biblical

Association in 1936 and subsequently to the publication of the Catholic Biblical Quarterly.

The early months of 1946 found Sr. Carmelita absorbed in planning the chapel of the new monastery. She wanted an open sanctuary with the altar to the front. When Mr. Shaughnessy brought some plans which she considered too modernistic, she told him that the sisters wanted a "prayerful" chapel. To her this meant arches. "Arch everything but the floor," she told him firmly. In May a railroad strike across the nation delayed progress on their building, as did the continual shortages of materials in the aftermath of the war. Other hours were spent planning an elaborate celebration of Corpus Christi that June. Bishop O'Hara carried the monstrance in a two-block procession from the monastery to the grounds of the Nelson Art Gallery where the second Benediction was given. The sisters reckoned that eight thousand people took part, including the Knights of Columbus, the Holy Name men and three hundred of their women Sentinels of the Blessed Sacrament.

In August the sisters were concerned about the epidemic of polio in the country with three hundred cases reported in Minneapolis alone. Happier news was that Pope Pius XII was consulting the bishops of the world about defining the dogma of the Assumption. As the Nuremberg trials continued, the sisters prayed for the souls of the ten Nazi ringleaders who died on the gallows, Herman Goering having committed suicide in his cell. In the U.S. John L. Lewis, head of the United Mine Workers, refused to call off a soft-coal miners' strike, with the result that for nearly two weeks the freight trains were not operating, passenger trains were curtailed and some industries had to close. There were dim-outs in twenty-one states whose electricity came from coal. As the year ended, Sr. Carmelita was helping Fr. Bernard Sause, O.S.B., of Atchison correct the page-proofs of his multi-volume work on the Rule of Benedict. Fr. Bernard was giving conferences on the Rule to the community at this time.

In March 1947 the community on Rockhill Road, along with other Benedictines, rejoiced when Pius XII issued an encyclical on St. Benedict. That Lent they prayed for the success of the Bishops' Relief Campaign for the victims of war, for which Bishop Fulton Sheen was making eloquent appeals. By April the sisters were worrying about the labor situation across the country. As more and more industries went on strike, it became a question of whether or not to proceed with the building of their new monastery. In June they had something else to worry about: the worst flooding in over one hundred years, with water rampaging through Swope Park in Kansas City.

It was August 15 when the actual work of construction began on the hill overlooking the Paseo. In September Mother Carmelita was consulting Bishop O'Hara about the feasibility of a hydraulic lift to reach the large stationary monstrance on the proposed high altar. Was this acceptable to liturgists? By this time the sisters were more concerned about the fate of Archbishop Stepinac, the imprisoned Yugoslav prelate. He had been one of the seminarians to receive aid from the CARITAS program. From every side they heard solemn warnings that the growing split between Russia and the west must be healed at all costs. That fall the government began a food conservation program: meatless Tuesdays and no poultry or eggs on Thursdays. Eighteen roosters were shipped from Clyde to the sisters on Rockhill Road just at this time. During unloading two of these roosters got loose and went running around the front lawn with the sisters in hot pursuit.

At the end of November the sisters were hearing about Pope Pius XII's latest encyclical: *Mediator Dei*. The chronicler noted that it "combats false mysticism and exaggerated archeologism in liturgy." As the year itself ended they felt their purpose in coming to Kansas City was being fulfilled as they saw the more than four thousand registered hours of nocturnal adoration kept in their chapel.

In January, 1948 the community was able to begin continuous exposition of the Blessed Sacrament, always a goal for a young foundation of the congregation. Then late in February the cement floor of the new chapel was poured and by May the sisters were able to go out in groups to see the progress on their future home. Mother Carmelita was worried about the lack of response to their appeal for building funds. It was apparent that diocesan funds would not sponsor this chapel and monastery, although individuals continued to be extremely generous. There was Mr. Dunn, for example, who donated both the choir stalls and the chimes, saying he wanted "the melody of the bells to float over the Paseo." In Europe at this time tension mounted over the Russian blockade of Berlin, but even at home Mother Carmelita had some lesser tensions. When she called City Hall to learn if any city ordinance prohibited the ringing of bells, no one seemed to know. She contacted one office after another without result. Finally she was referred to the Nuisance Department, which politely informed her that the bells could be installed.

By the end of September the chapel walls were up to the clerestory level and a firm had been found to make and install the hydraulic lift. For the cornerstone laying on October 3rd, the bishop insisted on English lettering, much to the disappointment of Mother Carmelita who, said the chronicler, "would much rather have had it in Latin."

1949 began with a number of concerns on the international front. Tientsin fell to the Chinese Reds, which, the sisters were informed, might be the final blow to General Chiang Kai-Shek. On February 8, Cardinal Mindszenty was sentenced to life-imprisonment in Hungary. Closer to home, Bishop O'Hara was seriously ill. Through all of this, work on the new monastery continued, gathering momentum as the opening date of May 17 was set. Then Mother Dolorosa asked Mother Carmelita to put aside her plans in order to accompany her to the first

121

meeting of all the American Benedictine prioresses, called by Abbot Primate Bernard Kaelin, to be held in Lisle, Illinois.

Forty-one prioresses met at the sisters' convent there. Abbot Bernard Kaelin made an urgent plea for help to finance repairs to the international college of Sant' Anselmo. He told the assembled prioresses that the abbots in America had pledged $100,000. According to Mother Carmelita's notes of this meeting, the prioresses did not hesitate to let the Primate know how little their sisters received for teaching in parochial schools, as well as how much it cost to educate them. Getting down to particulars, they informed him that shoes cost as much as $13.00 to $16.00 and a coif, $6.00. In the end they did promise him some help. Abbot Bernard cautioned them against letting communities grow too large and advised against over-large schools. Another plea he made was for help for diocesan communities of Benedictines who were not affiliated to other groups.

Back in Kansas City, the sisters were at the new monastery every evening now, scrubbing floors and cleaning up after the workmen. When it was dark enough for them not to be seen, they also leaned out to wash all the windows. A steady procession of borrowed cars began transferring their possessions to Paseo and Meyer in April. Great was the concern when the new altar arrived with the mensa broken in half. When the tester was smashed in an accident, the sisters began to wonder if the devil was at work.

Tired though they were, it was a real satisfaction for the community to welcome some eight thousand people who milled in and out on May 7 and 8 for their Open House. On May 16 Bishop Joseph Marling blessed the altar. That evening the sisters draped bunting over the still unfinished upper part of the chapel to conceal it for the 17th, on which Cardinal Stritch presided at the solemn pontifical Mass. The Conception Seminary choir sang for the occasion. Aware of the pace the sisters had recently kept and seeing their tired faces, Abbot Stephen Schappler urged Mother Carmelita to give them some extra rest.

In September the continuous track was installed behind the arches of the sanctuary from which hung the dossals in liturgical colors. Working in the chapel, the sisters often saw Bishop O'Hara showing visiting priests around. In December when they began the traditional baking of Christmas cookies for benefactors, Srs. Meinrada Dietrich and Justina Huppe arrived from Clyde with evergreen trees to be planted on the still bare lawns. The year ended with a private holy hour in the chapel led by Bishop O'Hara.

MUNDELEIN

On January 4, 1940 the sisters at Mundelein learned that Samuel Stritch, Bishop of Milwaukee, was to be the new Archbishop of Chicago. To honor the occasion they were allowed to listen to the ceremony of his installation on a radio broadcast from the cathedral early in March. When Mothers Dolorosa and Thiadildis (Edith Marie) paid the archbishop a visit in May, he told them: "When going to the seminary grounds, some people look at the powerhouse and are interested in that big smokestack. But I look over at your convent and think: that is the real powerhouse."

As the tulips, peonies and mock-orange blossomed that spring and summer, the canning went into full swing. The sisters had such an abundance of apples in the fall that they were glad to share them with the hospital. All this meant concern about getting the rest of the work done. It was important to this Mundelein community that all be done as perfectly as possible. This is evident in the chronicler's report on their Corpus Christi procession: "The procession went off so nicely, with no mistakes at all."

Abbot Stephen of Conception was there for the community retreat early in January 1941. Even during these days the sisters in the altar bread department had to work as the orders poured in. That Lent they sent out more than a million breads. They were never too busy, however, to take note of the seminarians, especially during Holy Week, when the chronicle described them as kneeling in the chapel "hands devoutly joined and motionless as statues." Late in June the sisters were happy to have a group of women pledge to make a weekly holy hour in their chapel and form a group known as the Sentinels, like those in the Tucson community. But there was no jubilation when Mother Dolorosa's letter in December announced that Mother Thiadildis was to become the Clyde community's prioress. Farewells to this loved superior were charged with emotion.

Early in 1942 the sisters were involved in sewing for the Red Cross. That same month an air-raid warden came to give them instructions. During a trial black-out the sisters huddled together in the side chapel with all the lights out. In April they began a first aid course and soon were donating blood to be used for wounded soldiers. They could not fail to notice how gas rationing was affecting the numbers who came to their chapel. That December the community furnished altar breads to the Great Lakes Camp which was so large it had become the most populated area in the state.

They continued to feel the effects of the war in 1942 as the government insisted the community convert from oil to coal heating. It took the sisters until June to convince the bureaucracy that their heating system was non-convertible. They were glad to forget about this when Mother Dolorosa arrived for one of her visits. Only with her were they allowed to walk as far as the bridge over Lake Mary, a few yards from the end of their property. Otherwise they never saw the manicured beauty of the seminary grounds. It was not beauty that disturbed the chronicler in September. She noted indignantly: "Some of our sisters nearly fainted recently at the sight of a woman coming from our chapel dressed in shorts!" She was somewhat consoled by the celebration of Catholic Chicago's consecration to the Sacred Heart with twenty-four bishops present. Another consolation was Monsignor Hillenbrand's promise to come to the community to talk about the concept of Christ's Mystical Body. Monsignor was a treasured friend, rector of the seminary and revered by many as a saint.

Again that summer the orchard bore heavily, the trees propped up to support their load of red apples. In early August Bishop O'Brien dropped in unannounced, as he liked to do. He came just in time for the evening meal. At this time butter was not served at table, so when a flustered sister passed the bishop some dried bread, a sort of rusk popular in the community, the bishop refused it with the wry comment: "No thank you. What I have is dry enough!" That fall the entire country was to experience the worst shortage of butter in nearly fifty years. In late August the sisters' attention was turned to peaches. One of their workmen was returning to the monastery with sixteen bushels of peaches for the sisters. When he had some car trouble, he got hold of the deputy sheriff, asking him to stay with the car, while he went off to get a new tire. When someone tried to steal the peaches, the sheriff promptly took care of him, then called the mayor to get a trailer to take the peaches to their destination. The sister in charge of the garden noted at the end of the month: "If the bishop deigns to dine with us, the mayor arranges for our peaches, and the deputy sheriff condescends to accompany our workman and then stand guard over the peaches for some hours, we won't be satisfied with anyone less than the Pope hereafter, and the president for our civic and domestic needs!" More important to the sisters was the appointment of Sr. Blandina Cummins as their new prioress.

1945 opened with many, many columns of names of those dead and wounded appearing in the Chicago papers. In March the sisters prayed for the thousands of Americans lost in the battle of Iwo Jima. More cheerful news was that Conception Abbey was to make a foundation not far from their own monastery at Antioch, Illinois, with Fr. Richard Felix, O.S.B. as prior.

One of the community's chief preoccupations that year was the consecration of their chapel which was to take place on November 21. When Mother Dolorosa arrived on November 11, she had made her first plane trip, having always before come by train or car. She was delighted with air travel: "Why, I don't even feel tired! I feel fresh and ready for work!" The day of consecration was a full one. The sisters rose at 4 a.m. and the ceremony itself took five hours. Among the many bishops present for the occasion was Charles Buddy of San Diego, who once again took Mother Dolorosa aside to beg for a foundation in his diocese.

As 1946 began, the German-born sisters in the community were receiving letters from relatives describing the devastation of war. Many wrote that they were grateful just to have a roof over their heads and something to eat, when so many were starving or freezing. Knowing this, the sisters contributed as much as they could to the National Catholic Welfare Council's drive for food for the war-stricken countries. Chicago alone contributed more than one million cans of food.

In February, with other American Catholics, the sisters' attention turned to the creation of four American cardinals. At a public consistory, thirty-two cardinals received the red hat from Pope Pius XII. For the first time in six centuries there were more non-Italian than Italian cardinals. Along with their Cardinal Stritch, Cardinals Mooney of Detroit, Glennon of St. Louis and Spellman of New York were honored. Cardinal Glennon was not destined to return to St. Louis as he died in Ireland on his way home. Another matter of ecclesiastical interest was the 25th anniversary of Chicago's seminary that fall. The chronicler noted that nine hundred priests had been ordained from St. Mary of the Lake.

1947 began quietly at the Mundelein monastery. The sisters followed with interest the progress of Conception Abbey's foundation which was located on an old estate at Benet Lake, Wisconsin, two miles northeast of Antioch. Prior Richard Felix was deeply concerned about the home missions and hoped his foundation would become a center for such missions. He had moved his "Defenders of the Faith" press to Benet Lake and was already turning out leaflets by the hundreds. In June a sister from the Benedictine community at Ferdinand, Indiana came to make a private retreat with the Mundelein Benedictine Sisters before taking up her assignment as novice director for a small group of women who hoped to begin a community of Benedictine Sisters for the home missions.

June brought many groups to pray in the chapel. The Christian Mothers' Association, the Association of Catholic Nurses, and small groups of Catholic Workers came from Chicago and Milwaukee. In August the community was host to Bishop Adolph Noser, S.V.D., who was ordained bishop of Accra, Gold Coast in Africa on the 23rd. Both his sisters, Srs. Tharsilla and Paschalia Noser, along with other members of the family, held a reunion with the new bishop pontificating for the community on December 8.

The community's aging benefactor, Mrs. Forschner, continued to visit them, bringing gifts of furniture, table linen and china. The sisters were increasingly concerned about her health and finally persuaded her to go to the hospital when she fell ill in October, 1948. When she had a stroke and lay in a coma, both Mother Dolorosa and Mother Carmelita made a hurried trip to see this old friend. Later in October the sisters were much involved with preparations for the

Abbot Primate's first visit to their monastery. This meant calling the seminary to find a sufficient number of seminarians to attend him, arranging for a throne and other items. The seminary's master of ceremonies got into the spirit of the occasion and secured the use of the late Cardinal Mundelein's favorite set of solemn vestments, made to order in France. Buskins and shoes were included with the set, along with the precious miter. As the solemn notation for October 31 reads: "This stirred us up and it sounded serious." In due course Abbot Bernard Kaelin came and remained for several days. Among other things, he told the community that more than half the Benedictine sisters in the world at this time were in the United States.

On November 2 Harry Truman was elected president against all odds. The chronicler could not find much to say, except: "We know the Russians were not much in favor of Truman, so that speaks in his favor."

Early in 1949 the sisters' table-reading was from a book by a young Trappist monk of Gethsemane, called Thomas Merton. They did not realize then the extent of the influence this American monk was to have on the monastic life of their day. Something they did realize was the rapid growth of the town they lived in: Mundelein, according to the mailman, had grown from the 900 people he served when he started his route to three thousand now. The chronicler recorded other growth with satisfaction: more than one thousand priests had been in retreat that June at the seminary.

In the fall the canning was heavier than usual. There were peaches, pears, tomatoes, grapes, pumpkins, squash and apples to take care of. Perhaps this explains the enthusiasm in the chronicle for October 24, after the sisters had asked the seminary rector to have services one half-hour earlier. "This change of time means about twenty-two extra hours for work for the entire community each week. Deo Gratias!"

TUCSON

By the middle of January 1940 the sisters in the Tucson community were going out in groups on Saturdays to see their new monastery. A month later they watched one hundred and forty men working on the site. One of these, a well-driller, on being told the sisters were praying for him, replied: "This is the first time in my life any prayers were said for my drilling. Usually all I ever hear is cussing!" On April 21 the cornerstone was laid and by the end of the month the cement floor of the roof deck had been poured. Generations of sisters were to enjoy this sunny deck with its spectacular view of the Catalina mountains.

The story is told in the community of the day when two sisters were working at the new building, where as yet no plumbing had been installed. Setting out to look for a bathroom in a nearby house, the poor sisters walked for blocks in the area without finding anyone home. The resolution of their difficulty is not recorded. All that summer work on the monastery continued steadily. By November the sisters were spending hours varnishing and painting, so that early in December most of the furniture from the Main Street house could be moved to 800 North Country Club Road. Hundreds of people turned up for the Open House on December 7 and 8, which the chronicler hoped "would be helpful to dispel ignorance and prejudice."

As 1941 began the sisters were busy in the altar bread department, at canning fruit and vegetables. They added sewing mantles for the Fourth Degree Knights of Columbus to their activities also. Next they planted a "Friendship orchard" of figs, dates and citrus, each tree bearing a plate with the donor's name. On Sunday noons the sisters liked to walk out into the desert around their monastery, admiring the strange shapes of the cacti. At this time Tucson had a population of some 59,000 people in its metropolitan area; 2,666 students were enrolled in the University.

A number of Catholic women joined the sisters' Benedictine Oblate program, technically affiliated through Conception Abbey in Missouri, but it was to the sisters they came for help. Though it meant much advance planning, the community was glad to host the first Knights of Columbus laymen's retreat ever given in Tucson. Attending to the multiple details involved, the sisters were careful to stay in the background, mindful of Mother Dolorosa's exhortation: "Work together cheerfully and in a spirit of gratitude to God that you do not have to take part in these public gatherings. We must surely be grateful that we do not have to mingle with the people of the world." Such advice was to become increasingly difficult for the community to follow. The sisters had many friends in the city who came for spiritual counseling. They had several associations of lay Catholics connected with them. They knew themselves to be much appreciated and were soon aware that they would be far more involved than the rural communities at Clyde and Mundelein.

This involvement increased when the U.S. entered the war. That December, 1941 radio broadcasts began requesting institutions and homes to volunteer for use as refugee shelters should American coastal cities need to be evacuated. According to these broadcasts, there would be no need to dig air-raid shelters or have blackouts in Tucson, but Arizona was offering to care for ten thousand children in case of emergency. By the end of the year, the Catholic Daughters of America were keeping a weekly holy hour for peace in the sisters' chapel. As Manila fell to the Japanese early in 1942, the monastery became a Red Cross center for Catholic women with most of the sisters signing up for the first-aid courses and a course in home nursing.

By July three sisters were attending Civil Defense meetings dealing with air-raids. In October there were regular air-raid drills and one city-wide mock alert. Each sister in the community was assigned certain tasks for this eventuality. When Sr. Elfleda Felten, who had been appointed prioress the year before, required surgery in December that year, it took many hours to arrange her transportation to Kansas City, since most trains were used for troop transport.

Bataan fell to the Japanese in April 1942. At home ordinary life went on as best it could. The community was relieved finally to be able to sell the Main Street property to the B.V.M. sisters who wanted it for a convalescent home for their aged and ill members. In their own community there were always several on the sick list. Any sisters in the congregation with tuberculosis were sent to the desert monastery in hope that the dry climate would afford relief, as were a number with arthritis. Of the thirty-two sisters then stationed at 800 N. Country Club Road, five were incapacitated.

In the spring the sisters set about planting a two-acre "victory garden" in the lot behind their building. Late in August they welcomed Archbishop Spellman who promptly gave them several "free days," such a bestowal being the privilege of a bishop at this time. In the fall, dates from their own palms were ready for picking and the sister-gardener proudly brought in a seventy-nine pound squash from the back lot. However, it was a sad Christmas that year for the German-born sisters with neither mail nor packages from their families. With typical understanding, Mother Dolorosa wrote each of them a personal letter.

As 1943 opened with the Casablanca meetings of Roosevelt, Churchill and General DeGaulle, the Tucson sisters had more immediate concerns: wild jack-rabbits were invading their victory garden and making off with the spoils. By March their south patio was a thing of beauty as the orange, lemon and lime trees blossomed. A little later the sisters were bundling up palm branches to send to the Clyde community for Holy Week. When an acute shortage of meat began to develop in the area, the sisters undertook to raise chickens and rabbits. The chaplain was a little confused when he blessed them since he took the blessing for birds. Apparently, he also named them since they had the Greek alphabet shared out among them: Alpha, Beta, Gamma. The canning room was a busy place those days with the results of the garden. They had lettuce, radishes, cabbage, peas, beans, turnips, spinach, tomatoes, carrots and onions, along with grapes. All this was written up in the local paper.

That August their table-reading informed the sisters that the Army Transport Corps had moved two million men overseas, along with twenty-million tons of cargo in its first year of operation. On the home front the gas allowance was cut twenty-five percent and meat was not allowed in many states on two days a week. At the end of the month the sisters took part in an air-raid practice. At the first alarm they were able to get to the basement in eight minutes, but they did wonder about the scorpions who also liked to invade that area at this time of year. They also worried about the bombers from nearby Davis-Monathan air base, which tended to fly all too low over the monastery and its tower that housed the five thousand gallon water tank.

In September the community expected to harvest three hundred pounds of dates from their own trees. Even more satisfying was Mother Dolorosa's permission to have exposition of the Blessed Sacrament every night of the week, which made the sisters feel they were now full-fledged members of the congregation. Had they had more sisters they might have been more interested in Archbishop Cantwell's invitation. He visited the community with his auxiliary, Bishop McGucken, accompanied by Bishop Gercke, and said he wished the sisters would come to Los Angeles to open a retreat house for women.

In early April of 1944 the pace in the altar bread department became more than usually hectic with orders from many prisoner of war camps in the U.S. Along with other Americans, the sisters were quite indignant when the postage increased for air-mail letters. On the other hand, they rejoiced when it became possible to buy bananas again as these had been almost entirely off the market since the war. Late in August when the Allies were freeing Paris, the sisters noticed young American soldiers joining in their own third Sunday processions of reparation. There was more cause for joy in September when they learned that the lights had come on again in England after five years of blackout. It was in September, too, that Sr. Placida Stephan celebrated the sixty-eighth anniversary of her entrance into the community. She entertained the sisters at recreation with recollections of loading her bed, washstand, and chair into her father's lumber wagon for the trip to Clyde. There was more good news in October: General MacArthur landed on Leyte.

In mid-January, 1945 the workmen were busy in the monastery basement, completing the large assembly room. Mother Dolorosa came in March to tell them it was time to concentrate their energies on altar bread making and sewing. They had too few sisters for so many endeavors; from then on there was to be no more chicken or rabbit raising and only a small garden. It was about the garden that their retreat director, Fr. Vincent Carey from St. Martin's Abbey in Washington, had a story to tell. He happened to be out in the garden one evening in August when Bishop Gercke came by with two priests. They looked at the watermelons, picked up a large one and went off with it. The bishop later told the community: "One of the priests knocked on it, said it was ripe, so we took it."

The new assembly room got plenty of use in 1946 with days of recollection for the Women Sentinels and Spanish Knights. Fr.

Dominic Lavan of Conception Abbey was the community's chaplain at this time. A man of considerable charm and drive, he devoted himself generously to the lay associations and Oblates. He was a great success with all, from the young girls who made up a group called "The Benedictine Doves of the Tabernacle," to the Newman Club students at the University. Conferences, mini-retreats, days of prayer multiplied under his direction. He even helped Sr. Leona Eichenhofer harvest six bushels of peanuts from her garden.

In May 1947 when the sisters held another of their annual "Family Gatherings" in the Friendship Garden, over four hundred attended. In June one of these friends remembered them with fresh grapefruit: three thousand pounds of it. On July 2 it was 110 degrees in the city, followed by dust storms so thick that even in chapel the sisters were almost blinded. However, by August they were able to enjoy recreations on the roof-deck, marveling at the brilliant beauty of the sunset and at the number of buildings which had sprung up around them in ten years. The end of this year brought Mother Thiadildis (Edith Marie) Kraus to the community as prioress, replacing Mother DePazzi Fink.

Early in 1948 the community welcomed two Benedictine sisters from the Philippines who were in the U.S. collecting money to rebuild their missions. They told of hiding in the hills during the war with Japan, living on a bowl of rice soup or one sweet potato a day. That May Mother Thiadildis brought an interesting story to recreation. A Jewish business man was making repeated calls to offer one million dollars for their monastery. When she invited him to meet with her, she asked why he was so insistent about it. His answer was succinct: "Because it's the most outstanding building in the southwest." It WAS a beautiful structure, pale rose-colored, with a style suited to the spirit and terrain of Tucson.

Early that summer the community decided to buy equipment for maturing and refrigerating dates from the Reid Fruit Ranch in Phoenix. These friends of the sisters were selling out, so they obtained the equipment at a fraction of its original cost. With the help of such equipment, the sisters were anticipating a harvest of some two thousand pounds of dates. What they did not anticipate was the first death in their community. On November 23 Sr. Jane Frances Hurley had lung surgery; after receiving five blood transfusions in the week that followed, she died of a pulmonary embolism on December 3. She was thirty years old.

Abbot Primate Bernard Kaelin visited the community early in 1949. This, he told them, was the fifty-ninth Benedictine house he had seen in the U.S. and Canada. He preferred small communities like theirs, rather than larger ones, for he felt monastic life as St. Benedict intended it was more easily lived with fewer numbers. Before leaving, the Primate checked to make sure the sisters took a noon siesta, "like in Italy," in the hot Tucson climate. He was hardly out the door when the pilgrim statue of Our Lady of Fatima arrived on an unscheduled visit to the chapel, which was filled to the doors as soon as the news spread.

Fr. Vincent Carey was the sisters' chaplain at this time. Trained in liturgy, he began teaching the lay Oblates how to sing Vespers with the community in an effort to bridge the "chasm" between the sisters' stalls and the pews. He also took charge of the sisters' singing practice sessions for he loved Gregorian chant. A vigorous and endearing person, he had the idea of starting a circulating library for the Catholic laity of the city. The Oblates and Sentinels would work on the project and the library could be housed in the assembly room. Losing no time, Fr. Vincent contacted the bishop along with various parish organizations. The Oblates took up the project with enthusiasm, holding raffles and rummage sales to obtain funds. By fall they had more than one thousand dollars plus two hundred books. Then Fr. Vincent set about making shelving for bookcases. There was no Catholic library in the city so he was convinced this one would fill a real need. A library association was founded with officers from the Oblates and Sentinels. A student from the university offered to help catalogue the books and make file cards.

By that fall the Knights of Columbus had been sponsoring a Friday night adoration program in the sisters' chapel since 1938. Two friends of the community, Fr. Arthur Kimball, state chaplain of the Knights and Andrew Grondona, long a prominent member, decided to apply for affiliation with the Archconfraternity of Nocturnal Adoration in Rome. Forty-five similar programs had been inspired by the Tucson undertaking. Toward the end of October, 1949, on the feast of Christ the King, fourteen Knights in full regalia, along with the "Benedictine Doves" in gold mantles and white veils took part in a splendid procession with the Blessed Sacrament.

This was fully appreciated by the sisters, but they had other concerns at this time. Mother Dolorosa had appealed urgently for funds from all the monasteries, as the debt on the Kansas City house weighed heavily upon her. So did the number of elderly and ill sisters at the motherhouse. With its 75th anniversary of existence in the U.S., the congregation now had a good many retired and incapacitated sisters.

The monastery and village of Maria Rickenbach, Switzerland

*The original statue of Maria Rickenbach
in a 14th century shrine*

The Clyde motherhouse and chapel, 1927

The pond and pine forest at Clyde

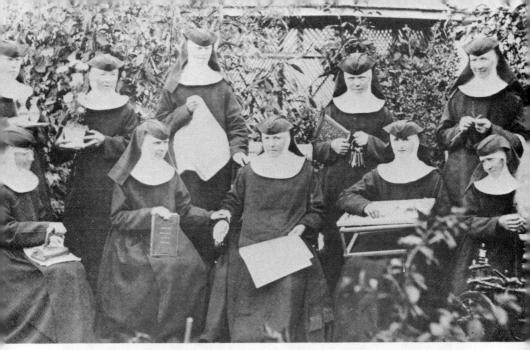

The community at Maria Rickenbach around 1870, with Sr. Joanna Gretener, Mother Gertrude Leupi and Mother Anselma Felber in center front.

Mother John Schrader

The chapel at Clyde with four sisters kneeling in adoration, 1942

*Benediction in the Mundelein monastery chapel, 1938 &
Monastic Choir*

*Mothers Thiadildis Kraus, Dolorosa Mergen and Carmelita Quinn,
1952*

A group of postulants at Clyde, 1952

The Tucson chapel and monastery

The Kansas City monastery chapel

*The San Diego
monastery chapel*

*The St. Louis
monastery chapel*

The Sand Springs ashram

A group of sisters at prayer

Bread means life

*They live by the work
of their hands*

Moments of solitude

Chapter Eleven
1950 – 1960

The Catholic Church in the U.S. began to come of age in the 1940s, and continued with an accelerated pace into the 1950s. Statistics alone are revealing: from 1940 to 1960 the American Catholic Church grew from twenty-one million to forty-two million. For the first time, this increase was due not to immigration but to natural increase, along with a considerable number of conversions. This was one of the reasons the astute Pius XII appealed for help to U.S. Catholics, not only for war-torn Europe, but also for the church in Latin America. Another factor in this was the media. The nation's first generation of television watchers were enchanted with Monsignor Fulton Sheen's lectures on Catholic philosophy and theology. He piloted dozens of prominent Americans into the church.

One of the single most important factors in the position of Catholicism in this decade was the continuing concern on the part of Catholics about atheistic communism. Catholic rhetoric reinforced national fears, helping to expand the "cold war." As a result, Catholics gained increased attention and respect on the part of some. Sensing this, Hollywood produced a series of movies with Catholic themes. Notre Dame's Knute Rockne was followed on the screen by Boy's Town's Father Flanagan, and then by the fictional Father O'Malley immortalized by Bing Crosby. Presidents and politicians consulted such churchmen as Cardinal Spellman on the Palestine issue, Cardinal Ritter on desegregration, Cardinal Cushing on Catholics as social justice advocates. Thomas Merton began attracting the attention with his books about monastic life.

This kind of expansion had a modest parallel in the Congregation of Benedictine Sisters. Here, too, there was a reaching out not previously experienced. In September 1950 as part of the American Benedictine Prioresses' Holy Year pilgrimage, Mother Dolorosa, Mother Carmelita and Mother Thiadildis (Edith Marie) traveled to Rome. This pilgrimage had been suggested by the Abbot Primate at the Lisle,

Illinois meeting the year before. On September 24, 1950 the group sailed on the Mauretania. On their schedule was an audience with Pope Pius XII, a visit to Monte Cassino and Subiaco and the opportunity to see the European motherhouses of their respective communities. The Abbot Primate hoped that all this would unite American Benedictines more closely, giving them a deeper sense of identity and roots.

Since this was the first such venture for the Clyde Benedictines, it was carefully checked with Bishop LeBlond of St. Joseph, Missouri and Abbot Stephen Schappler of Conception Abbey. With the blessing of obedience obtained in this way, the three prioresses were intent on sharing as much of their pilgrimage as possible with the sisters back home. Mother Carmelita was the scribe. Often she wrote her letters perched on the edge of a bathtub in a small hotel or monastery room, wrapped in a blanket to keep warm, with her little portable typewriter on her lap. Around her was their personal wash, draped on radiators or hanging out the window at night.

There were twenty-seven Benedictine prioresses in their group, Mother Carmelita wrote, and no one had been seasick. They had a life-jacket drill soon after steaming past the Statue of Liberty. Mass, office and rosary were prayed in common, after which the Mothers enjoyed the keen air, wrapped in blankets on the deck-chairs. On October 7, 1950 Mother Carmelita was writing from Cardinal Faulhaber's residence, describing the ravages of the bombing still very evident in Munich. Next the pilgrimage went to Switzerland, where a cable car took the three prioresses from Clyde up to Maria Rickenbach. They stayed overnight there in their original motherhouse, keeping an hour of adoration in the chapel. Later their chartered bus narrowly escaped a few collisions with several herds of brown Swiss cattle, while it was passing trucks loaded with huge rounds of cheese. Winding up and around the passes between Switzerland and Italy, the prioresses saw tiny villages, each with its church steeple, clinging to the mountainsides. In Milan, Mother Carmelita wrote, they watched experts working on Leonardo Da Vinci's painting of the Last Supper, trying to repair the damage caused by dampness during the war years. By October 14th they were passing fields of alfalfa and the mulberry trees of the silkworm industry. Later their bus took them by the olive and orange groves of the Tuscan Hills.

As they neared Rome, their bus passed ox carts side by side with great vans transporting material for repairing the roads bombed out in the war. That same week the prioresses were in the basilica of St. Mary Major, watching a Dominican priest hear confessions as he leaned against a pillar. Mother Carmelita wrote that the ceiling of this chapel had been gilded with the first gold brought from America. She described a real Pentecost of pilgrims at the basilica of St. Paul-outside-the-Walls, with people singing in German, French, Spanish,

Italian and English. Afterward she made the Scala Sancta on her knees, "which is not recommended for anyone with heart trouble." A tour of the Coliseum with its memories of early martyrs was overshadowed by the prioresses' first visit to St. Peter's. The American Benedictines stood around the confession of St. Peter and sang the Creed "at the top of their lungs."

October 19th brought Mothers Dolorosa, Carmelita and Thiadildis the highlight of their entire pilgrimage: a private audience with Pope Pius XII. This was arranged for them by Mother Pascalina, later to be known to the unfriendly as "La Popessa." A personal friend of Cardinal Faulhaber's, Mother Pascalina had taken care of donations sent from Clyde to the Cardinal, when these could not be forwarded to Germany during the war. She also disbursed some of the Pope's private charities. A Bavarian by birth, Mother Pascalina met the future Pope when he was a sickly young prelate in a German clinic. By this time she had been looking after him for thirty-five years, both as nurse and housekeeper. Cardinal Faulhaber had asked her to obtain if possible a special private audience with the Holy Father for the three prioresses of the Clyde congregation. After a large public audience, Mother Pascalina arranged for Mothers Dolorosa, Carmelita and Thiadildis to see the Pope alone. She begged them not to tell the other prioresses about this, since the pontiff had cancelled most audiences due to the pressure of preparing for the proclamation of the dogma of the Assumption. Kneeling before the Vicar of Christ in Castel Gandolfo, they listened in awe as he asked about the participation of lay Catholics in their work of adoration and begged them to pray for the Church. Before Monsignor Montini motioned them to rise, the Pope told them to found more sanctuaries.

After this everything else was a kind of anti-climax, even though they delighted in Mother Pascalina's further kindness in obtaining a personally signed blessing from the Holy Father for their Christmas gift to benefactors. In this way she repaid them for Mother Dolorosa's gift of a prize dairy bull-calf, shipped to the papal herd to help rebuild it, and ever after known at Clyde as the "papal bull."

On October 21 the Benedictine pilgrims visited Monte Cassino which now resembled a ghost town. About twenty-five monks remained at the site, helping to reconstruct the monastery with some government aid. The following day the Mothers were able to sing Vespers at Sante' Anselmo, where the students told them about studying in bed, wrapped in blankets during the winter cold. While visiting Subiaco a few days later, Mother Carmelita took a few leaves from the famous thorn-bush as a memento. The pilgrims traveled through Turin, Grenoble, Lyons, Orleans and Lourdes, visited the famous cathedral of Chartres and various churches in Paris, before returning to the U.S. By November 19 they were back in Clyde.

On New Year's Day, 1951, at the motherhouse there was a festive dinner, whose main course was the goose Sr. Romana Moritz had slaughtered for the occasion. Then the sisters' attention turned to the Chapter which was to begin in February. Many of them realized that it was time for a change, yet who wanted to think of Mother Dolorosa being out of office, after she had been prioress for more than thirty years? On February 21, Mother Carmelita Quinn was elected the second prioress general of the congregation. She had been an influential figure in the community from her novitiate. Secretary and disciple of Fr. Lukas, she helped him plan the Mundelein foundation. She was both designer and first prioress of the Tucson and Kansas City communities. A woman of vast drive and determination, Mother Carmelita combined a strong spirit of prayer with foresight and the ability to read the signs of the times. Though not loved as Mother Dolorosa was, she inspired reverence and admiration. It was a difficult and delicate thing to take over from a revered predecessor, but Mother Carmelita managed it with skill and tact, making Mother Dolorosa her first councilor and obtaining permission for her to retain the title of Mother. Next she appointed the well-loved Mother Thiadildis Kraus as prioress at Clyde.

Immediately after her election, Mother Carmelita set to work at a building and renovation program. Workmen began to clean and paint both the monastery itself and the printery building. Linoleum was laid in rooms and halls. The large refectory got this new flooring, besides a huge mural at one end, painted by Srs. Cyrilla and Angelica to complement the crucifix at the opposite end. This painting meant that the community had to eat in the narrow refectory-hall for more than six weeks, with table-serving becoming a feat to baffle Houdini.

The novices worked into the night sanding and painting the old novitiate chairs a dazzling white. The kitchen was renovated and a new gas oven installed in the bakery in which, as the chronicler noted enthusiastically, "forty pies can be baked at once." There was new equipment for the laundry and the infirmary. Water coolers were placed on the different floors. Another blessing was a loudspeaker system for the refectory which eliminated having to shout to make oneself heard throughout this one hundred foot room. The old coal shed became a garage. An inter-communicating phone system put an end to the portress having to run around the house looking for someone, while her guardian angel coped with any callers at the door. The bell-ringers were delighted when the bells were electrified in 1954 as this meant no more straining to pull heavy bell ropes during services. It also meant no more giggles for the postulants when they watched a small bell-ringer's feet leave the floor during her exertions on a feast day.

Major renovations during this decade included a huge new reservoir to help solve the perennial shortage of water. With so many at Clyde, they needed twelve thousand gallons daily. During the drought years of 1953 and 54 water had run perilously short, to the point where baths could be taken only once a week and that with half a bucket of water. Day after day groups of sisters went to the site of the reservoir to help tie reinforcing rods and save money, under the genial supervision of Henry Lange who had returned from Oregon to oversee this work.

Next Mother Carmelita set about planning a new cemetery to replace the old one which they had outgrown. After endless correspondence with both civil and religious authorities, she succeeded by November 1955 in having all the graves moved to the new site south of the laundry building. Now only the grave of Fr. Lukas remained at the old site. In July 1952 Mother Carmelita was telling the sisters about her plans to remodel what was called "lower Hall," and to excavate under the east wing to obtain more space for various uses. Then courtyard porches were enclosed with glass blocks to create new bedrooms and workrooms. Lastly, excavations under the south wing made room for new freezer space, dining rooms and a much-needed additional elevator to bring the sick to the chapel.

In 1955 the printery was renovated. This meant taking steel wool to the press room where the grime had been undisturbed for nearly half a century. Before this the roofers had put on a new roof, beginning their work at five a.m. to avoid the intense heat. In 1957 the workmen's house was partially converted into a new guest house. By the end of this decade when most of the renovations were completed, Mother Carmelita was heard to say wryly: "I have been accused of shaking the foundations, raising the roof and moving the dead."

For those who found all this unsettling, there was a reassuring sameness about the Clyde farm. Despite the heavy flooding along the Missouri River in 1951 the crops were good, especially the apple crop. By October 16 the sisters had picked 1600 bushels of Jonathans, along with red and yellow Delicious. They still worried about flooding in the spring of the following year. By April 1952 nearly eleven thousand families had to be evacuated from suburban St. Joseph, Missouri. Hundreds of people were working on the levees, as thirty-five thousand families fled their homes in Omaha and Council Bluffs.

Everywhere farm workers were demanding higher wages. The community purchased a new tractor, combine and baler in these years. By June 30, 1952 the heat wave had built to a new high. The sisters heard that asphalt streets in St. Louis were buckling as the temperature stayed over 90 degrees for three weeks. Heat-related deaths were occurring all over the country. Despite the heat, some sisters enjoyed a ride around the fields in the new combine on the 4th of July. Sunday walks often took them to the chicken yard to see the baby chicks, which one sister described as "2,500 fluffy marshmallow balls." That August they bought a truck-load of fresh pineapple at a great reduction. By the end of the week, there was scarcely a sister without bandaged fingers. In the fall it was time for apple-picking again. A painter would have wanted to set up a canvas in the orchard that September to capture the red and yellow fruit on the trees, the black-aproned sisters beneath and the white-veiled novices perched on the topmost branches.

The drought in the midwest continued into 1956. On January 18 that year the chronicle noted: "We have had less than six inches of rain for the past six months." By May the ground was drier than it had been in thirty-two years. It was mid-June before the first rain fell. A hint of what might befall the farm came in a letter from Bishop John Cody to Mother Carmelita in January 1957. He questioned the wisdom of the community being so involved with heavy farm work and suggested getting rid of "high-bred cattle."

Whatever the future might bring, the sisters were busier than ever at this time. Apricots were plentiful, the June total of strawberries was 1,560 gallons. In July as the heat rose like steam from the damp ground, the bean-pickers had to change every stitch of clothing before going to Vespers. In June 1958 something new was added to the Clyde scene: thirty-five sheep, which the farm manager hoped would help keep down the brush in the pine woods. The sisters who liked to pray their rosary in the woods were not all that delighted with this addition. Some of them, however, did remember back in 1955 when they had agreed to pasture six goats for an old farmer who called himself "the infidel," since he practiced no religion. Appreciating the way Sr. John Meyer cared for these goats, the infidel had decided there must be something to this religion business and proceeded to take instructions in the Catholic faith.

Recurring epidemics of flu in the winters during this decade led to a farm inspection by the state board of health. Their recommendations were serious: the slaughter-house must be renovated, the water purified and refrigerated drinking-fountains installed. Above all, the milk must be pasteurized.

While the farm went on its accustomed way, other aspects of life at Clyde began slowly to change. Despite her unswerving adherence to traditional pieties, Mother Carmelita was well aware that Pope Pius XII had repeatedly urged religious to adjust to modern times. She attended the first National Congress of Religious in the U.S. at Notre Dame in 1951. Convinced that the sisters needed more schooling in the area of theology and spirituality, she felt she had to move carefully as there was a strong element of anti-intellectualism in the congregation. With Thomas a Kempis, many of the sisters believed that to leave the enclosure was to risk harm to the spiritual life. Some of the older sisters, in fact, had rarely been off the Clyde property. Sr. Romana Moritz was 75 years old when she accompanied Mother Dolorosa to the Mundelein monastery in 1955. That was the first time she had ever had a purse or suitcase in her possession.

138

Gradually, while the sisters continued to enjoy familiar things like picnic suppers in "Subiaco Park," or down by the laundry pond, less familiar things were introduced. Political awareness was encouraged by a better choice of newspaper items read at table. Now the sisters heard more of the Korean war. Mother Carmelita urged them to vote. "We don't want you to vote like a flock of sheep, but to use your own intelligence. If Catholics had exercised their privilege in Germany, men like Hitler would never have gotten into power." She had representative Democrats and Republicans come to the monastery to keep the sisters informed about the party platforms.

Unfortunately, along with other Catholics, the sisters were duped by Senator McCarthy's anti-communist activities. The chronicle for November 11, 1954 refers to a pro-McCarthy demonstration in Washington to protest a Senate investigation of his witch hunts: "The sisters are praying the collect to frustrate the enemies of our holy religion." The community at Clyde heard about the first unmanned artificial satellite launched by the Russians on October 4, 1957, stumbling over the new term, "Sputnik." When the American "Explorer I" was launched by rocket-power on January 31, 1958 few of them realized that the space-age had begun.

Toward the end of August 1959 the sisters learned that Hawaii had become the fiftieth state. A few weeks later in mid-September they were keeping two days of silence so that Premier Krushchev's visit to the United States would have no evil effects. Something else unfamiliar to them kept appearing in the newspaper clippings, a new word, "integration." The congregation had no black sisters. There were no blacks in the vicinity of Clyde. But the sisters remembered being told what Bishop O'Hara had said when he preached at a Labor Day Mass in Kansas City: nowhere in the metropolitan area was there an accredited and properly equipped hospital where a Negro doctor could take a private patient for care. They also heard that Cardinal Ritter was working toward integrating the Catholic schools in St. Louis.

Workshops were next on Mother Carmelita's list. The prioresses, councilors and novice directors began attending these. With Mother Thiadildis, Mother Carmelita herself flew to Rome for the first Congress of Superiors General in September, 1952. With some seven hundred other major superiors, they heard pleas for more collaborations between congregations of religious, more insistence on charity, poverty and obedience, more training in doctrine for younger religious. Worried about the drop in membership for religious communities of women in Europe, the Pope pleaded for greater simplicity of life, including a simpler habit. Mother Carmelita was pleased to note that the Clyde congregation's habit was voted one of the simplest by the other superiors at this meeting.

In October 1953 the American Benedictine Prioresses' retreat and novitiate workshop were held at the Clyde monastery. Preparations began months ahead. Painting, cleaning, re-arranging went on apace. The sisters doubled up in bedrooms and dormitories to make room for the forty-three prioresses and thirty-eight novice directors who began arriving on October 19. For the first time the sisters gained a little privacy in these dormitories, with cubicle curtains now surrounding each bed, plus the addition of a chest of drawers. There were six priest moderators at this meeting, which meant that masses were going on simultaneously at three altars, with another in the Relic Chapel for sisters who had given up their choir stalls to the visitors. The priests were served separately, but all the others ate in the community refectory. This was done with due ceremony in entering and leaving processionally. There was considerably less ceremony for the community's younger members as they scrambled around behind the scenes, washing dishes in relays. The days were crowded with lectures and the evenings made enjoyable by programs of slides with commentaries from the various prioresses, showing the communities represented at the meeting.

After this Mother Carmelita girded herself to undertake a major project. She planned to bring Fr. Conrad Louis, O.S.B. of St. Meinrad's Archabbey to Clyde to give the entire community a six-week Scripture course. This project took both courage and patience as lamentations resounded on all sides about work piling up while more than two hours daily were devoted to his lectures. Fr. Conrad arrived on June 21, 1955 while the canning season was in full swing. How would they ever get the work done? Mother Carmelita prevailed. The lectures would count for meditation and spiritual reading; the community would rise half an hour earlier to pray Lauds.

Her choice of Fr. Conrad was a wise one. He managed to charm the community before the first week was over. "The Bible," he told the sisters, "used to be kept with the Sacrament in the early Church." He explored the Covenant theme in both the Old and New Testaments. Bibles were everywhere now. Each sister could have one and it was permissible to make notes in one's own bible. When Fr. Conrad returned for a second session the following year, it was like welcoming an old friend, as he led them through the psalms and the Pauline letters. He taught the community to sing Psalm 116 in Hebrew, and cheerfully mopping his forehead as the temperature in the lecture hall passed the 90 degree mark, assured them that they, too, were now "whole burnt offerings." As a follow-up on this, Fr. Ignatius Hunt, O.S.B., of Conception Abbey came to the community in December 1959 for a series of lectures on the place of the Scriptures in the Church. Fr. Conrad was there again in 1960 for a course on the prophets.

After her re-election in 1956, Mother Carmelita decided it was time for the next step. God was blessing the congregation with many vocations at this time. Further training in spirituality, theology, scripture and some basic psychology was definitely needed for forma-

140

tion directors. Armed with ecclesiastical approbation from the bishop, Mother Carmelita won her council's consent to send Srs. Pascaline Coff and Matthias Igoe to St. Mary's College in Indiana, where Sr. Madeleva C.S.C. was dean. On learning that the two were to study for doctorates in theology, Sr. Euphemia Staudt from her infirmary room asked Sr. Matthias when she expected to offer her first Mass.

In 1959 the Abbot Primate, Bernard Kaelin came to Clyde to meet with the presidents of the American Federation of Benedictine Women. They discussed founding a Benedictine Institute of Theology, having previously voted during their 1957 meeting in Ferdinand, Indiana, to locate such an institute at St. Benedict's College for women in St. Joseph, Minnesota. Fr. Paschal Botz, O.S.B. of St. John's Abbey in Collegeville, Minnesota was to be the dean, assisted by Sr. Anthony Wagner, O.S.B. of St. Benedict's. A substantial financial gift from the Clyde congregation was instrumental in readying the Institute for the summer of 1958. Mother Carmelita sent Srs. Rosalita (Audrey) Jones, Dolores Dowling, Damien (Paula) Thompson and Maureen Truland to work for a master's degree in sacred studies during the next five summers. Sr. Damien had previously had a three-month course in psychiatric nursing with Sr. Annunciata McTague. There were also chant courses for some of the senior organists, along with frequent lectures by Edmond Kestel, O.S.B. of Conception Abbey for the entire Clyde community. Mother Carmelita by now was entitled to think that she had done the best she could to prepare for what the future might bring.

At this time the future of religious life in America looked very bright. Vocations were pouring into most communities: novitiates were bulging. Sister Formation courses were offered in many locations. In the summer of 1952 twenty young women applied for entrance into the Clyde congregation, and by that November there were eighteen postulants in their neat black dresses and capes. The novitiate had thirty-three sisters with temporary vows, as well as ten novices in May 1953. Toward the end of 1955, there were one hundred forty sisters at Clyde; the congregation total was three hundred eleven. The chapel was so crowded by now that seating had to be found for the postulants in a side sanctuary. Two colorful figures swelled the Clyde numbers that April. Mother Dolorosa Shanley and Sr. Joseph Szelongowski; foundress and first novice-director of the Handmaids of the Precious Blood, came to make a formal novitiate under Mother Carmelita's supervision. They wore rose-colored habits with white veils and were preparing to establish a new religious community in connection with the work of the Paraclete Fathers in the rehabilitation of priests. Later, they set up their own novitiate at Jemez Springs, New Mexico.

In June 1956 the General Chapter had decided that five years were to be spent in temporary vows before final vows could be made in the congregation. This, coupled with the previous Chapter's decision that the novitiate itself would last for two years, meant considerable work for the novice director and her assistant. In March 1959 there were twelve postulants. It was that September that Mother Carmelita was able to appoint Sr. Pascaline Coff as novice director. She had her doctorate in theology and was fully capable, Mother Carmelita believed, of guiding these young women, under, of course, her own close supervision.

During these years the community at Clyde continued its customary work and prayer. Their chaplain, Fr. Anselm Coppersmith, O.S.B. gave the novitiate a course in the theology of the Eucharist just before he was appointed prior of his abbey. He was succeeded by an older monk, Fr. Innocent Amhof. In 1953 Fr. Frederic Shindler came as chaplain. He had worked at Clyde as a seminarian and was known to many of the sisters. Fr. Frederic was to remain for nine years and to endear himself to the community. His conferences on the mystical body of Christ later in this decade helped the sisters to a deeper understanding of church.

The summer months continued to bring hundreds of visitors to see the chapels, as well as relatives to enjoy a few days with the sisters. The sister-guides to the chapels took modesty seriously, to the point where women in shorts were liable to be draped in some sister's black underskirt before being admitted to the adoration chapel. It was not unusual for busloads of Knights of Columbus to arrive on Sundays. Dignitaries visiting Conception were often brought to Clyde at a moment's notice. Mother Carmelita liked to remind the community that "all guests were to be received as Christ," according to the Rule. She asked the sisters to receive them in a spirit of faith with warm hospitality.

The seasons came and went. Spring meant violets in the woods and a drift of apple blossoms in the orchard. It meant habit-hems wet with dew when the junior sisters returned from letting hundreds of chickens out for the day. Summer meant peonies lining the roadways and banked on the altar for Corpus Christi, while the vegetable garden shimmered in the heat. Fall meant trees that were a mass of gold, scarlet and tangerine against the spruce and evergreens. The seasons were like old friends changing as they endured.

Appointments of new prioresses were made on the traditional date of November 21 every three years. The much-loved Mother Cornelia St. Cin came to Clyde as prioress in 1956 with Sr. Lucy Carter as her assistant. Sr. Lucy had grown up in the Clyde area. She knew everyone and everyone knew her. She also knew every nook and cranny of the Clyde buildings, which was a great advantage for the auction planned for December 12. The sisters scoured the attics and basements for anything that would attract antique hunters. Three hundred items were auctioned off that day, including a child's rocker that Sr. Martina

142

Born had brought with her when she came to the monastery more than half a century earlier. Old choir stalls found stored away in a remote basement were given to the Trappists at New Melleray in Iowa.

For Mother Carmelita the climax of 1957 came on December 16 when she was able to announce to the community the possibility of Fr. Lukas Etlin's cause for canonization being introduced. The following February a postulator was appointed for his cause. It was the extensive CARITAS program and Fr. Lukas' proven devotion to the Blessed Sacrament that were to be the mainstay of promoting this cause. Even Bishop Cody's caution to proceed very carefully could not dampen Mother Carmelita's enthusiasm. The sisters themselves were more enthused about the arrival of Marie Freehill on October 25, 1958 to be house-mother at the guest house. Marie was to become an institution at Clyde, remaining at her post for more than twenty years and known to hundreds of guests.

When the sisters heard the Abbey bells ring out in the crisp autumn air on October 28, 1958, to be joined in a moment by their own bells, they knew what it meant. The Catholic world had a new pope. As 1959 progressed they learned more about Angelo Roncalli, now Pope John XXIII. Seventy-four years old, but younger in heart than many half his age, he did things recent popes had never dreamed of: visiting hospitals and prisons in Rome, leaving the Vatican to walk among his people. When Abbot Stephen told the sisters at Clyde about the Benedictine Abbots' Congress to be held in Rome that fall, he said that each abbot was to describe what his monastery was doing to promote the work of the Ecumenical Council called by the Pope. The Abbot intended to promise the prayers of all the Clyde congregation for its success.

In June 1953 the congregation celebrated its 75th anniversary of perpetual adoration in the United States with a pontifical mass and other festivities. This anniversary brought home to them that their members were living longer; there were now a good number of elderly and ill sisters who required much nursing care. They had twenty-three golden jubilarians. During this decade many younger sisters took turns working night shifts in the Clyde infirmary. Others rose early to help dress the elderly and take them to the infirmary chapel in time for mass. This mass was celebrated by their resident infirmary chaplain, Fr. Sisbert Burkhardt who was himself in his eighties.

Mother Carmelita had been in the hospital in Tucson in 1953 for several months, suffering from a back injury received in Rome the previous year. When she attended a superior's workshop in St. Louis in 1954 where the speakers urged that the sisters be allowed more fresh air and exercise, she began looking seriously at the health situation of the Clyde community. Flu epidemics in the winters meant as many as thirty extra trays had to be carried to the victims, along with the regular thirty to the usual patients. She decided to hire a night nurse for the sick. Then Mother Carmelita changed the daily schedule to give the sisters a chance for more rest. Priests and doctors who knew the community had been urging this for some time. They recognized the strong work-orientation that contributed its share to illness in the younger as well as the older sisters. At this time the bell rang for rising at 4:35 a.m. Few had the opportunity to rest at noon, even in the intense heat. The canning season made extra demands on the sisters late into the nights in summer.

When Sr. Mechtilde Hilgert died in 1954 after seventy-five years of monastic profession, a link with the past was broken. She was the last sister to have known Mother Anselma Felber. The following year Sr. Teresa Willier died. She, too, was a survivor of the community's earliest years. When a younger sister visited her in her sick-room shortly before her death, she asked Sr. Teresa if she might have her profession ring as a memento. "Yes, my dear," said the irrepressible 86 year-old, "and you can have my teeth, too. They're right over there in that tumbler."

A sadder death was that of Sr. Sennorina Zavadil. She had left the congregation in an effort to establish a Benedictine community which would combine catechetical work with liturgy. Failing in this, she had returned to the congregation, only to die of cancer a few months later. A brilliant teacher and influential, she was ahead of her time and would have fitted easily into the decades after Vatican II.

On September 26, 1957 Sr. Modesta Steil died suddenly while at Clyde to celebrate her golden jubilee with her nine companions. The following year Mother Carmelita was in a car accident which resulted in a badly smashed right leg that took months to heal and left a legacy of pain which she was to endure for many years. Another shock to the community was the sudden death of Sr. Josephine Gruenes, the farm-manager. She had a serious heart condition but insisted on keeping to her work. She was in the implement shed one June day in 1959 when a fatal attack occurred. One of the workmen saw her collapse and called for help. Fr. Frederic grabbed the oils from the sacristy and ran straight to the shed to anoint her, as the workmen, some of them in tears, knelt around her. This was a sobering reminder that though the congregation was blessed with many young vocations, the elderly, for the first time in their experience, were very numerous. Provision for future care began to loom large on the horizon.

During this decade one man played a role of some importance to the Clyde congregation. This was Bishop John Cody. Appointed auxiliary to the ailing Bishop LeBlond of St. Joseph, Missouri in 1954, he came to visit Clyde that June. Wondering what so many sisters did with their time in this rural place, he was taken on a tour by Mother Carmelita, which left him asking how so few managed to do so much. As he began to take over the reins of the diocese, Bishop Cody conducted the canonical visitation of the community in February

1956. It took him more than a year to return to give the results of his interviews. He stressed the need of more relaxation for the sisters. Bishop Cody insisted that one period a day should be taken for recreation, no matter how much work there was and nothing should interfere with this period. "Recreation," he told the sisters, "is just as much a part of your obligation in your training for spiritual perfection as is meditation." In a meeting with the superiors the bishop added: "When everything is routine, the nervous system cracks." He demanded that Mother Carmelita set a deadline of September 1 to inform the Abbey that the sisters would no longer do the monks' personal laundry nor that of the seminarians.

In late August 1956 the diocese of St. Joseph became the diocese of Kansas City-St. Joseph, with Bishop Cody as ordinary after the death of Bishop LeBlond. Bishop Cody now wished to preside at the professions and jubilees in the Clyde community. This became something of a joke for the sisters as more often than not, the bishop had to cancel his appearance at the last moment. This led to the hasty taking down of the episcopal throne or its equally hasty erection when he did appear. It was with some satisfaction that Bishop Cody presided at the investment and profession of eleven sisters at Clyde on March 12, 1959. That evening he watched a volley-ball game between the "Doves" and the "Ravens," no doubt feeling that his advice about recreation was being followed.

During this decade the sisters' liturgical life mirrored the slow advances in the church. Having rejoiced at the proclamation of the dogma of the Assumption in 1950, the community was more delighted to be able to celebrate the Easter Vigil in the evening on March 11, 1951. Some of the sisters were not at all ready, however, to give up adoration of the Blessed Sacrament on Good Friday. It was on Ash Wednesday in 1955 that they experienced the use of English in a liturgical rite for the first time, when the ashes were distributed with the solemn warning: "Remember that you are dust and unto dust you shall return."

A spiritual highlight for many of the sisters in 1952 and 1953 was the ceremony of the Consecration of Virgins. Formerly allowed only to papally enclosed nuns with solemn vows, this privilege was obtained by the Abbot Primate, Bernard Kaelin, for all North American Benedictine Sisters in 1950. Mother Carmelita worked out some difficulties while in Rome for the International Congress of Superiors in 1952. The Clyde community was the first in America to experience this ancient rite. Seen in an almost mystical light by Mother Carmelita, the ceremony was carefully prepared for. Eighty-nine sisters who had been professed the requisite ten years were consecrated in a marathon rite by the Abbots of Conception, Collegeville and Mt. Angel, Oregon.

By 1956 the sisters were practicing parts of the Requiem service in English. They regretted the suppression of all octaves except those of

Easter, Pentecost and Christmas, since this meant they had to give up the beloved octave of Corpus Christi. That Holy Week they heard the Passion sung in English and experienced the Holy Thursday Eucharist in the evening. By the following Holy Week, they had the Easter Vigil before midnight, instead of the early evening. On Mother Carmelita's feastday in 1957, July 16, they prayed the table prayer in English for the first time.

At this time neither television nor newspapers were allowed in the communities, but the library was now open to all. Increasingly better books appeared as more sisters were trained in theology and scripture. Over-all, a spirit of simplicity and hunger for God remained a mark of the congregation. When Abbot James Fox, O.C.S.O. of Gethsemane had preached in the Clyde chapel the day after the ceremony of the Consecration of Virgins, his theme was: Is Jesus really *real* to you? The sisters felt that this was the heart of the matter.

SAN DIEGO

In this decade the major thrust of the congregation's expansion was the founding of the fourth daughter-house in San Diego, California. From his installation as first ordinary of the new diocese in 1936, Bishop Buddy had been pressing for such a foundation. As early as June 1951 Mother Dolorosa with Mother Carmelita had made a special trip to San Diego to talk this over with him. The bishop wanted them to open a chapel of perpetual adoration at the diocesan seminary, while also taking care of the cooking and laundry for the seminarians. He was politely but firmly informed that this kind of work was not the aim of the congregation. Next Bishop Buddy proposed that they locate in the university complex. Looking at each other, the two Mothers explained carefully that it would be difficult to maintain a monastic house of prayer next door to a sport's stadium. Undaunted, the bishop had them driven around the city to look for a suitable location. They left with a fair idea of the layout of San Diego, but with no commitment to a foundation.

In the fall of 1953 Bishop Buddy was passing through Kansas City and spoke to Mother Carmelita about the possibility of a diocesan-owned building in Old Town, San Diego, for their use as a temporary location. It was in good condition and next door to the church of the Immaculate Conception. After consulting her council and a good many of the sisters, Mother Carmelita accepted this offer. Taking with her Sr. Cecilia (Claire) Bock who was a native Californian, Mother Carmelita set out for San Diego. They were warmly welcomed by Bishop Buddy. "Oh! I have waited for this so long, so long!"

On January 17, 1954 a special travelers' blessing was given to the fifteen sisters assigned to this newest house. A copy of the gospels, of the Rule, a particle of the true Cross and a relic of St. Benedict were given the superior, Sr. M. Cecilia. Then in a heart-shaped lamp, which Mother Anselma Felber had brought from Maria Rickenbach, a flame from the Clyde sanctuary lamp was enclosed. Sr. Cecilia and Sr. Dymphna (Elizabeth Mary) Meyer, who were the first to leave for the coast, carried this lamp, safely burning, all the way to their new monastery in San Diego.

When the rest of the sisters arrived, the house was formally opened on March 25, 1954. Though ill with laryngitis, the Bishop insisted on officiating. The chapel was in the basement of the tall, narrow house. The only way into this basement from the other three floors was through a door on the street or via a fire-escape which the sisters called "Jacob's ladder." In the rear of the building was a garage which became the community laundry, also a small lawn surrounded by a fence over which a glorious bougainvillea spilled its crimson flowers. The sisters slept dormitory-fashion on the third floor. Extra mattresses belonging to the diocese were still stored in various rooms. Going to adoration at night meant squeezing by one another or toppling a mattress.

The bishop's sister, Mrs. Daniel Redmond, took the community under her wing, often coming to 2610 San Diego Ave. with a little gift for the sisters of some freshly baked cookies. Another good friend of those early days was Mrs. Marie Coniff who ordered the first set of vestments made by the sisters for a priest-friend. Mr. Geary, who worked at a large commercial garden-farm, was unendingly kind, often appearing very early in the morning at the back door, laden with the finest fresh strawberries, tangerines, grapefruit, dates and prunes. At other times the sisters would open this door to find the small porch covered with boxes of vegetables. Once when Mr. Geary heard one of the sisters coughing in the chapel, his next gift included fresh lemons and honey. Mr. Riviera, whom the chronicler referred to as "our kind baker friend," regularly brought them dozens of rolls, bread and buns. The Sisters of Nazareth were generous with gifts of fresh eggs. Mr. and Mrs. John Pruett with their family of twelve children also became staunch friends at this time. They came regularly to make a holy hour in the chapel, leaving dozens of eggs for the sisters, as Mr. Pruett owned a chicken ranch.

On Holy Thursday that year the sisters held a public holy hour from nine to ten p.m. The little chapel was filled to capacity. This was further encouraged by Bishop Buddy who urged all the pastors to inaugurate holy hours in the sisters' chapel during this Marian Year. Even though he was busy moving to the magnificent new university and chancery buildings on the commanding site known as Alcala Park, the bishop always found time to visit the community. He continued to take great interest in Mother Carmelita's search for a permanent location.

147

By this time the sisters were settled enough to follow the customary monastic routine of the congregation with Sr. Cecilia as their prioress. There were enough sisters to keep two nights of adoration a week. They supported themselves by making vestments and first-communion veils. By that September their chapel register could show three thousand names for the five months it had been used. There were fourteen groups keeping holy hours. One sister was kept busy answering appeals for prayers that poured in via letter and phone. San Diego's Catholic population was growing. On a tour early in 1955, Bishop Buddy confirmed more than two thousand children and converts. Appeals to Ireland brought the Irish Mercy Sisters from Sligo to staff two schools in the diocese, where already many priests and sisters from Ireland were at work.

The sight of Navy busses filled with service men and women coming for holy hours in their chapel reminded the sisters of the grim possibility of war. Despite an Easter appeal from Pius XII in 1954 that atomic warfare be banned, except for defense, the U.S. was nearing success in developing atomic missiles that could be guided from North America to Russia. In June 1955 the Russian foreign minister was demanding that the U.N. seat Red China. Knowing that San Diego was a key point and might be one of the first places attacked, the sisters listened carefully to two men from the Civilian Defense Commission who spoke to them about "measures of precaution" should war break out. Most of the community enrolled in a first aid course soon after.

With Sr. Cecilia, Mother Carmelita continued her search for a permanent site. It would be important that this location be available for a good segment of the city's Catholic population, which now numbered some 200,000. San Diego had 135 parishes, 314 priests and 75 educational institutes. Mother Carmelita weighed all this carefully. Bishop Buddy then made an offer of some property in the San Bernardino area, which at this time was part of the San Diego diocese. This property consisted of 280 acres with a large ranch house in a beautiful mountain setting. The donor had given it to the bishop, stipulating that it must be used for a religious group. Knowing that the community at Clyde was bursting at the seams with one hundred forty sisters and twenty novices, the bishop offered this to Mother Carmelita as a place where girls too young for the postulancy could be trained in an aspirancy.

Though the community in San Diego was barely on its own feet, this offer seemed too good to turn down. Mother Carmelita accepted it and began making plans to renovate the ranch-house, which she wanted to name San Benito. She had some anxiety about the water and certain restrictions in the deeds. Mother Carmelita also worried about what the future might hold, when she read that the U.S. had exploded its first hydrogen bomb in 1954 in the mid-Pacific with a burst of brilliance greater than the sun.

In August 1956 Mother Carmelita was in San Diego to conduct their visitation before going to San Benito for the opening ceremonies at the new aspirancy. Five young girls were already there, neatly attired in their blue jumpers and white blouses. Besides these aspirants, there were eleven sisters and an elderly monk from Conception Abbey as chaplain. Sr. Henrietta Kaiser had been appointed superior of the little group.

At the General Chapter in November 1956 Mother Henrietta became prioress of the San Diego community, because by then it was obvious that San Benito was not destined to endure. The water problems turned out to be insoluble: the bacterial content in the wells on the property meant that drinking water had to be hauled from San Jacinto. By December the foundation was closed. Two of the sisters assigned to San Benito were now able to go to the San Diego community, which brought their number to sixteen by March 1957. Watching the population of the city grow to nearly 500,000 at this time, Mother Carmelita continued her methodical search for the right place to build a permanent monastery and chapel.

Various diocesan priests served as the sisters' chaplains, among them Fr. John Quinn who was later to be Archbishop of San Francisco, and Fr. Philip Straling who was destined to be the first bishop of San Bernardino. When the St. Meinrad Benedictines began a foundation near Oceanside, California in 1957, they were the confessors to the community and helped direct the Oblate groups. By 1958 the sisters were beginning to overflow the crowded little house on San Diego Avenue. Bishop Richard Ackerman, the auxiliary to Bishop Buddy, came one day to have some buttons sewn on his cassock and asked if the sisters were getting enough fresh air. This led to some volleyball games on the back lawn for the younger sisters, but space was severely limited.

In May 1957 Mrs. Redmond drove Mother Carmelita to see a property in the developing Clairemont area. They kept going back to it, until slowly Mother Carmelita grew certain that this was the location they had been seeking. From the top of the undeveloped hill there was an amazing view of Mission Bay and the Pacific Ocean. In the surrounding area there were already over 40,000 residences, with plans for 20,000 more. St. Mary Magdalen's, a new parish, was in the vicinity. When Mother Carmelita talked to Bishop Buddy about the location he promised to donate another property which could be sold to help purchase the one in Clairemont. By December 20 the matter was settled in probate court: now they had a site to build on. They also had a new prioress in Sr. Paschalia Noser, who replaced the ailing Sr. Henrietta.

1959 was an exciting year. It began with the proclamation of Alaska as the 49th state. On January 25 Pope John XXIII announced plans to hold the 21st Ecumenical Council, the first in eighty-nine years. At the end of May the sisters were awed to hear it predicted that by 1970 metropolitan San Diego would have a population of one and a half million people. California already led the country in the number of registered cars: over eight million. In July the city was 190 years old, having been founded by Fr. Junipero Serra in 1769 as the first link in his chain of missions. By September the newspapers were talking about a visit to the U.N. by Pope John to balance that of Krushchev. That December President Eisenhower did meet with the pontiff in the Vatican.

Amid all this, the five-year old Benedictine community in San Diego went on its monastic way. The sisters canned vegetables and dealt with thirty-one pounds of tuna given them by the fishermen of Portuguese descent, whose numerous boats made the San Diego harbor the base of the largest tunafish operation in the world. With other Catholics they were proud when two more American cardinals were created and rejoiced in the dedication of the national shrine of the Immaculate Conception in Washington, D.C.

MUNDELEIN

During this decade Chicago was the largest archdiocese in the United States. A LIFE magazine article offered some statistics: the Windy City had 414 parishes, 2,270 priests, 8,766 sisters, and 529 Catholic institutions. All this was under the guidance of Cardinal Samuel Stritch whom Bishop O'Brien once called "the intelligence of the American hierarchy." The LIFE article described the Cardinal as "a rare mixture of tough-minded practicality and unworldly piety."[1]

In this same article there was a large picture of some of the Benedictine sisters at the Mundelein monastery engaged in sorting altar breads. The sisters would have preferred a picture taken in their chapel. After all, had not the Cardinal himself written them on January 4, 1952 to say: "On our way home Friday morning we dropped in to say a prayer in your church . . . To me your work is one of the great things in our archdiocese." Still, the large room where the altar breads were made did symbolize many aspects of the community's life. It was the hub of the house's work. Sometimes in rush seasons such as Lent and Advent, it taxed the sisters to the limit. The work meant more than physical weariness. It was their ministry, part of their dedication to priests, whose consecrated hands, they were often told, would offer this bread "as the food of eternal life." So they worked in the bakeroom and the sorting-room uncomplainingly through many a recreation and rest period, often late into the night. They had no time as the chronicler noted on March 31, 1950, "even to mend their clothes."

Though scarcely a half-hour's drive from Chicago, the sisters lived in almost rural solitude, protected from the road by broad lawns. Their property adjoined the vast acres of the diocesan seminary with its carefully tended grounds and pleasant lake. The seminary staff looked after the sisters with paternal care, supplying chaplains, altar-servers, advice, and on occasion, assistance with snow-removal and garden plowing. In return the sisters prayed for the seminarians as class after class entered and graduated. Besides this, they made vestments for the priests and surplices for the students. In 1950 thirty-three deacons were ordained and that fall a class of one hundred and one began their studies. On May 1, 1952 it was fifty-three deacons who were ordained priests and then began to come to the chapel to celebrate Eucharist for the sisters, giving them their priestly blessing. Fr. Paul Cull came from the seminary for a weekly conference on prayer, the sacraments, the Eucharist and continued this throughout the decade. Msgr. Kush was often there during these years helping the sisters with the chant and the new organ.

After the General Chapter of 1951, Mother Mildred Wachter was appointed the new prioress. Mother Carmelita had chosen wisely. Nearly half the sisters at the Mundelein monastery were over sixty; even in 1955 there were only three sisters under forty years of age. They were a peaceful, settled group, perhaps more closely knit than any of the others. Very work-oriented, the sisters were busy with the altar breads, the vestment-making or the canning. If that did not fully occupy them, they might be seen on a warm day brushing out their woolen habits or attacking some cleaning project. Mother Mildred fitted in easily. Calm and simple in tastes, with a systematic, orderly mind, she was maternal, interested in the sisters' welfare and a fine manager.

That winter the sisters were happy to move from room to room as the house was repainted. Another cause for rejoicing was the appointment of Msgr. Meegan as pastor of Santa Maria del Popolo parish in Mundelein. He was present for the solemn blessing of their new pipe organ in the fall of 1952 with Cardinal Stritch presiding and Fr. Edmond Kestel of Conception Abbey playing. At Christmas, Msgr. Meegan sent over three turkeys and eighteen bottles of wine. When the ceremony of the Consecration of Virgins was held in the Mundelein chapel in January 1953, he donated a huge sirloin roast and innumerable groceries. That day was a gala event in the annals of the community. Forty-one sisters were consecrated in the ancient rite, which began at 8:30 a.m. and lasted until 12:30 noon. The deacon class from the seminary took care of the singing. There were fifty visiting sisters present, along with some sixty of the clergy. Besides decorating the altars with dozens of roses and calla lilies, the ladies of Msgr. Meegan's parish served all the meals, while the men of the parish acted as ushers.

This was not the end of Msgr. Meegan's efforts. Feeling the effects of the hard wooden benches in the adoration chapel, he wrote a letter to his parishioners who kept regular holy hours there. Under the title of "calloused Catholics," he asked them to donate money for padding all the kneelers. When Sr. Hildelita Mergen did not seem to improve after three months' bed rest in the community's infirmary, it was Msgr. Meegan who brought in a tuberculosis specialist to check on her. He was a constant visitor to Mother Mildred when she had surgery in 1953. During a flu epidemic that summer, he sent over a special medicine for the sisters: twelve bottles of whiskey.

Order and meticulous attention to detail characterized the hardworking Mundelein community. Even a chronicle notation about the sisters who were picking chokecherries and apples that summer ends with: "It freshens up all the sisters and they will be able to work better tomorrow." There were satisfied notations all through the chronicles about house-cleaning: "Everything looks so orderly!" The sisters' liturgical life was as orderly — and as strenuous — as other elements in their schedule. The Christmas horarium shows the sisters praying Vigils on Christmas Eve, retiring about 9:45 p.m. Before the Midnight Mass they prayed Matins, getting back to bed at 2:30 a.m. At 6 a.m. they were up praying Prime and Terce, followed by three low Masses and breakfast. The high Mass was celebrated at 9 a.m. followed by Benediction and Sext. Dinner was at 11:45 with Vespers at 3:30 p.m. And this was followed by Compline, Benediction and Matins.

Along with a number of parish holy hours, the community annually welcomed a group of the elderly from the Libertyville home for a holy hour and a visit with the sisters. This, of course, was arranged by the indefatigable Msgr. Meegan. It was he who began the custom of bringing one hundred disabled children to the monastery each summer. These crippled, retarded youngsters were his special love. He would help carry them into the monastery himself or assist the sisters in feeding those who could not help themselves.

The Monsignor was also on hand for the celebration of Fr. James Madden's first solemn Mass in the sisters' chapel. Fr. James was the first priest to be ordained from Mundelein and Libertyville, so the people went all out to make it a genuine celebration. There were twenty boys and girls in their first communion attire. There were Knights of Columbus in full regalia, along with the clergy and a hundred relatives. A sadder occasion was the death of the sisters' great benefactor, Mrs. Forschner, on June 15, 1954.

For the Marian Year of 1954 the community undertook its most ambitious vocation project. In May they sent letters to all the Catholic high schools in the Chicago area, inviting girls to spend "a cloister weekend" with them, praying the Liturgy of the Hours with the sisters, having periods of adoration before the Blessed Sacrament and, in general, getting a taste of Benedictine life. These weekends were held in August. Twenty-eight girls attended the first weekend and thirty-two the second. The sisters were a little taken aback by some of the pillow fights which enlivened one evening, but hoped just the same for good vocations from the groups.

The early months of 1955 brought the sisters several reasons for gratitude. The first was the new altar bread equipment that arrived in March, which would cut down working at night. The second was the good parishioners of Msgr. Meegan, who presented the community with a handsome set of chairs for the sanctuary, plus fifty folding chairs. A visit from the famous Bishop Fulton Sheen in May was another cause for gratitude. While giving a retreat to priests at the seminary, the bishop dropped in to see the sisters. He predicted to them that in another hundred years, Africa would be what America was then. He went on to congratulate the older sisters, remarking that the nearer we grow to the source of life, the younger we become.

That fall the sisters were grateful to the many who helped them pay for the new driveway and parking lot near the chapel. Not to be outdone, Msgr. Meegan had his people donate new lights for the entire area. 1955 ended with a remark that could be found only in the Mundelein chronicle: "Our pre-Christmas rush is going along smoothly."

1956 began as usual but was soon to be clouded by Mother Mildred's illness. When she entered the hospital that May, the doctors thought she had a cerebral hemmorhage, but on her transfer to Mercy Hospital in Chicago, a malignancy was found. After a coma lasting for several days, Mother Mildred died on June 7. It was the beloved Mother Dolorosa who replaced her as prioress late in November.

The Lent of 1957 was a busy one for the sisters. Over a million altar breads were sent out weekly. That May brought the long-awaited ordination of Billy Nemers. The Nemers were good friends and neighbors. Everyone worked to make his first Mass in the sisters' chapel a very special occasion. Mother Carmelita heard all the details when she arrived on one of her periodic visits. She brought something quite new to the community this time: balls and roller-skates. With new equipment in the altar bread department and in the canning room, she hoped that the sisters could take more time for fresh air and exercise.

In many ways 1958 was to be a year of departures for the church and for the Mundelein Benedictine community. In March the sisters learned that Cardinal Stritch had been appointed pro-Prefect for the Congregation of the Propagation of the Faith, which meant that he would be going to Rome, after eighteen years as leader of Chicago's two million Catholics. His reply to Mother Dolorosa's letter of congratulations was characteristically simple: "My dear Mother Dolorosa: thank you for your kind letter! Obedience is sweeter when it asks something hard. Pray for me."[2] The sisters did not know then that their Cardinal was to die in Rome only two months later.

The day of Cardinal Stritch's death, Sr. Victoria Kohlleppel died suddenly in the Mundelein monastery. This was a shock to the sisters and the cause of much sadness as Sr. Victoria was well loved. Not two months later the sisters heard about Mother Carmelita's traumatic injury in a car crash. Typically, Msgr. Meegan flew to St. Louis to check for himself that she was going to recover.

On September 24th, the sisters learned the name of their new Archbishop: Albert Meyer, who had been bishop of Milwaukee since 1953. On October 9 word came that Pope Pius XII had died. As the sisters prayed for the repose of his soul and for the conclave which would elect his successor, they heard that Cardinal Mooney of Detroit had died of a heart attack in Rome. On October 28 their telephone kept ringing with the news that the new Pope was Cardinal Angelo Roncalli of Venice. Knowing nothing about him, the chronicler merely remarked: "As he is 76 years of age, no doubt his pontificate will not be too long."

November brought Mother Thiadildis Kraus and Sr. Irene Prugger with Mr. Alexander Barket to the community. He owned a construction company in Kansas City, Missouri, and was there to consult with the sisters about the planned addition to the north porch. Immediately after, he flew to St. Louis to check the plans with Mother Carmelita in the hospital there. Another visitor to the community was an old friend from the seminary, Msgr. Grady, who was now the rector of the shrine of the Immaculate Conception in Washington, D.C. He brought slides to show the sisters, telling them that the shrine would be the second largest in the U.S., that it had already cost eighteen million dollars and would take another ten to twenty years to complete.

On December 1, 1958 Mother Dolorosa asked the sisters to pray for the grade-school children killed in the tragic fire at our Lady of Angels parochial school in Chicago. Ninety-two children were known to be dead, with another two hundred in the hospital. Three B.V.M. sisters had also perished in the fire. Though ill, Archbishop Meyer got out of bed to anoint the dying children and console the parents at the site of the fire. Four hundred prisoners in the Cook County jail offered to donate blood for transfusions. The sisters had a requiem Mass for the victims on December 4. It was the end of the month before their new Archbishop could pay them a visit. He particularly asked that there be no formal reception as he liked things simple. "I hope to see you in your aprons," was the way he put it. It was the following March, 1959 that the sisters read about a similar simplicity on the part of the new Pope. It was reported that he had told the Vatican gardeners not to run off when they saw him walking in the gardens: "I do not wish to be the sovereign of a cemetery or a penitentiary!"

In May, 1959 the sisters celebrated a typical feast of Corpus Christi. The Catholic high school graduates of Mundelein were there in their blue caps and gowns, along with six monsignors, twenty-seven priests and thirty-two seminarians. Bishop Hillinger presided in the sanctuary with deacons and sub-deacons. Twelve seminarians alternated

154

with the sisters' choir. Knights of Columbus held their swords aloft as the Blessed Sacrament was carried to the outdoor shrine, with the St. Vincent de Paul men of the parish acting as marshals and ushers. Bridal wreath in full bloom lined the walks with other shrubbery donated by Mr. Albert Fiori, another good friend of the community. A few weeks later Mother Dolorosa was appointed to her second term as their prioress, much to the sisters' joy. By then the plans for the new addition had been approved. Foundations for a new garage had been dug in September and by December the workmen were laying bricks and cement blocks for the addition to the north porch.

TUCSON

Many of the values, as well as the spirit of Catholicism in this decade were reflected in the chronicles of the Tucson community. The Church was on the march and it liked to record big numbers. When the diocese sponsored a giant Holy Name rally on May 10, 1953, twelve thousand Catholics attended. A May crowning in the Marian Year of 1954 drew ten thousand. Similarly, when the sisters celebrated the 75th anniversary of perpetual adoration in their chapels on June 18, 1953, more than one thousand people crowded their chapel, overflowing onto the lawn. The chronicler kept careful record of days of recollection which were attended by large groups: at one time one hundred women from one parish, at another, two hundred and four high school boys. By this time the Knights of Columbus' Eucharistic Guard numbered two hundred and fifty-six men who kept an hour of adoration each Friday night. The chronicle notes that one hundred and seventy-five of these men left a New Year's Eve party to keep their Holy Hour in 1951. These Knights of Tucson had been instrumental in setting up other such Guards in twenty-two different cities. There were one hundred and eighty-seven Spanish-speaking women Sentinels and one hundred and forty-five English-speaking, who kept weekly holy hours in the chapel. Seventy-nine young women made up the "Benedictine Doves," keeping regular hours of prayer. By 1957 the circulating library had a collection of ten thousand volumes and a circulation of over eight thousand. It was, in fact, becoming a Catholic information center, staffed by lay volunteers. Among those who donated books to this library was Senator Barry Goldwater.

In 1950 the Korean war began; this made little impression on the sisters until Fr. Patrick Veil came to visit his sister, Sr. Fidelis. Then his scarred hands and back told them a story of imprisonment and torture. On March 5, 1953 the chronicle says only: "My Jesus, mercy! Stalin is dead!" The sisters were wondering at this time how Eisenhower would fare as the first Republican president after twenty years of Democrats. Besides this, the community occasionally welcomed visiting priests and sisters from Mexico. Some Benedictine sisters from Mexico City told them that they could wear their habits only in their own chapel. To satisfy government regulations they had to refer to their monastery as a library.

The spirit of that time was evident in the assigning of a squadron of Sabre jets to the Davis-Monathan AFB in Tucson to protect the defense industry and military installations. Some twenty young airmen from this base were among those who faithfully kept hours of adoration at night in the sisters' chapel. Planes from the base could be heard directly over the monastery in their daily flights. Even when the Korean war ended, the community agreed in August, 1953 that their building could serve as a casualty clearing unit. With this in mind, twenty-five sisters undertook a first-aid course.

When the sisters came to Tucson in 1935 the population numbered about 57,000. By 1952 it was 190,000. The water problem grew along with the population. A well dug in 1939 at the monastery found water at 114 feet; in 1952 it was 145 feet. This well water was used to irrigate the garden, though Sr. Leona Eichenhofer also, the sisters were sure, used a little holy water. The chronicle records that in 1951 the sisters harvested 350 avocados from their tree, as well as 300 pounds of dates from one tree. Each March the orange trees bloomed, filling the house with their fragrance. In December, 1954 the orange trees yielded over three thousand oranges, with the result that many a recreation was spent squeezing orange juice. By 1958 the date palms were producing so abundantly that the sisters went out daily during October to pick them, their long skirts hampering them as they climbed the twelve foot ladders. Besides this, Sr. Leona watched over peanuts, onions, spinach and lettuce in her garden, carrying around a big clock in a half-gallon can to keep her on time for the Hours of liturgy. Mrs. Brady gave her Mr. Brady's wristwatch when he died. The Bradys were old friends. James Brady had been one of Tucson's pioneers, having come to the city in 1899. Mr. Brady had served on the Mexican border with General Pershing when Pancho Villa was active.

Many other loyal friends were among God's blessings to the Tucson Benedictines. When the Conception Abbey monks could no longer serve as their chaplains, the diocese supplied priests. Fr. John Burns was their chaplain in 1954 and was to have a long association with the sisters. He was succeeded in 1957 by Fr. Robert Fuller who had often served Mass as a boy in their chapel. Arthur Lensing came to work for the community in 1953 and was to remain for many years. He helped build "St. Joseph's House" on the grounds, which served both as a workmen's and a guest house. For years the Ellingers spent the winters in Tucson, devoting days to running errands for the sisters. Other friends spent long hours helping with the shopping, in the garden, or with electrical and plumbing needs.

During this decade, Sr. Blandina Cummins and Sr. Tharsilla Noser were the prioresses of the community. Bishop Gercke, who had celebrated his golden jubilee of ordination, continued to drop in for formal and informal visits, usually accompanied by Duke, a large dog, who frisked about while the Bishop was talking. It was for the consecration of Bishop Gercke's auxiliary, Bishop Francis Green, that the sisters had their first experience of watching television. During the winter months, they spent hours finding housing for visiting relatives and friends or offering hospitality to other religious.

By 1955 work on the chapel was completed. A statue of Christ the King was placed in a niche over the chapel door. A new permanent altar was installed, surmounted later by a baldachin. The entire chapel was painted for its solemn consecration on March 21, 1955. Since they were up at 3 a.m. that day, the sisters, with other Catholics, thanked God for the fact that since January of 1953, water no longer broke the communion fast. But rubrics still dominated, as two sisters discovered who arrived from San Diego still fasting in the hope of receiving communion. Since it was after twelve noon by then, the priest in the neighboring rectory felt he must consult a theologian about the matter. He was told that it was not permissible to give communion after twelve o'clock, except in a case of emergency. Fr. Burns heard confessions on Holy Saturday at the cathedral in 1956 all afternoon. There was no time for supper before celebrating the Easter Vigil with the sisters, so he fasted until the end. The chronicle notes: "He felt very weak by the last alleluia."

There was little real recreation for the sisters during this period. All through Lent many extra orders for altar breads kept them working from after breakfast until, often enough, close to midnight. The rest of the community came to help sort the breads during the noon and evening recreation periods. At other times these periods were spent covering the grapes to keep the birds from getting the fruit. If not this, then they were involved in the massive housekeeping common in religious institutes at this time. Often enough, a dust storm would follow on the heels of this cleaning covering everything with a thick layer. At least twice a year they had a deluge of rain which flooded the basement. On Sundays the prioress led the sisters in a thorough study of a booklet called "Points of Observance." This little manual detailed the right procedures in almost every area of their lives. The goal was congregational uniformity. The chronicler referred to it with considerable satisfaction: "Questions are asked, doubts are cleared, order and peace result."

After San Benito was given up, there was still a need for a place where girls too young to be postulants could be received. Tucson was decided upon as the best place for such an aspirancy. Two years later in 1959 the community had four girls there, with five more interested.

These were girls of fourteen, fifteen and sixteen, some of whom had not finished 8th grade.

The sisters watched television for the second time when Pope John XXIII was made Vicar of Christ. They did not realize that they were watching the end of an era: that this "interim Pope" would set in motion a series of events which were to change the church. When he visited them on St. Benedict's feast day in March 1959, Bishop Gercke told the sisters that this Pope might summon something called an "Ecumenical Council." Bishop Gercke was excited about the possibility. "This is one of the greatest things we've had in years! It's a great thing in the history of the Church!"

KANSAS CITY

1950 opened for the sisters in the Kansas City monastery with a holy hour in their chapel led by Bishop O'Hara. By March 1950 their chapel was all but completed: the ever-generous J. E. Dunn having donated the side altar of St. Joseph with all its furnishings. As elsewhere in the nation, there was increasing assurance for Catholics in Kansas City. Public displays of faith became more and more numerous. It was nothing for the sisters to stay up until 2 a.m. decorating the repository for Holy Thursday when people flocked in for visits to the Blessed Sacrament. Their adoration chapel became the diocesan focus for the celebration of the feast of Corpus Christi.

In June 1950 Kansas City celebrated the centenary of its founding with a month of civic observances. The diocese entered into this celebration with a will. A log replica of the first Catholic church in the area was erected on the monastery lawn, illuminated at night with a neon sign. On the feast of Corpus Christi there was a procession from Bishop Hogan high school to the chapel. Torches lit the night. Contingents of Holy Name men from every parish in the city marched beside a car draped in white, in which Bishop O'Hara rode holding the Blessed Sacrament. An umbrellino wired to the side of the car shielded the Sacrament. While the choir of St. John's Seminary sang, the Bishop gave the first Benediction at the log cabin and the next at the chapel portico. A crowd estimated to be between eight to ten thousand took part. Later in August one of the innumerable Holy Year pilgrimages to the sisters' chapel was made by four hundred religious women, representing all the congregations in the diocese. As the Korean War continued and the reserves were called up, followed by the drafting of one million men between the ages of twenty-five and thirty-five, a holy hour for peace in the chapel attracted five hundred Catholics.

In February 1951 when Mother Carmelita was elected prioress general of the Congregation, Sr. Loyola Churan became the prioress of the Kansas City community. As usual, that Lent was a strenuous one for the sisters working in the altar bread department. They took turns baking the breads during dinner and supper in order to meet the extra demands. After Passion Sunday the demand was such that they had to work late into the night.

July brought other concerns: travel between the Clyde and Kansas City monasteries was becoming dangerous because of the flooding along the Missouri River. By the middle of that month, they were filling buckets and tubs with water as the supply was endangered. Conditions became increasingly hazardous: there were people trapped on the top floors of office buildings. They all were warned to stay off the streets. The downtown offices and stores were closed, except for drug stores. The Red Cross was busy finding shelter for people from north Kansas City. Hospitals postponed all but the most necessary surgeries. Now all water had to be boiled. The stockyards were under water. Out of 6,000 cattle only 800 could be saved. Gradually things began to return to normal. The next year, however, there was another history-making flood of the Missouri.

As the war got worse, with eighteen-year olds being called up, the sisters prayed urgently for peace and the safety of American soldiers. Their own life went on its ordered way on top of the hill overlooking the Paseo. Friends of the community continued to do their shopping for them, as at this time the sisters neither owned nor drove cars. So friends took them to medical appointments, and made bank-deposits for them. Monthly the big truck from Clyde arrived, bringing meat, butter, milk, fresh fruit and vegetables. Butter was selling for 75 cents a pound, which meant that the sisters used peanut butter and saved the butter for the chaplain. As their garden began to produce abundantly, the community was glad to share melons with their friends and to can such things as beans, peas, and squash.

By April 1953 there were thirty-three sisters living in the Kansas City monastery. They welcomed Cardinal Spellman late that month. He offered Mass for them and left a donation with Mother Loyola for a treat of ice cream. The next visitors were Abbot Stephen Schappler with Mothers Carmelita, Jerome Schmidt of the Yankton Benedictines and Rosamond Pratchner of the Benedictines of St. Joseph, Minnesota to confer about the request of the Sacred Congregation for Religious that a school of higher studies be established in Rome for women religious. The Mothers were opposed to their sisters being away from their communities for three years. Their discussion, however, did result in the permission for the Kansas City sisters to read for a half-hour after Night Prayer. This concession was overdue because the chronicler was telling the truth when she noted: "Our days are full and we have little time for reading."

1954 began with a new prioress, Mother Cornelia St. Cin. Then there was the excitement of loading the van with items for the new foundation in San Diego, California. The generous Ellingers were

159

kept busy making reservations and checking trunks for the sisters assigned to this far-off monastery. In May Bishop O'Hara dropped in to check on the progress of the crypt beneath the adoration chapel where he wished to be buried. He was on his way to Rome for the canonization of St. Pius X. Later the sisters heard that Pius XII had given their bishop the personal title of Archbishop.

January 1955 brought a blizzard. The over-worked sisters in the altar bread department felt that the blizzard continued all through Lent. Relief came the following year when the threat of competition from a commercial firm in Rhode Island led to buying four large stoves for baking and two mixers, besides renovating the department. The sisters in the correspondence department sent out over nine hundred invitations to their Corpus Christi celebration that May. Fifteen hundred people came for the solemn high Mass and outdoor procession. That fall their chaplain, Fr. Hugh Farrington, O.S.B., began a twice-weekly course on the liturgy. When Fr. Patrick Peyton was in town for a Rosary Rally which attracted 25,000 Catholics, he came to visit the Benedictines. On leaving he remarked: "You are such a happy community. You must have a lovely superior!" The sisters agreed with him about Mother Cornelia, as the chronicler noted: "Her direction is full of that confidence and holy liberty which the love of Christ gives."

All through 1956 the Kansas City house was a kind of depot for the sisters of the congregation coming and going to the other monasteries. Never was there any lack of opportunity to practice the Benedictine virtue of hospitality in the Kansas City monastery. As so often happens, however, the sisters felt that the bread they cast upon the waters returned to them a hundredfold. One instance of this was the formation of the "Eucharistic Guild" in July 1956. This was a group of Catholic women who worked together to help the community pay off the considerable debt on their building. With Mrs. Herman Tarwater as their first president, these energetic women held teas, dinners, bridge parties and other events for the sisters. Their support was to continue for many years.

On September 11, the sisters were shocked to hear that Archbishop O'Hara had died of a heart attack in Milan, Italy. He was the American hierarchy's representative at the first International Conference on Pastoral Liturgy held in Assisi. This meant that the crypt beneath their chapel in which he wished to be buried had to be hastily completed. On September 18 after a funeral Mass in the cathedral, an escort of thirteen motorcycle police brought his body to the monastery, where some three hundred people watched Archbishop Ritter of St. Louis officiate at the burial service. It was Bishop John Cody who was installed as first bishop of the newly formed diocese of Kansas City-St. Joseph.

On November 17, 1956 Mother Cornelia went to Clyde for the Fourth General Chapter of the congregation. She was not destined to return, being appointed prioress of the Clyde community, while Mother Eulalia Wagner took her place as prioress in Kansas City. The year ended with the reassuring sight of loads of tile arriving to begin the completion of the unfinished west wing of the monastery. Additional bedrooms were much needed since the sisters were losing sleep in bedrooms designed for only one, which had to hold two, with alarm clocks ringing for night adoration hours.

In March 1957 the midwest was in desperate need of rain. "In Kansas," the chronicle related, "the dust lies in drifts like snow." On their hill the sisters could still rejoice in the sight and smell of lilacs and apples trees. May brought several tornado warnings, so that more than one night had to be spent in the basement, with the Blessed Sacrament on a stand in a small room as ambulance sirens shrieked until dawn. All this month and the next, work continued on the unfinished wing, as the sisters spent hours cleaning tile. By the end of August some of them could move into the new third floor rooms. That same month Fr. Hugh began a new series of conferences on the Fathers of the Church. At the informal beginning of one of his talks, he told the sisters that Pius XII had recently exhorted the Jesuits to greater poverty and austerity, urging them to cut out smoking and costly vacations. Some of the more scrupulous sisters were worried, as a result, when the community received no less than eleven turkeys that Thanksgiving. To their relief, many of these were promptly given to the poor or sent to the community at Clyde.

January 1958 brought a paralyzing snowstorm to the city, the worst in half a century. This was forgotten by May when the sisters were indignantly discussing the latest hike in postal rates: now first class letters required 4 cents! That June men of the Serra Club again sent out appeals for donations to cover the cost of flour for the sisters' altar breads. Substantial returns were received almost immediately. Other news was less happy: in Washington by mid-July Eisenhower was sending troops to Lebanon because of the tension over a coup in Iraq and an attempted one in Jordan.

None of the sisters were quite sure what the *Kansas City Times* meant by its headline on January 25, 1959: "Pope calls Unity Parley." Their year went on as usual: much work in the altar bread department and at the canning. Hardly a week went by without the sister-infirmarian having to take someone from Clyde or the Kansas City house to the hospital. Endless hospitality was offered to visiting priests and sisters. How could something called an "ecumenical council" affect this ordered routine of monastic life?

NOTES

1. Dec. 26, 1955. Special issue on Christianity.
2. Letter of March 21, 1958, in the Benedictine Sisters' archives, St. Louis.

Chapter Twelve
1960–1970

The decade that was to turn the country and the Church upside down began quietly enough for the Benedictines in Clyde, Missouri. In January, Michael Marx, a monk of St. John's Abbey in Collegeville, Minnesota, directed the annual retreat for ninety sisters. Before leaving he said he found a hunger and thirst for God in the community that he had not found in other places. On a more earthy plane the following month saw many parts of the house being fumigated with sulphur in a desperate effort to halt the flu epidemic which was sending fifteen sisters at a time to bed. More than fifty trays had to be carried to flu patients at the height of the invasion, while Mother Carmelita was busy going from room to room giving chest-rubs until she herself succumbed.

In the summer and fall of 1960 Ignatius Hunt, O.S.B. came frequently from Conception Abbey to lecture on biblical theology and show his fine slides of the Holy Land. In July the weekly table-reading from newspaper clippings informed the sisters that John F. Kennedy had won the Democratic nomination on the first ballot. Lyndon Johnson was to be his running mate. Closer to home, the community was host to twenty-six young women at a "Eucharistic Seminar" which began on August 12. Bishop John Cody came to address them since the seminar was his suggestion. Another bishop, Fulton Sheen, wrote at this time to thank the community for encouraging the readers of their magazine to pray and sacrifice for the missions.

That Christmas Mother Carmelita presented two significant gifts to the sisters. One was a set of the Collegeville Press "New Testament Reading Guides." The other was the blueprints for the new San Diego monastery. Soon after, the sisters in the correspondence department were busy addressing fifty thousand appeals for this fourth foundation from Clyde.

In January 1961 while the country's youngest president was inaugurated, the Clyde community began a massive overhaul of the infirmary wing of the building on all three floors. This entailed sending several patients to other houses and moving the rest to different quarters, while the healthy slept in every conceivable nook and cranny. The work started out to be of three month's duration, but inevitably took a good deal longer. Then in early February, a new dining room for the thirty-two workmen employed by the community was installed in the basement of the workmen's house. With a couple hired to do the cooking and cleaning, the sisters were relieved of serving the meals and the long waiting for the men to return from the fields in the hot summer evenings.

Mother Carmelita played a tape of President Kennedy's inaugural address to the sisters and applied his famous line: "Ask not what your country can do for you . . ." to the spiritual life. She went on to urge the community to pray for the world situation, particularly in Laos, Cuba, and the Belgian Congo where Communist take-overs were feared. This was further impressed on the sisters when a County Extension agent lectured them on rural civil defense, warning about possible "fall-out" from Kansas City and Lincoln, Nebraska in case of attack. The Clyde Press had a more immediate cause for gloom in the removal of St. Philomena from the calendar of saints that April, since they had just reprinted fifty thousand copies of her popular booklet.

This was forgotten in the excitement of Cardinal Joseph Ritter's visit. He told the community that in St. Louis the Carmelites and the "Pink" Sisters had many lay people visiting their chapels to participate in their adoration of the Blessed Sacrament. He added that he would like a chapel of perpetual adoration in south St. Louis. "Here and now I invite you to my see! Get the contract ready and I'll sign it!" Cardinal Ritter said he had studied at St. Meinrad's seminary and felt at home with Benedictines. Just a few days later Mother Carmelita received a letter from the Cardinal, proving that he meant what he said, since he asked her to meet with Fr. Joseph McNicholas, the spiritual director of the two "Legions of 1,000 Men" already established in St. Louis. This energetic priest wasted no time in coming to Clyde to talk about a foundation in the archdiocese. His uncle, Peter Tallon, had left a considerable bequest for the building of a chapel. On June 1 Mother Carmelita and her council voted to accept the Cardinal's invitation, though she made it clear that there could be no immediate foundation until the one in San Diego was closer to completion.

That August Mother Carmelita returned from a spirituality institute at Notre Dame to tell the sisters about the church's Latin American thrust. The Apostolic Delegate had asked each congregation to pledge one-tenth of its membership to that area for the next ten years. Fr. Gerald Fitzgerald, founder of the Paraclete Fathers, replied at once that if he had the fare he could send two men immediately. Mother Carmelita sought him out and wrote him a check for the amount. By September 12 two of the Paraclete Fathers were on their way to the missions of Latin America.

At table the sisters were listening to Pope John XXIII's encyclical *Mater et Magistra,* which was to be termed one of the finest statements on social conditions ever written. Then Bishop Cody came for a visit in September. He had been appointed co-adjutor bishop of New Orleans. He told the sisters he was "out campaigning to build new churches, schools and seminaries . . . The best civil defense I know is the state of grace!" Bishop Cody also told them that the Pope for the first time had appointed observers to the meeting of the World Council of Churches. "He is bringing people closer together." A week later the community, along with peace-loving people everywhere, was saddened to learn of the death in a plane crash of U.N. Secretary General, Dag Hammarskjold. "A noble servant of peace is gone," said President Kennedy addressing the U.N., "but the quest for peace lies before us . . . In the development of this organization rests the only true alternative to war . . . So let us resolve that Dag did not die in vain."

October was a busy month with work beginning on enclosing the porches which overlooked the central courtyard. At the same time the new library was nearing completion. All such work was interrupted when Abbot Stephen Schappler died of lung cancer. His body was brought to the Clyde chapel for a special requiem on November 9. A few weeks later the community rejoiced at the election of Anselm Coppersmith as the fourth abbot of Conception. He had been the sisters' chaplain ten years before.

Just before Christmas, blizzards struck the area with drifts of snow that were more than five feet high in places. This resulted in stalled cars, but also some glorious sledding for the novitiate sisters. Carroll Stuhlmueller, C.P. directed the first retreat of 1962 and was to become a treasured friend of the congregation. At the end of that January when Bishop Charles Helmsing was appointed Bishop of Kansas City–St. Joseph, the sisters heard that there was considerable satisfaction among the priests of the diocese, who felt he would "pay more attention to building up a spiritual structure." A structure closer to home was of particular interest to the sisters at this time. The clerestory windows of the adoration chapel had just been equipped with long metal chains so they could be regulated from inside. Sr. M. Teresita Parra had special reason for gratitude. "What a relief," she wrote, "that we won't need to go outside any more in a storm! Three of us had an experience out there in one storm and we are grateful to God and our guardian angels that no one has yet been killed. Two sisters got blown clear to the edge of the roof, but fortunately their feet got caught in the gutter and they managed to hold on . . . One night I was out there for fifteen minutes trying to keep my balance, crawling on the roof because the west wind was like a whirlwind. The wind strikes the wall and then pulls you away from it and there is nothing to hold onto as you go from one window to the other to close them. My veil and headdress were pulled right off . . . I was down to my apron strings."

The spring of 1962 brought the usual arrival of new life, this time two thousand baby chicks, along with forty baby pigs and fifty-two Black Angus calves. The infirmary chaplain, Fr. Sisbert Burkhardt, O.S.B., blessed the lot. More exciting was the news that the astronaut, Lt. Col. John Glenn had orbited the earth three times on Feb. 20. That May Russian and American scientists were talking confidently of sending men to the moon via rocket in just a few years. The Clyde chronicler noted: "These rocket ships cost approximately two million each. God grant they be used only for peaceful purposes."

In October, the sisters began a novena of prayer, fasting and night vigils for the success of the Ecumenical Council which was to open on October 11. On the day itself the entire community rose before 3 a.m. so that their Mass might coincide with that of the Council Fathers in Rome. At 9 a.m. all the tower bells rang for ten minutes to proclaim the beginning of the Council. The sisters were the more motivated for this because of Dom Jean Leclercq's lecture a week before, when he spoke to them of the necessity for contemplatives to have a universal outlook. Then they learned that Pope John had visited Assisi to pray for the Council, the first such trip for a Pope outside of Rome in more than one hundred years. The community also enjoyed Bishop Helmsing's visit before he left for the Council. "The Council will work from Tuesday to Saturday," he told the sisters. "Sunday will largely be taken up with ceremonies and on Monday we do our wash . . . I bought myself some drip-dry underwear, so when you are doing your wash on laundry-day, think of your bishop in Rome doing the same."

On October 14 the one hundred and eight sisters of final vows chose the six delegates who would represent the Clyde community at the Chapter. By the end of the month their chaplain was telling them that the Council Fathers were discussing liturgy. Many of these Fathers favored greater adaptation of the liturgy to the needs of the people, along with some use of the vernacular languages in the liturgy of the Word. As the congregation's delegates began to arrive for the Chapter on November 15, Mother Carmelita received a letter from Archbishop Cody in New Orleans. He thanked her for the prayers offered for him, which he said had helped give him the courage to proceed with the integration of the Catholic schools there.

On November 21, 1962 Sr. Cecilia Bock was elected the third Prioress General of the congregation. A few days later Sr. Tharsilla Noser was appointed prioress of the Clyde monastery. Mother Cecilia was a woman of quiet strength and courage. She had given herself generously to all the responsibilities Mother Carmelita had delegated to her over the past twelve years. Capable of great self-sacrifice for duty's sake and with a calm, practical grasp of affairs, she subdued a warm, social personality to the demands of an office she did not want, at a most difficult time in the history of religious life. It was Mother Cecilia who began to open the congregation to the realities of the rapidly turning world of the sixties, away from the rather Cluniac view of monasticism that had prevailed. It fell to her lot to change and adapt many of the supernaturalized and sacralized codes of behavior that had been confused with the Rule itself over the years.

One of the major decisions of this Chapter of 1962 was to dispose of the Holstein dairy herd, except for the number necessary to supply the community's daily milk needs. By March of 1963 permission had been obtained from the Holy See to dispose of all the cattle, including the Black Angus. This amounted to a saving of at least $800.00 monthly. Joseph Gemmeke, the capable herd manager for so many years, helped in the sale of the cattle to private buyers. The poultry were the next to go, as it was becoming clear even to the most resistant that it was cheaper to buy meat, chicken and milk rather than keep the farm. When the last pony was sold, the chronicler noted on September 14: "We realize that our congregation is moving from one era into another. Our older sisters can recall riding side saddle on ponies to teach school and driving teams of horses hitched to the farm wagons." At this time more than 800 acres of pasture land were rented out to the Merrigan brothers, stock dealers in Maryville.

Next the apple orchard was thinned out to save on labor, spray and the sisters' time. Gradually, even the farm implements were sold off. It took frequent explanations and exhortations from both Mothers Cecilia and Tharsilla to convince sisters born and raised on farms that this was the right thing to do. The superiors pointed out the prohibitive cost of maintenance and labor, the difficulty of hiring good help, the saving of money. They told the sisters that the Jesuits at St. Mary's, Kansas, had sold their farm, so had the Benedictines at Atchison, Kansas, and Collegeville, Minnesota.

With the farm more or less disposed of, it was time to concentrate on the magazine, *Tabernacle and Purgatory,* which also needed a drastic updating since, as the chronicler put it, "it had suffered a great decline in subscribers." The altar bread making also came in for some attention. The department was renovated, and that fall letters went out to pastors and religious houses asking them to buy from the sisters rather than a commercial firm.

With Catholics everywhere, the sisters worried about Pope John XXIII that May of 1963 as his cancer worsened and hemmorhages became more frequent. One afternoon at the end of Vespers everyone in the choir swung to the center aisle as Fr. Sisbert stalked in, announcing in his great voice that the Pope was in a coma, with peritonitis setting in. That evening the entire community gathered to offer the prayers for the dying. On June 3, the pope who had brought a new Pentecost to the church died on Pentecost Monday. A few weeks later the sisters learned that Cardinal Giovanni Montini, the first

167

cardinal Pope John had made, was to be his successor. It was generally believed that he would carry on John's dream for the Council.

Mother Cecilia had her own worries during this time. Besides the disposal of the farm, the proposed foundation in St. Louis met with a great deal of resistance, particularly as the San Diego house had barely been completed. Yet the promise to Cardinal Ritter had been made. By November Mother Cecilia was telling the sisters that the Cardinal had approved a tract of land bounded by Morganford and Union Roads. Within a two-mile radius of the site lived an estimated sixty-four thousand Catholics, something very important for a shrine of adoration. Before the end of 1963, an architect was engaged and plans made to build the monastery in the form of a quadrangle enclosing a central courtyard. The chapel was to have a central altar, with the sisters' choir-stalls on one side and pews for the laity on the other. Happy with all this, the Cardinal was ready to announce that soon the Legion of 1,000 Men South would be a reality.

During the summer of 1963 the sisters prayed earnestly for the racial problem in the U.S., which Abbot Anselm told them was daily becoming more serious. At table they listened to the American Bishops' pastoral on race. Hours of adoration were also being offered for the second session of Vatican II. Fr. Louis Meyer, O.S.B., their chaplain, took the Constitution on the Liturgy as the topic of his Sunday conferences to the community, bringing up the possibility of praying the Divine Office in English. That Christmas for the first time the familiar carol, "Silent Night" was sung in English instead of German at the Midnight Mass.

Christmas that year was a subdued one because the community, along with most of the country, was still shocked by the assassination of President Kennedy. November 22 was also Mother Cecilia's nameday. It had been in the midst of a festive dinner in her honor that the unbelieving community learned that the Camelot days had ended with a bullet to the brain of America's first Catholic president.

The year 1964 opened with Pope Paul's trip to the Holy Land and his unprecedented meeting with the Orthodox Patriarch Athanagoras. In a similar ecumenical vein there were numerous tours of the Clyde chapels by students and teachers of other denominations. Meanwhile, the staff in the editorial department of the monthly magazine was busy revising and removing from circulation a number of booklets which might offend the spirit of ecumenism or whose theology needed an updating. At this time, Ignatius Hunt, O.S.B. of Conception Abbey offered to write some biblical articles, which was the beginning of writers other than the sisters appearing in the periodical. By that August Mother Cecilia was asking the sisters to suggest a new name for the fifty-five year old publication as part of the effort to modernize it.

Drawing a deep breath, as she afterwards told some, Mother Cecilia announced to the congregation toward the end of March that the general council had voted to remove the residence of the generalate, the novitiate, and the postulancy to the new foundation in St. Louis. The blueprints had been adjusted to allow for a third story on the building. Transportation in and out of Clyde was becoming increasingly difficult for the many trips the council needed to make, Mother Cecilia explained. Mail service was very slow. St. Louis could provide improved educational facilities for the novitiate. It might be a better source of vocations, since the city was known as "the Rome of the west." Then, too, this move would provide badly needed space for the overcrowded Clyde community, particularly for the infirm and elderly. Clyde would remain the motherhouse; St. Louis would be called the "central" house.

This announcement stunned the sisters. Clyde was the heart of the congregation. The early training for all the members had always been there. What would such a move mean to the community? A stubborn, if quiet, resistance to the entire plan developed and continued for several years. The almost weekly bulletins issued by the council detailing each step of the progress on the St. Louis monastery did nothing to quell this, but served as something of an irritant. It was a relief for Mother Cecilia to take time off to accompany Srs. Dolores Dowling and Maureen Truland to Collegeville, Minnesota in May to be present when they received their degrees in theology as part of the first graduating class of the Benedictine Institute of Sacred Theology; the other two students, Srs. Rosalita Jones and Damien Thompson, received theirs in absentia.

At this time the sisters were vaguely aware that the Civil Rights Act had been passed on June 19. From the table reading they understood that this bill contained strong barriers to racial bias in employment, public facilities, business and federal aid programs. Mother Cecilia kept urging them to pray about the danger of outbreaks of racial violence, especially in the slums of America's big cities. That month the Clyde chronicler noted: "May white people realize that Negroes have a just cause and recognize their moral obligation to treat them as equals." A recorded talk by John Howard Griffin, who had colored the pigmentation of his skin in order to see how Negroes were actually treated, brought this home to the sisters, most of whom had no real concept of the extent of racial prejudice in the country.

When the third session of Vatican Council II opened in October, there were almost daily releases from Catholic news services about the proceedings. The sisters applauded when Pope Paul VI invited women auditors to attend for the first time. With other Benedictines, they rejoiced on October 24 as the Pope dedicated the totally rebuilt abbey Church at Monte Cassino, declaring St. Benedict the patron of Europe. They were fascinated by other reports indicating considerable debate on the decree dealing with the church in the modern world, with "liberals" and "conservatives" battling it out, to the delight of the press. Fr. Sisbert, who considered it his duty to keep the community informed on political issues, told the sisters on November 4 that President Johnson had won a smashing victory. Then interest swung back to the Council as the Pope promulgated the decrees on the Church and on Christian Unity. More alarming were the reports filtering back from the Belgian Congo about persecution of clergy and religious of all faiths.

The sisters felt the most immediate effects of the Council in their liturgy. On Palm Sunday they heard the Passion read in English for the first time. That July the formula for the sacrament of Penance was also said in the vernacular. Later that month Cardinal Ritter told the crowd assembled for the ground breaking at the St. Louis site, "The sisters will carry out their adoration linked to the liturgy." In October they began to sing the familiar Benediction hymn, "O Salutaris" in English. Early in November, 1964 the intercessory prayers were introduced into the Mass. Mother Cecilia read the American bishops' "Guide for the Mass in English" to the sisters, telling them she was planning for portable altars in each of their chapels. On the first Sunday of Advent, Mass could be said facing the people with as much vernacular as the bishops allowed. That Christmas the sisters received communion standing, each one having placed her host in the ciborium, while strains of the English propers composed by Fr. Edmond Kestel, O.S.B. rang through the chapel.

During these same months several sisters were working far into the nights preparing an English translation of the Divine Office, now to be called the "Liturgy of the Hours." Fr. Godfrey Diekmann, O.S.B. had carried the American abbots' petition to the Abbot Primate in Rome in April, asking that he take action so that the hours could be prayed in English. By July 24 the sisters were practicing to recite Compline in the vernacular. By mid-November the community was able to pray all the ferial Hours in English.

Slowly this understanding of the Hours deepened and personalized the sisters' liturgical prayer. Experience convinced them of the truth of the statement in the Document on Revelation: "There is a growth in the understanding of the realities and the words which have been handed down. This happens through the contemplation and study made by believers, who treasure these things in their hearts."(#8). Such personal study was helped when the community gave up common spiritual reading and allowed each sister to do her own private lectio.

1965 began at Clyde with the first discussions in the community of a possible change of their religious habit. The Ursulines in nearby Kansas had already done this. The Daughters of Charity had given up their cherished white-winged headdress. In September Mother Cecilia

170

wrote to the community about a Major Superiors' meeting in Denver, where the Undersecretary of the Sacred Congregation for Religious had stated that Rome wished religious women to modify the habit. The head should not be "enveloped" in linen; long, flowing veils should be eliminated; the amount of material in the habit should be reduced so that it did not sweep the ground. The forehead and ears might be uncovered and there should be a minimum of adornment, such as cords, crucifixes and rosaries. Mother Cecilia went on to ask the sisters for suggestions about a changed headdress that she could take with her to the Benedictine Mothers' Retreat that October. The chronicler felt "that this is a very great sacrifice that is being asked of us." But she did understand that there was a general dearth of vocations to religious life. Over two thousand dispensations had already been granted. "We are experiencing this at Clyde," wrote Mother Cecilia, "for there is much instability among our postulants, novices and younger sisters." It was true, for although set after set was invested or made profession, by the end of this decade not many remained. There were twelve junior sisters in 1965; only four were to continue in monastic life.

Late in January, 1965 Fr. Sisbert told the sisters about Winston Churchill's death at the age of ninety and of the millions who lined the sidewalks of London to watch the greatest state funeral ever accorded to an Englishman. However, it was the Vietnam crisis that absorbed American attention. Most of the sisters had to look up that little country on a map when it first came to their notice. A few of them knew that a military coup had overthrown the Diem government in Saigon in the fall of 1963 and that U.S. military personnel there kept increasing. By 1965 U.S. forces were carrying out bombing raids on North Vietnam: America was once again at war. This was not a popular war; already there was a ground swell of disapproval which kept escalating in the months that followed.

For table-reading at this time the sisters were listening to the Council decree on the Church in the Modern World. Mother Cecilia thought it an appropriate time to announce the new title of their magazine. From then on it was to be called *Spirit & Life*, and would have more photos in an effort to give it a new look. The table-reading about the race crisis was more somber. The sisters heard of the civil rights demonstration at Selma, Alabama. In their monastic refectory they listened to descriptions of nuns wearing their black and white habits marching arm-in-arm with denim-clad youngsters in the group of four thousand demonstrators, guarded by carbine-carrying troops. They marched to a pasture eight miles from Selma on the first leg of that historic freedom march in a mile-long procession that had to pass by jeering crowds of white people. In front of Browns Chapel Martin Luther King, Jr., spoke to his people: "Walk together, children; don't you get weary ... it will lead you to the promised land ... and America will be a new America."

Something new to the Clyde community began that April: discussion groups. The sisters could choose among three topics: monasticism, liturgy and the vows, led by Srs. Dolores Dowling, Matthias Igoe, and Helen Barrow. This was "a real means of dialogue among the sisters," noted the chronicler with satisfaction. That summer the schedule was adjusted to give the sisters a little more rest and some time to enjoy the outdoors. There was the inevitable strawberry picking and the enjoyable Sunday evening outdoor meals. At one of these Sr. Cunegunda Eikelmann, aged 90, had her first experience of ice cream in a sugar cone. She ate the ice cream with a spoon and then someone told her that she could also eat the cone. "Think of that," she said, "first you eat the dessert and then you eat the dish!"

That September the community had a more searching visitation than the ones they were accustomed to. This was conducted in the name of Bishop Helmsing by two experienced priests of the Kansas City diocese. After reassuring the sisters that the financial resources of the congregation were adequate for the new foundation in St. Louis, they went on to speak very directly to the superiors. They must, said the visitators, lighten the workload of the sisters. The sisters must be assured of some time for themselves — a free noon period was suggested. Real efforts were to be made for greater collegiality: the sisters should be consulted before any significant undertakings. As a result of this, Mother Cecilia asked all the departments to close at noon for at least an hour. She said: "We are trying, though it will probably take some time, to work toward a normal day when you can accomplish your work without having to take your meditation early in the morning ... The community owes you this! You should be able to pray without cutting down on your time for sleep."

On September 17, 1965 the Second Vatican Council took up, the sisters learned from their table-reading, the decree on religious liberty, which was largely the work of the American Jesuit, John Courtney Murray. The sisters were proud to hear that Cardinal Ritter had told the two thousand five hundred prelates in the great hall that "if we do not approve this document, we run the risk of being enemies of the Gospel."

On January 3, 1966, Mother Cecilia asked the sisters to begin studying the present constitution of the congregation with a view to the revision that would have to be made in light of Vatican II. By this time the decision had been made to modify the habit somewhat by shortening it to ankle-length. Odd-looking headgear was appearing at evening recreations as the sisters experimented with various designs. In February a series of taped lectures on religious life in the contemporary world were begun; such input having been suggested by the visitators. Mother Cecilia's next question to the community dealt with work. What did the sisters think should be done in the St. Louis monastery for self-supporting work and what could be done to lessen the work-load at Clyde? This was not an academic question since the novitiate did the bulk of the cleaning chores in the house.

On April 11 the first group assigned to the St. Louis monastery departed. By April 28 all those destined for the newest monastery had driven off in a cavalcade of cars. Those left behind waved goodbye and then looked at each other as they returned to the house. An era had just ended. Clyde was still the motherhouse, but would no longer be the center of decision and formation. Now there was the excitement of forging a new approach: their own prioress would have greater authority. Perhaps there would now be closer cohesion in the community. On the practical level, there was the thrill of each one having her own bedroom. To eliminate some work, formal serving in the refectory was given up and cafeteria-style introduced. There would now be only one sister at night adoration rather than the customary two.

Late in June the renowned moral theologian, Bernard Haring, whose work was having such an effect at the Council, came over from Conception Abbey to speak to the sisters about renewal in the church. That November in a new venture for them, two of the sisters from Clyde attended a diocesan council of women religious. More were excited about the multilith machine donated to the Clyde Press by Fr. Alphonse Sitzman of the Abbey. He also trained two of the sisters in its use.

In September truck-loads of furniture were still heading toward the St. Louis monastery. From the General Council there came another permission: the sisters could eat a meal with relatives when they came to visit. When the community heard that the American bishops had lifted the Friday abstinence, except on Fridays of Lent, they were convinced that the old order was indeed changing. The final excitement of 1966 was Sr. Marietta's brother, Pat Crahan, a bomber pilot, who flew over the Clyde monastery three times, each time lower than the last. He told the sisters this was his salute for the prayers they had offered for him. He was convinced these had saved him all the time he was in Vietnam, where he had flown over forty bombing missions.

1967 was dubbed the year of the questionnaire. In preparation for the renewal Chapter of 1968, Mother Cecilia sought the sisters' opinions on a variety of topics. One set of questions dealt with identity. Sr. Georgia Nacke summed up the older sisters' bewilderment with all this when she asked: "Are we first finding out now who we are? I thought I knew all the time!" Privately and in discussion groups, the sisters struggled with such questions as: What are we? Why are we? In what ways are we effective in the church? Are we relevant to the needs of the church? If not, how should we change? How should we return to the spirit of our founder? Are there new works we could undertake? Should we accept sisters who wish to transfer from other congregations? Should we offer facilities for retreats to other sisters? Do you favor hair showing in the new headdress?

As a result of these questionnaires and of attendance at various institutes on religious life, Mother Cecilia set about changing some of the time-honored customs of the community, those largely inherited from their European origins. Now the sisters could write to relatives and friends as they chose; there would be no censoring of letters. Customary Lenten penances were dropped. Attendance at diocesan institutes on religious life was encouraged, as was sharing about these with the rest of the sisters.

Lent began that year on February 12. The community's new chaplain was a little confused about the ashes. As the newsletter writer told it: "Our imperturbable Fr. Joseph administered the ashes. He seems to believe in the Vespers' Scripture text: 'Between the porch and the altar,' for he put the ashes square in the center of our starched linen bands. And he was liberal, the fall-out drifted to our noses. In all, nearly seventy-five bands went to wash that day."

As Lent continued some of the sisters listened to tapes from a workshop on Teilhard de Chardin. They also had discussions on monastic poverty, which the chronicler felt were "helpful in that they give the sisters an opportunity to learn to express themselves." March brought the election of Sr. Domitilla Dirig as the Clyde representative on the team which was to revise the constitutions for the General Chapter's approval. Amid all this, the work at the altar bread department continued to be very heavy, with the sisters there working during Matins and supper to fill all the orders.

Worry about the situation in Vietnam grew steadily. The chronicler noted that more than ten thousand Americans had died there since 1962. That fall Sr. DePazzi Fink received two letters from her nephew, Jeff Olsen. The first one was dated from Vietnam in October, 1967:

> About a week ago I was able to get to Mass and communion. The chaplain set up his little altar in a wet field . . . This marked the first time in four months that I was able to receive the sacraments . . . Every few nights we go out on ambush patrol, ten men armed heavily with machine guns and other weapons. Then we lie in wait for the Viet Cong to come our way . . . The night is very long and often rainy. It gets very difficult to stay awake . . . I found a way to do it. I pray the rosary . . . My ten fingers definitely have been very helpful in the past week."

The second letter was dated November 27:

> "Already Thanksgiving has passed and things just don't look that good. On Thanksgiving we were flown in some decent chow by a chopper. About 11:30 that night we were mortared by the Viet Cong and had some casualties. One of the infrantry men, Chalkie, was killed . . . It was strange that Chalkie had attended a service and when the minister asked

him what he was grateful for, old Chalkie told him he was thankful to be alive and healthy. But only five hours later he was dead . . . On the tank I am now riding, Grinnell, whom we call 'chief' because he is part Indian, was hit in the back and I helped him as much as possible. He kept saying: 'Swede, I'm scared! Help me!' He was bleeding pretty badly and I'm sure he was in shock . . . I really feel the need of God in this situation . . . I am still wearing your medal and glad to have it. However, it is getting worn and I would like you to send me another. In fact, send as many as you are able, because a lot of men have asked me to get one for them."

June was a busy month at Clyde. Five sisters celebrated their golden jubilee of monastic profession with more than one hundred guests present for the occasion. Six sisters were attending an institute at Conception Abbey at the end of June, where Fr. Charles Curran, the controversial moral theologian from Catholic University, was the main speaker. Three others went to the national liturgical week in Kansas City, while two more were at the American Benedictine Academy meeting at St. Meinrad's in Indiana. Even though Mother Cecilia herself had given permission for this, many of the older sisters were confused and disturbed by these exits from the enclosure. Perhaps that is why discussions in July concentrated on how to create a better family spirit. The chronicler's summing up is ambiguous: "One would say the discussions went well — better than usual for Clyde."

Events on the national scene took the sisters' attention off local issues. Sr. Benedicta Faistl's brother, Fr. Clem, came to visit her and told the community about his participation in the march at Selma, Alabama. On July 17 the sisters heard about the gunfire and fighting for the fourth consecutive night in Newark, New Jersey, as the race riots continued. Property damage in Detroit alone, they were told, was supposed to have soared beyond the one hundred million mark.

In March, the prioress, Mother Irene Prugger, bought a table for each sister's room. Before this, the austere bedrooms had only a bed and a chair. Then Mother Irene led the community in discussing the first version of the revised constitution. When the Clyde community sent in its suggestions for further revision to the committee working in the St. Louis monastery, Sr. Domitilla wrote that they weighed three pounds. Slowly, the sisters were taking hold of their future, learning to express their opinions, to ask for changes. One of these changes was later rising, now at 5 a.m., and one hour's recreation at noon.

At the end of September, 1967 the sisters learned that for the first time an American had been elected Abbot Primate of the Benedictine order. He was Rembert Weakland formerly co-adjutor abbot of St. Vincent's in Latrobe, Pennsylvania. Only forty years old, he was a musician, composer and accomplished organist. Now he was accountable to more than thirteen hundred Benedictine monks. Interest in him, however, took second place to interest in the new headdress. For the first Vespers of All Saints in November the sisters appeared in the new look. According to the chronicler, "we were proud of our sisters as there was a one hundred percent change to the new headdress. We rose ten minutes earlier so that those who needed time might have it!" There were no mirrors at that time but all kinds of substitutes were used. The new soft nylon band and collar left some of the senior sisters feeling almost naked after years of wearing the stiffly pleated and starched linen band and coif. The last excitement for 1967 was the election of delegates from the Clyde community to the Chapter. There was a feeling that this would be the most important Chapter the congregation had ever held. After a tense morning, the eighty-three sisters eligible to vote, chose four to represent them at the Chapter: Srs. Raymond (Josephine Marie) Roos, the subprioress, Paschalia Noser, Domitilla Dirig and Dolores Dowling.

The delegates left for St. Louis on February 4, 1968, sent off to the tune of the community band, which included guitars, ukeleles, drums, cymbals, a melodica and an accordian. Soon after this departure, Sr. Margaret Mary Belinski received permission to go home to be with her dying mother. Everyone knew that this matter of home-visits was due to come up at the Chapter, so this experimental permission was a return to a custom that the older sisters remembered, but the younger had never known.

After the election of the fourth prioress general, the sisters waited anxiously to learn who would be their local prioress. A phone call on March 6 told them it would be one of their own: Sr. Benita Luetke-meyer, with Sr. Lucilla Scurlock as her assistant. The entire community lined up at the kitchen steps to welcome these two home on March 23. Mother Benita gave them a copy of the revised constitution, telling them there would be ongoing discussions to familiarize them with it. She also explained the integrated program of formation, as well as the committees to be set up in each monastery to further community living and the purposes of the congregation. Other changes had soon to be implemented: lay employees for the altar bread work, a weekly "free night" during which the sisters could do what they wished to relax, three home-visits in a sister's lifetime and at the serious illness or death of a parent. In a subsequent chapter the home visits were extended to one week a year or two weeks every two years.

At this time, the chaplains to the community at Clyde were three Conception monks: Frs. Lucian Bianchi, Marcian O'Meara and James Jones. Fr. Edmond was still giving organ and chant lessons, as well as playing on occasion for solemn Vespers. By May the chronicler was writing: "We do have a wonderful little family here, serving God by loving each other and being faithful to prayer and work." Two other Conception Abbey monks began to help the sisters learn the new sung

Liturgy of the Hours composed at the Abbey. With Frs. Marcian and Lucian, these two formed part of the team for the annual retreat. This was something new, as were the conferences on community and personal responsibility.

Then the classes and lectures began. There were Scripture courses by Fr. Augustine Stock, O.S.B. Fr. Basil Rechenberg began a series of lectures on psychology. Sr. Dolores arrived from St. Louis to speak to the sisters on the new approach to the vows. The pace increased in 1969. There was a whole-hearted, if not particularly integrated, effort to achieve the "aggiornamento" urged by the beloved Pope John XXIII. Time and again in the past, various authorities had urged the superiors to keep the sisters better informed, to help open their minds and hearts to the advances in spirituality and theology. This effort begun by Mothers Carmelita and Cecilia now shifted into high gear.

There were classes in creative writing for those interested. The Conception Abbey seminarians began coming over once a week to talk about social problems, poverty, "hippies," inner-city strife, etc. There were group discussions on taped lectures by Bernard Cooke, S.J. on the Eucharist. The director of the state hospital came to help the sisters on the retirement committee in their work with the aging. Another first for the Clyde community was their retreat given by a layman, Dr. Thomas Francoeur of Montreal, Canada. A lay theologian and psychologist, he insisted that "our eucharistic responsibility is to become food for one another." Following on this, Fr. Lucian began a series of talks on the mystery of the church, which was followed in turn by the St. Louis University scripture scholar, Dr. Irvin Arkin on scripture subjects. The sisters themselves began sharing the fruits of their studies. Sr. Paula Thompson lectured on "body-person and community life." Sr. Valeria Scott developed some lectures from a seminar on gerontology. In December Sr. Teresa Bertolotti shared some of her University of Notre Dame courses from Dr. Josef Goldbrunner with his theme of "holiness is wholeness."

In between life went on. It was a severe winter with Clyde "one block of ice" according to the chronicle. Corpus Christi brought Abbot Anselm with sixty of his monks to celebrate with the sisters. On July 20 there was a special liturgy with frequent mention of the moon in both psalms and readings to commemorate the moon-walk of the astronauts. One of the most appreciated innovations was the "hermit-day" each month, a day on which the sister could omit the usual schedule to pray, read, or rest. One small indication of the depth of these changes was the general acceptance of Fr. Lucian's homily at the end of the year. On the feast of St. John, he told the sisters that each one should have a St. John in her life, "someone we love very much, just as Jesus loved John." Slowly the old fear of "particular friendship," with all the loneliness and emotional isolation it had fostered, was being laid to rest.

ST. LOUIS

In April the few sisters already at the St. Louis monastery were hosts to an Open House which drew three thousand visitors the first day and nearly thirteen thousand on the second, which was a Sunday. As usual in a new building, when the builders finished their work at 5 p.m., the sisters went on working until midnight, cleaning up, washing windows, waxing floors. The monastery was large, of a rather indeterminate style. There were grounds enough around the building to plant trees and have a tennis court. The chapel had walls of grey marble with high, narrow windows full of stylized symbols. A silver monstrance supported by the hands of two adoring angels rested above the altar. This was a cause of controversy from the first and was settled a few years later by the removal of the angels, much to the relief of the more liturgically inclined. At the back of the chapel stood racks of devotional candles whose fumes soon necessitated the installation of a vent. These lights, together with a statue of the Sorrowful Mother and the Infant of Prague were a great source of satisfaction to some of the visitors to the chapel.

As early as May 5 Fr. Joseph McNicholas had invited fifty southside pastors to the monastery for a noon meal. He asked them to appoint outstanding laymen from their parishes to work with the moderator of this new Legion, Frank Maroon. Both Cardinal Ritter and Bishop Flavin attended the meeting. On June 9, the feast of Corpus Christi, Cardinal Ritter was principal celebrant of a pontifical Mass, which officially opened the chapel. The Legion of 1,000 Men South was now a reality. By August 1, over one thousand visits a week had been registered. Careful records were kept of all this, which was merely one more example of the tremendous efforts made by the sisters over the years to involve the laity in their adoration of the Blessed Sacrament. Each monastery had a sister assigned to keep a record of the number of visits by various associations of the laity. The sisters considered this to be part of their eucharistic apostolate, a way of sharing what Mother Carmelita had called "the great gift of the Father: Jesus in the sacrament of love." Others also shared by their goodness to the community. Dick Poehling and Rich Pinter served Mass almost daily. So did Gregory Bockius who also was on hand whenever needed to act as chauffeur.

On September 17 the community experienced the first profession services in their new chapel. The changes suggested by Rome were already in evidence. There was no more bridal attire for the novices; no more lying under the pall for those making final profession and no tolling of the bell. Parents, brothers, or sisters accompanied those to be professed into the sanctuary, symbolizing their gift of one of the family to the Lord. Because of the importance of Christian baptism, the name given at that time could be retained if the sister wished.

By May 17 the representatives from each monastery assembled in the central monastery to begin the work of revising the Constitution, collating the hundreds of suggestions sent in by the sisters. They often consulted Fr. Paul Boyle, C.P. a canonist. There was a second such session in October, after the first revision had been discussed in all the monasteries. Between sessions the sisters mourned the death of Cardinal Ritter on June 10. They also prayed fervently for an end to the race riots and the Vietnam war. By now most of the community knew a priest or sister who had marched in protest against it. Then their attention turned to the Middle East, where Israel was becoming a major power after the shattering collision with Arab forces in the "Six Day" war.

Mother Cecilia's letter from a superiors meeting in Denver that August amused them all with its description of the new look among the twelve thousand superiors gathered there. "You should see the styles: short skirts, high heels. I don't think we have seen any other Benedictines yet — but, then, how can we be sure?"

While the sisters on Morganford Road rejoiced at the introduction of English into the canon of the Mass, they worried about the vocation situation. True, they had fourteen postulants, but at the same time seventeen sisters were in various stages of withdrawal from the congregation. 1965 had been the peak year for vocations to the religious life in the U.S. Now the slide had begun. In less than five years, fifty thousand sisters would have left their congregations. Anxiety about these departures was one of the reasons for an announcement that shook the congregation of Benedictine Sisters of Perpetual Adoration late in October, 1967. Mother Cecilia wrote that the special General Chapter mandated by Vatican Council II would take place in February, 1968, and it would be a chapter of election as she planned to resign at that time. With her usual clear-sightedness she saw the need for younger leadership. Reading the signs of the times with the detachment that was one of her gifts, Mother Cecilia felt that the new constitution on which so much time and labor had been spent deserved new insights and fresh approaches to make it a lived reality.

It was this sixth General Chapter which absorbed much of the energy of the St. Louis community in the early winter of 1968. After what seemed like endless preparation, the Chapter finally opened on February 6, but not quite as planned. The assembled delegates had another shock on the first morning, when they learned that the Apostolic Delegate had appointed Fr. Conrad Louis, O.S.B. to supervise the negotiations of the Chapter. In the bland phrasing of the official letter to the congregation it was stated that this was done "so that an experienced priest could be present to assist in the Chapter's approach to the problems of renewal." The letter to Fr. Conrad himself was more to the point: "The Benedictine Sisters of Perpetual Adoration have been experiencing some agitation in their approach to the renewal of their religious life as prescribed by the second Vatican Council. I am certain that the presence of a qualified priest at their forthcoming Chapter ... would furnish precisely the elements of wisdom and peace which these sisters require."

What the majority of the delegates did not know was that this appointment had been precipitated by the Tucson community. Worried about the departure of so many younger sisters, concerned that the preparations for this renewal Chapter were not extensive enough, they wrote both to their own bishop and to the Delegate in Washington, D.C. The result was that for the first time the congregation's Chapter was presided over by someone outside the congregation. The Apostolic Delegate had chosen well. Fr. Conrad was known to all the sisters. With considerable skill, tact and sensitivity to the group of twenty-three delegates, he helped guide them toward renewal.

The main business of this Chapter, besides the election of a new prioress general, was to approve the revised constitution. The revision committee had produced a completely different version. No longer did their constitution follow the chapters of the Benedictine Rule point by canonical point. Instead it was divided into four main sections dealing with worship, community, formation and government. The spirit of the Rule was intact in this document, while the spirit of Vatican II was incorporated with numerous quotations. Fr. Conrad, who said he was there to provide, not preside, encouraged the delegates to aim for something workable and flexible, a useful tool, not a finished one, since this was the time for experimentation. The sisters struggled to define their role in the church: they were monastic contemplatives, but not strictly cloistered. Their dedication to the Eucharist was not only a devotion, it was a ministry.

Section by section the Chapter members labored over this constitution, trying to make its theory come to reality in the directory. They wanted to encourage interpersonal relationships: community bonding was an important goal. They wanted the prioresses to foster the personal contribution of each sister to the welfare of the total community and the church. Because of this the delegates took a second look at the advantages of a discriminating use of newspapers, periodicals and television.

By the day of the election, March 2, 1968 the delegates were almost unanimous in the choice of Sr. Pascaline Coff. Forty-one years old at this time, she had been novice director, carefully tutored by Mother Carmelita and also sub-prioress. Open-hearted, enthusiastic, with a good sense of where the congregation was and where it needed to go, she accepted the office generously. Next, the delegates chose Srs. Maureen Truland, Reparata Hopp, Gertrude Gross, and Dolores Dowling as the general council. True to Mother Cecilia's vision, the leadership age had dropped from the sixties to the forties. The council appointed younger prioresses to each monastery as well. Then they

180

chose Sr. Damien (Paula) Thompson as postulant director with Sr. Regina Arnold as novice director.

In March the Chapter recessed for a year. Almost immediately a number of experimental changes were introduced. There would be less formality in liturgical prayer, with the "Little Hours" prayed on a conversational tone. The organists were to attend classes in liturgy. Dr. Mario Salvador, the well-known organist at the St. Louis Cathedral, helped the community obtain a pipe organ and began coming weekly to give organ and choir lessons.

Classes began in real earnest. The directors attended mental health workshops, the nurses gerontology seminars, because "it is imperative to make older religious feel needed and useful, since the life-span for women had increased a good ten years already." Ten sisters who had entered the congregation very young began work on their high-school equivalency diplomas. There were classes on nutrition for the cooks, on arts and crafts for those who wished. Any sister who wanted to do so now had the opportunity to make a privately-directed retreat. Rank was abandoned as far as the refectory went with no more formality in the cafeteria-style meals.

On April 4, 1968 many in the community were horrified to hear that Martin Luther King, Jr., the compelling black leader with his magnetic eloquence, had been assassinated. On April 8 some 30,000 St. Louisans marched from the Gateway Arch to Forest park to honor his memory. On April 23 the sisters were praying for the two hundred and fifty American bishops assembled in the city to draft their letter to Catholics, warning against racism in housing, education and employment. At this time, Bishop Green from Tucson came to visit the sisters, telling them about the serious problems facing the hierarchy in the many departures from the priesthood and the diminishing number of seminarians. This was not news as the Catholic papers were busy expressing dismay at the extent of the losses from the ministry and religious life.

That fall did not bring better news. As the sisters knelt before the Blessed Sacrament in their chapel, some felt they were praying for a world gone mad. Hubert Humphrey, Robert Kennedy and Eugene McCarthy had been vying for the Democratic nomination. It was Humphrey who officiated as vice-president at the dedication of the Gateway Arch, with a crowd of some 200,000 standing in the rain and a regatta of hundreds of boats on the Mississippi. In June there had been the horror of Robert Kennedy's assassination just after he won the California primary. Then the sisters read about the violence which flared at the Democratic convention in Chicago with people being clubbed and dragged from the hall.

There was some unrest also in the congregation about their eucharistic charism. Even as Archbishop Carberry, Cardinal Ritter's successor, came to celebrate the community's second anniversary in his diocese, a letter from Mother Pascaline referred to this. "Properly understood," she wrote, "devotion to and adoration of Christ in the Eucharist is conceivable only as an extension of the worship offered at Mass, into which context our devotion to the sacrament must fit. The theology of the tabernacle is meaningless if separated from the mainstream of eucharistic theology."

That same June Mother Pascaline wrote again about her interview with the Abbot Primate, Rembert Weakland, at St. Gregory's Abbey in Oklahoma. She told the sisters he had spoken of the pitiful condition of many contemplative nuns in Europe who had neglected any apostolate for the good of the church and so had become irrelevant to its life. The Abbot Primate felt that Benedictine sisters had full permission to experiment with the Liturgy of the Hours. In his judgment, he told Mother Pascaline, no Hour should exceed forty-five minutes. When she asked him about the traditional separation between novices and the professed sisters, his reply was emphatic: "We Benedictines have taken on the Jesuit idea in this which was never intended for monastics. Today's young people have a great need for recognition and should be given attention!" Rembert Weakland went on to suggest that reasons of charity should be stressed in the practice of silence, not ascetical reasons, and above all, "give people time for that integrated thought which leads to prayer." In this the Abbot Primate echoed the plea of America's foremost monk, Thomas Merton, who urged monastic people to lead a deeply-experienced life, so that those most alive in the world outside the monastery would spontaneously come to share in monastic silence, leading to a fruitful exchange of ideas.

The sisters on Morganford had no realization at the end of July 1968 of the impact Pope Paul VI's teaching on birth control would have. The Pope held to the traditional view that no artificial means of birth control could be used by Catholics. It became apparent that many of the world's half-billion Catholics did not agree with this teaching. It gave promise, in fact, of becoming an issue, that would split the church. Prominent theologians in the U.S. and elsewhere dissented from the Pope's view. There were debates, imposed silences, and bitter wrangling.

In September Mother Pascaline was in the Kansas City monastery with the junior sisters of the congregation for the formal opening of the juniorate there. This was another result of the Chapter. There were to be special courses for these young professed preparing for final vows, as well as time to study with a director to help them. Mother Pascaline urged them "to become real women of prayer, women concerned about world conditions: famine in Biafra, the migrant workers in our own country, the yippies in Chicago, the elections in November." Late in August Mother Pascaline was again asking the sisters to pray, this time for an end to the hijacking of planes and the appalling upsurge in the use of drugs. She told them about thirteen young people in St. Louis, all from good homes, who had been arrested at a "dope-party."

The sisters were not sure what to make of it when they learned that Bishop Helmsing of Kansas City had publicly disassociated himself from the popular independent Catholic weekly published in his diocese and soon to be known as the "National Catholic Reporter." They heard that renowned theologians like Hans Kung and Edward Schillebeeckx had been called to Rome to defend their writings against charges of heresy. In the U.S. the well-known Berrigan brothers, Phil and Dan, were arrested for burning draft cards as part of the "Catonsville Nine."

The community prayed in gratitude that November when the president ordered a halt to all air, naval and artillery bombardment of North Vietnam. In December they were praying with the rest of the Catholic world for the repose of the soul of Thomas Merton, accidently killed in the Far East at a religious conference. One of the most influential monastic figures of the century, Merton had been a sponsor of the Catholic Peace Fellowship. The thousands of Americans dead in Vietnam, along with the uncounted Vietnamese, also cried out for a peace that remained elusive.

As the sisters opened their chapel doors at 6 a.m. in the early months of 1969 there were always people waiting to begin their day with a visit to the Blessed Sacrament. An average of two hundred visits daily were made. At the end of the month, the doors were opened to welcome the delegates returning to the second session of the renewal Chapter. These Chapter sessions, the delegates agreed, would be open to any sisters who wished to attend. Experts in theology, spirituality and psychology spoke to the delegates in the first days of the Chapter, helping them achieve a more cosmic view of the Eucharist, a deepened understanding of human relationships in community and the more practical necessity of good screening of candidates for monastic life. Commissions of delegates worked on position papers outlining a basic approach to their charism, to worship, community living, government and formation. One very appreciated decision of this Chapter was that of allowing the sisters to drive cars, which put an end to the incessant calling on friends for this service.

As the Chapter ended and February turned into March, the sisters learned that Fr. Joseph McNicholas had been named auxiliary bishop of St. Louis, while another friend, Fr. Marcian O'Meara, O.S.B. was installed as the prior of the Benedictine monks at Pevely. Then in May word came of the new Roman missal, which eliminated the prayers at the foot of the altar before Mass and included some new canons. The ruling that women must have their heads covered in church was abolished. Now there could be considerably more spontaneity in planning liturgies. It was the era of "creative" offices, with copying machines breaking down regularly under the load.

That summer the community sent sisters to Notre Dame University, to San Francisco University and to St. Louis University. Closer to home, Sr. DeSales Markert resigned as editor of "Spirit of Life," after thirty-three years and was warmly welcomed to the St. Louis monastery. It was the Prayer Institute they were sponsoring at the end of July that absorbed much of the sisters' time and energy that summer. So much washing and waxing of floors went on in preparation that one sister wrote: "Our coat of arms should be a polisher rampant on a field of heavy traffic wax." The three-day institute was a great success with over two hundred and fifty registrants daily to hear talks by Frs. Carroll Stuhlmueller, C.P., Luke Rigby, O.S.B. and Sr. Margaret Marie Vitt, O.S.U.

Toward the end of August St. Louis suffered even worse air pollution than usual, to the extent that the chronicler noted: "It was feared that industry and business would have to shut down with cars and buses." It was in August that the sisters began to hear and read about a three-day music festival at a place called "Woodstock" in New York state. Newspapers talked about the crowds of young people, the open use of drugs, the rock and pop stars. Editors wondered if this was a mass drop-out or a new kind of peaceful revolution. They were groping for terms to describe a generation in which remembrances, ideas and experiences were universally shared, with music as the conductor.

In September 1969 the sisters had a first-hand experience of the House of Prayer interest in that era, when Sr. Aelred, a Precious Blood sister, came to spend a year with the community in preparation for establishing a house of prayer in her own congregation. She was just one of the many from other congregations who were interested in the Benedictine life of prayer. At this time the congregation was receiving requests for transfer from other sisters who wanted a life of more intense prayer or whose own congregation's house of prayer failed in its purpose. After a period of adjustment several of these transfer sisters went on to make valuable contributions to the congregation. It was easy to remember the Abbot Primate's vigorous optimism at the end of this decade. When asked if monasticism would survive, he had replied: "Why not? We have everything going for us: prayer, liturgy, community!"

MUNDELEIN

The year 1960 began for the Benedictines in Mundelein with the long awaited pouring of concrete for the new wing. By August this was complete, but for the next five years at least, this "annex," as it was called, leaked badly. The chronicles are full of complaints about the rain coming in whenever the north wind blew.

At the end of March Cardinal Meyer dropped in for a brief visit. He came from the seminary in all the splendor of his red robes because, he said, he wanted the sisters to see him "in his glad rags." Early in April the civic elections occupied the sisters' attention. "Mayor Daley," noted the chronicler, "is said to be a good Catholic and an excellent mayor." In November she commented on the presidential election: "We have asked advice from various persons and all seem agreed that both Mr. Nixon and Mr. Kennedy are exceptionally fine men and that whichever one becomes the next president, the government should be in excellent hands." After Kennedy's election, there is only the rueful remark: "Some Protestants still seem to feel that now we have a Catholic president, all Protestant churches and public schools will be closed."

In the fall there were more apples on the trees than the sisters knew what to do with. The spring of 1961 brought the prioress other worries: too much to be done for the forty-five sisters to do it. There was the ever-busy altar bread department, the large garden and orchard. There were vestments to sew and the annual order from Quigley Preparatory Seminary for between four hundred and six hundred surplices. The sisters rarely had a genuine recreation. Only Sundays were available for rest, recreation, and fresh air and "quite a few of the sisters are elderly and cannot help as they did in former years."

Although the sisters lived in almost rural solitude, the community had many faithful friends. They phoned and wrote; they brought gifts of food and flowers; they did all kinds of driving, shopping and other services. These friends kept the sisters somewhat informed about what was going on in the local community and the nation. The sisters knew that in New Orleans, Archbishop Rummel had excommunicated three Catholic segregationists for interfering with his parochial school integration order. They themselves, however, scarcely saw a black in the Mundelein area of some thirteen thousand people. They prayed for the race crisis without real awareness of what it meant. They did wonder about Billy Graham's statement at his huge rally in Chicago on June 3, 1962, for the chronicler noted: "He says the world is in its last days."

That summer and fall the devoted Monsignor Meegan was at hand for any need. Gifts of food and money were showered on the community through him. It was owing to him that the annual celebration of the diocesan priests' silver jubilee was held at the monastery. The sisters served the banquet while the Monsignor personally arranged the menu, supervised the seating, showed the sisters how to fix the more elaborate dishes and chose the wine. He was on hand to mourn with the community when they reluctantly gave up their beloved Mother Dolorosa as prioress, and to rejoice when Mother Thiadildis was appointed to succeed her, since she had been prioress there before and fitted in comfortably with Mundelein ways.

In January of 1963 the sisters were praying for Pope John XXIII who was dying of cancer and who had offered his life for peace and the success of the Ecumenical Council. In a much more modest way Mother Thiadildis made a bid for peace when she decided that the vestment-making had to be given up. This helped, but the garden work remained heavy. While the rest of the sisters picked cherries, currants and strawberries, Sr. Emerentia Koening picked something she did not intend: in the trap she set for a marauding racoon, she caught a skunk instead. As the year ended, the chronicler noted that the community was still receiving Mass stipends for the repose of the soul of John F. Kennedy. The following November the Republican candidate would not have appreciated her comment: "We have been advised to be careful about Senator Barry Goldwater as he is so radical, he is liable to get us into war."

It was Cardinal Meyer that the sisters worried about early in 1965. On February 25 he was operated on for a malignant brain tumor, from which he never recovered. His death on April 9 brought sincere grief to the entire archdiocese. His had been an early and firm insistence on racial justice in Chicago. According to an updated clipping preserved in the chronicles from the *National Catholic Reporter:* "In another generation, Chicago might have given the Roman Catholic Church her first American Pope. Of such stuff was Cardinal Albert Meyer made . . . For a brief period of the Council's third session he frequently served as the main spokesman for the U.S. bishops." It was June 16 when the sisters learned that a very different man was to be their new ordinary, Archbishop Cody.

The liturgical changes resulting from the Council were slow in arriving at the Mundelein community. Fr. Wojcik of the seminary composed music for the Eucharist and ran off copies for the sisters. In August there was a call from the chancery advising the sisters that there should be only one Benediction daily. On September 22 for the first time, the community prayed the entire Liturgy of the Hours in English. There were other changes: Sr. Bertha Nortmann was appointed their prioress in November. There was also the slowly growing realization of the extent of the protest against the Vietnam war, as the sisters heard about the twelve thousand who picketed the White House late in the month.

Just before March 24, 1966 the sisters heard about another historic change: the meeting between Pope Paul VI and the Anglican Primate, Archbishop Michael Ramsey of Canterbury, England. This meeting ended in a joint statement announcing that their two churches would begin a serious dialogue that could lead to that unity in truth for which Christ prayed. The sisters themselves were busily dialoguing all that spring and summer on the constitution. The notation in the Mundelein chronicle about this is very typical: "May the Holy Spirit give us light to see and grace to accept, leaving all in the hands of our dear superiors and those who will make the final decision." Perhaps that is why Mother Cecilia wrote them on September 8 to say: "We are receiving quite regularly and in a most satisfactory quantity written suggestions for the revision of the constitution from all our convents except Mundelein."

Late in August the sisters were horrified to hear about the Catholics involved in the terrible race riots of Chicago, which Martin Luther King, Jr. said showed a worse hatred than any he had seen even in the deep south. The newspapers referred to "mobs of howling Catholics." The National Guard, the sisters heard, had to be called out to patrol Cicero, Illinois during a civil rights march.

By 1967 which opened with the Chicago area digging out from a record snowfall, the changes set in motion by Vatican II were affecting the Mundelein community more and more. Now the theologians from the seminary were coming weekly to the monastery to practice homiletics and to get to know the sisters. Sr. Bernard Vidal was the first in the congregation to enroll in an L.P.N. course at St. Mary's Hospital in Kansas City. That August Sr. Bertha resigned as prioress. By then some of the younger sisters were leaving the community, while many of the familiar structures slowly eroded. "It was just too much for her in this time of unrest," noted the chronicle. Toward the end of the month, Sr. Flora Schuster was appointed prioress with Sr. Corona Boylan as her assistant. It was Sr. Corona, along with Sr. Eulalia Wagner, who were elected delegates to the coming General Chapter.

At the end of January 1968 Fr. Wojcik asked the sisters to pray for the success of the bussing of black school children from inner-city parochial schools to the suburban ones. He told the community that Cardinal Cody was taking a great deal of abuse about this issue. Happier news came in February that Sr. Flora had been re-appointed prioress with Sr. Rosalita (Audrey) Jones as her subprioress.

In April the main topic of interest in the community was pentecostalism. The sisters knew that it was spreading from campus to campus throughout the U.S. David Garrets, O.S.B. of Benet Lake Abbey, brought a woman to the monastery to witness to the sisters about a healing she had experienced when prayed over. On April 21 the sisters had their first pentecostal-type prayer meeting. Almost all attended, having listened to a tape from Notre Dame about this charismatic movement. When she heard that one sister received the "baptism of the spirit" at this meeting and that later five sisters were speaking in tongues, Mother Pascaline grew concerned. She spoke about it to Fr. David on her first visit to the Mundelein monastery at the end of May.

That summer the sisters enjoyed much greater freedom in the use of the extensive seminary grounds that adjoined their own. A walk around St. Mary's lake became a must on any visit to the community. Courses in scripture and theology began for all the sisters. The year ended with Monsignor John Gorman's moving homily at Midnight

Mass. He spoke of the three astronauts in Apollo 8 orbiting the moon on Christmas Eve, reading from the book of Genesis: "In the beginning God created the heavens and the earth." He told the sisters of the television scenes of our earth taken by the astronauts. "Our world floats small, blue and beautiful in the eternal silence."

In 1969 one of the sisters' main concerns was the experiment involving the altar bread making. They decided to buy the breads from a commercial firm for three months, so they did not bake the breads, but repacked and distributed them to their patrons. At the end of the experimental period it was clear that this was not financially feasible. Besides it left many of the sisters at a loss without the familiar work which had so long occupied their time and energy.

TUCSON

When Abbot Stephen Shappler visited the sisters in Tucson in January 1960, he had not been there for sixteen years and was amazed at the view from their roofdeck. Where before there had been only desert, now he could see thriving residential developments on all sides. At this time the sisters were cleaning up after the completion of the infirmary wing. While the younger members of the community carried uncounted buckets of sand for the plastering, the other sisters had been busy making date confections from the year's harvest of more than seven thousand pounds of dates. Two sisters in full habit had their picture taken for a local paper as they climbed the tall scaffolding to reach the fruit which hung high on the date palms.

On March 22 Dorothy Day visited the community. The chronicler commented: "Whether one agrees with all Miss Day's radical ideas or not, it is certainly necessary to bow to her untiring zeal and courage." In May the chronicler took note of Alan Shepard's fifteen minute hop into space in a 6 × 9 ft. capsule. "Boy, what a ride!" he exclaimed. As in Tucson the sisters were harvesting twelve thousand pounds of grapes from their vines, in Germany the East Germans closed and fortified the Brandenburg Gate to prevent migration into the western section. With that kind of news the community was not surprised in late September when work began on a fall-out shelter in one of their basement rooms.

Lent in 1962 meant the usual hectic pace in the altar bread department with the sisters working until midnight to fill the orders. A cause for rejoicing was the success of their week-end retreat for young women that March, which was attended by twenty-one who were interested in monastic life.

That October the sisters obtained a television set to watch the opening of the Ecumenical Council where one hundred and fifty thousand people stood in the rain outside St. Peter's to see the procession of cardinals, bishops, patriarchs and others into the basilica, followed by Pope John XXIII in his chair. They listened to the accounts of the Catholic Press at table, detailing the struggles between the progressives who wanted more decentralization in the church and the traditionalists who objected to an expanded role for the laity and the extensive readjustment in many church practices.

Late in November the sisters elected Srs. Hiltrudis (Margaret Marie) Schmidt and Rosalita Jones as their delegates to the General Chapter. On December 2, Sr. Irene Prugger arrived to be their prioress for the next three years with Sr. Cornelia St. Cin as her assistant. Her welcome was slightly less exuberant than Bishop Green's, who was greeted on his return from the Council's first session by the mayor, some two thousand people and a group of Yaqui Indians who did a ceremonial dance for him.

As 1963 began the chronicler recalled that in 1962 Pope John XXIII had been declared Man of the Year by TIME magazine. He was the first churchman to be so acclaimed in more than thirty years because as the article pointed out: "Pope John has given the world what neither science nor diplomacy could provide: a sense of its unity as a human family." By that March the chronicler was noting something else: it had been so cold that "the cabbages froze in the ground." One day there was three inches of snow. "A snowman appeared on practically every block in Tucson as the children had the time of their lives." A different kind of delight was experienced by the sisters on Holy Thursday when for the first time their chaplain celebrated Eucharist facing them. There was no celebration at the end of May when the aspirancy was closed. Of the twenty-nine young girls who had taken part in the program, only two continued on in the monastic life. They were too young and the tendency to treat them as children was too strong, with docility and conformity rewarded rather than maturity.

According to the chronicle, the population of Tucson in the summer of 1965 had reached 234,600. Now there were houses in every direction around the monastery. The desert had been pushed farther and farther back. In July the community's bookkeeper learned that there was to be a new coinage, the first major change since 1792. There would be no more silver in quarters and dimes; the new coins would be nickel-covered copper.

That August after a major superiors' meeting in Denver, where she heard that U.S. sisters were asking for a voice in the Council for those deliberations which affected their lives, Mother Cecilia wrote to all prioresses asking them to keep the sisters better informed of world events. Mother Irene got a television set so that the community could watch Pope Paul VI on his visit to the U.N. But it was to be the new prioress, Mother Cornelia St. Cin with her subprioress, Sr. Damien Thompson, who were really to set things in motion. These two free spirits made a team which caused interesting developments.

Encouraged by Mother Cecilia, the sisters were deep in discussions of the revisions of the constitution as 1966 began. However, the decision to shorten the habit, which was the result of some of these discussions, upset a few sisters in the Tucson community. This was not the case for Sr. Celestine Holl who asked the seamstress only: "Are you sure my underskirt is not looking out?" In August Mother Cecilia wrote that Rome wished all religious communities to have a Chapter within three years. Later she wrote again about an interview she had with Cardinal Ritter. She quoted from his remarks on religious renewal: "More personal responsibility! Not so much that is automatic or routine. It must be my own commitment day after day. Do your Rule and constitution lead to, or hinder charity? We must be true Christians, genuine in our Christian life!"

When Bishop Green came to celebrate Sr. Evangelista Lange's golden jubilee with the community, he found them listening to tapes by some of the best theologians. They told him the younger sisters were playing volleyball at noon now or using an exercise bicycle. They did not show him some of the experimental headdresses. He suggested that they take one day a week during Lent to dialogue with each other in order to deepen community bonding. Later Mother Cornelia returned his visit to discuss with him the updating of their eucharistic organizations in an effort to make them more vital.

In March Sr. Damien was elected the Tucson community's representative on the revision committee and by May was hard at work with the others on the committee in the St. Louis monastery. As they finished their work in the first session, some of the suggestions received were put into effect. Now the sisters were free to suggest topics for local council meetings, to choose the table reading and to recommend retreat directors. With the rest of the congregation that fall, the Tucson sisters began wearing the new look, although the unstarched nylon headband was never a favorite with them. They did favor very much the air-conditioned chapel they had been enjoying since the summer, after a two-year wait for the extensive work required to install it.

Preparations for Mother Cornelia St. Cin's golden jubilee of profession began early in 1968. Hordes of guests descended on the community for the happy day and the sisters' orchestra performed for the reception which followed the Eucharist. The community retreat began on January 15 under the direction of Fr. John Hampsch. He centered his conferences on renewal with a dynamism that caught the sisters' interest. They began writing letters to Mother Cecilia and her council, expressing their hopes for a genuine renewal in the congregation, as well as their concern about the number leaving it. Fr. Hampsch counseled an "aggressive patience" to try to bring about whatever reform was needed. When thirty-one of the community signed a letter asking why the Chapter agenda had not been received and making three pages of other comments, Mother Cecilia replied tartly that the agenda was late because they had been late sending in their suggestions.

When the sisters learned that Sr. Pascaline Coff was their new prioress general, there was rejoicing and hope that fresh air would now blow through the congregation, with a lessening of artificiality and over-structuring. The chronicler relates that every time the phone rang the following week everyone jumped, expecting the announcement of their new prioress. On March 6 they learned it was to be Sr. Matthias Igoe with Sr. Philip (Kathryn) Neville as her subprioress. Sr. Matthias began going over the Chapter minutes with the community as soon as she arrived. The sisters were enthusiastic about praying the Hour of Matins on a conversational tone, rather than the traditional "recto tono." This was particularly true of those "unblessed with the talent of praying on the high tone our congregation has always maintained, and who consequently feel they have been excommunicated from participation in the Office."

A further result of the Chapter appeared in the white habits the sisters in the altar bread department wore for the first time in April. Next, two of the German-born sisters took advantage of the permission to make their first home visit in many, many years. Discussions on significant books began in the community; two sisters undertook the Famous Artists' course; a cantor from the local synagogue came to lecture on Jewish culture. Many watched the movie "A Raisin in the Sun" for a better understanding of racial prejudice. At this time also the decision was made to close Christ the King library. While the community was sorry to see it go, they could understand the board's position since the library had outlived its original purpose.

On the delegates return from the second session of the renewal Chapter in February,1969, further changes went into effect. Committees were set up to help the community function more collegially. The sisters could now drive cars, as well as go on outings to museums and other places of interest, with considerably more freedom than before. A more creative approach to liturgy was the vogue. For the most part, the sisters found this meaningful, "that poor, overworked word," as the chronicler put it. She also noted that "community discussions are now part of our way of life and we feel they are productive of much good." However, she was nostalgic about some of the changes, particularly the falling off of attendance at the evening Benediction. The chronicler considered this "part of a widespread disenchantment with Benediction and other formerly revered devotions." It was the same with First Fridays: "How different the liturgy from formerly! Sometimes we do ache a little for the loved devotions that are no more. But we can't go back."

Other changes were evident in the number absent from the community that summer of 1969 because of summer school. There were mixed reactions to this but the sisters tried to accept it, remembering what Mother Pascaline in her letter of July 14 had quoted from Eugene McClory, Vicar for Religious in Chicago: "Young people today expect deep sharing of goals and ideals, not just watching television in the same room. Sisters are still leaving religious life because communities are cold, aloof and unsupporting."

On July 20 the chronicler was fascinated by the moon-walk. "We were privileged to watch the entire program throughout the day if we wished. It was thrilling! Especially when Armstrong actually put his foot on the lunar surface, soon being joined by Aldrin. They remained there for two hours, picking up samples and demonstrating that the gravity (which is only one sixth of the earth's) was no obstacle ... as Armstrong planted the first human footprint on the lunar crust he said: 'That's one small step for man, one giant leap for mankind!' Outside their vehicle the astronauts found a bleak world. It was just before dawn with the sun low over the eastern horizon behind them and the chill of the long lunar night still clinging to the boulders, small craters and hills before them." On July 29 she wrote again: "When we look up at the moon riding so serenely through the skies these nights, how can we believe that an American flag is planted there and that human footprints have marked its soft surface?"

On September 3 the evening paper brought the news that the diocese would be divided, with Phoenix now separated from Tucson. Another kind of separation worried the chronicler in October: those leaving the congregation. "There are more outs than ins in our congregation! While painful, this is better than their staying around unsatisfied and confusing others." She also noted that coming to recreation each evening was becoming a vexed question. "We cannot impute unworthy motives or we shall be labeled 'judgmental.' Well!" It was at the end of November that two astronomers at Kitt Peak observatory spotted Apollo 12 as it circled the earth. "May the heavens and all that is in them praise the Lord!"

KANSAS CITY

As the new decade began on what the sisters stationed there affectionately called "holy hill," there were forty of them living there. The city itself was experiencing what the TIMES called the second snowiest winter in history. At one point there were forty-two inches of snow to contend with. The sisters' good friends helped them shovel snow, besides many other services. Mr. Roos, Mr. Battle, Mr. Carnelia could be called on at any time. By now the Eucharistic Guild had contributed thousands of dollars to the community with its card parties and other socials. Some of the priests of the diocese, in fact, called these women "the finest group in the city."

192

That June 1960 more than twelve thousand Catholics attended the Corpus Christi celebration on the monastery grounds with a candle-light procession, an outdoor Mass and three Benedictions. July brought the sisters many requests for prayers for the situation in Cuba, as well as the Congo. The revolt in the Congo was so bad that Dag Hammarskjold had been authorized by the U.N. to send troops there.

In July 1961 the sisters were hearing about Pope John XXIII's encyclical "Mater et Magistra." The chronicler preserved a clipping from the Kansas City TIMES of July 14, which referred to the encyclical as "wide-ranging on social problems. John XXIII calls for industry to limit profits and make sure the workers receive a just wage that allows for a life lived with dignity. A fruitful and lasting peace is not possible if there is too great a difference between people's social and economic conditions. In helping underdeveloped nations there must be no plan to predominate in a new form of colonialism."

Late in January 1962 the sisters heard that their new bishop was to be Charles Helmsing. He liked informality as they discovered in April when he dropped in for an unannounced visit. "Isn't it silly for a truck driver's son to have a coat of arms?" he had remarked. The bishop asked them to pray about the race situation. In September this grew increasingly ominous as the chronicler noted on September 30: "There is a serious crisis in Mississippi due to the refusal of the governor of the state and other officials, including those of the University of Mississippi, to admit a Negro student. The cause of integration in our country has been making steady progress the past few years. Archbishop Rummel and his successor, Archbishop Cody, have been heroic in their stand for integration in the Catholic schools of Louisiana ... The present situation is particularly alarming due to the contempt of the governor for federal authority. President Kennedy today gave an excellent address to the nation. He has ordered federal troops to handle the situation in Mississippi."

Early in March the sisters watched the arrival of a truck-load of supplies from the Civil Defense Commission: 88 cartons of survival biscuits, 86 water-drums, along with sanitation, medical and radiological kits. They also read about the tempest in the teapot at the Catholic University in Washington where four leading theologians had been refused as speakers in a lecture series: John Courtney Murray, S.J., Gustave Weigel, S.J., Godfrey Diekmann, O.S.B., and Hans Kung. Closer to home that fall, the sisters began experimenting with whole wheat flour for the altar breads, which became very popular. Another first was the ordination by Bishop Helmsing of several young men to the diaconate in the sisters' chapel, to give them opportunity to see such a ceremony. Shortly before this, two sisters had attended a forum on Cardinal Suenen's challenging book "The Nun in the Modern

World," which was causing some shock waves in religious communities.

Their New Year's Holy Hour for 1964 stressed ecumenism. Less ecumenical in every way was the placing of Missouri's first ICBM in firing position on January 16. The arrival of this Minute Man missile was cloaked in secrecy, but it was only the first of many. By April the sisters' attention was again on the race question. On April 7 the chronicler noted: "All the sisters voted for the public accommodations bill, which we pray will pass so that we may truly say that justice rules." The bill did pass, but with such a narrow margin, "that it was a shock to all in Kansas City to realize that they do live in so prejudiced a city, which has always proclaimed itself free and tolerant."

It was the following March their chaplain turned to the sisters after Benediction to say that he was leaving for Selma, Alabama to assist in a civil rights demonstration. "The conscience of every American," wrote the chronicler, "must find a way to assist the Negro in this time of racial strife, which is generally agreed to be THE great issue of the nation at this time. It is for us to pray and sacrifice." On March 13 she noted: "A terrible crime has been committed by four white men who killed a minister, who was in Selma to assist in the civil rights cause. His murder has shocked the nation into a new awareness of the seriousness of the situation and the necessity to recognize the Negro as a human being and to realize their worth and dignity."

The liturgical changes resulting from Vatican II began to be felt in the community at this time. Now the priest remained at his chair until the Gospel of the Mass, with one of the sisters reading the first lesson. Renewal was a general topic of discussion as was the ceremony at the Truman Library in Independence, Missouri, on July 31, 1965 when President Johnson signed the Medicare bill, making the health-care of all over sixty-five a national law.

There were further changes in 1966. Mother Jerome Moore had replaced Mother Bertha Nortmann as prioress of the community, with Sr. Matthias Igoe as her subprioress. The two were leading discussions in the community on the documents of Vatican II, as well as their own revised constitution. They decided to discontinue the book-bindery as the time and labor required were no longer warranted. That spring Mother Cecilia asked that the garden be kept to a minimum. Instead she wanted outdoor exercise for the sisters with games and more time for rest, as the canonical visitation had suggested. Late in September the sisters were alarmed by some vandalism in Archbishop O'Hara's crypt, as well as an attempted break-in to the offering slots in the back of the chapel. This was to become an increasing concern as the neighborhood deteriorated. Their chaplain struck a lighter note during the intercessory prayers one November morning when he included a fervent petition that Notre Dame win over Michigan State.

More changes in the accustomed ways continued in 1967. No longer was there strict observance of rank. Lay help was hired for the altar bread work. A psychologist came early in February to spend a day with the community talking about communications and interpersonal relations. One of the Rockhurst College Jesuits began giving a course on the sacraments. There were tapes on renewal in religious life; Leonard Bernstein's films on music appreciation were shown at recreations. The sisters then formed their own "orchestra" with a violin, saxophone, ukelele and recorder.

On June 15 that year the long-awaited air conditioning for the chapel was turned on and promptly blew a fuse. This kept happening with dismal regularity as the stifling summer heat continued unabated. When Bishop Helmsing dropped in for an informal Sunday evening patio supper, Mother Jerome, in desperation, took him to the basement to bless the stubborn machine. Even the episcopal blessing had no effect; the air-conditioning never did work.

Early in February, 1968 it was time for the General Chapter. Mother Jerome left for the St. Louis monastery with the two elected delegates, Srs. Matthias Igoe and Tharsilla Noser. It was not until March 6 that the sisters learned their new prioress was to be Sr. Bernard Vidal with Sr. Clarita (Rita) Downey as her assistant. Sr. Bernard had been taking an L.P.N. course in the city and was, according to the chronicle, "in a state of shock" at the appointment. With characteristic verve, however, she went to the St. Louis monastery for an orientation to her duties.

Welcomed back by the sisters with a twelve-piece band, Mother Bernard made energetic plans to renovate the chapel and the basement assembly-room. She invited sisters from the neighboring Hogan High School to dinner to share with the Benedictines about their work. Then she asked a nutritionist to come and speak about better dietary habits. Soon she had arranged a "family room" with more comfortable furniture and a bulletin board so the sisters could share items of interest. Next hospital sisters began coming to lecture on health, hygiene, menopause. Community sisters were dispatched to local hospitals to learn about dietetics. There were lectures on mental health; encounter groups were set up. Often, Mother Bernard had music at table instead of the customary table-reading. She invited friends in to teach the sisters how to play cards, so that canasta became the new craze on Holy Hill. She also set up departmental meetings for the sisters to be able to plan their work with more coordination. Her determination that no area of their lives be neglected as far as renewal went, left the community out of breath but struggling valiantly to keep up.

By April, 1968 the racial tension in Kansas City had reached a new high. Parish Holy Hours were canceled in the sisters' chapel. At the Landing shopping mall, just down the hill from the monastery, plate-glass windows were regularly smashed. A 7 p.m. curfew was ordered throughout the city. Rioting and looting spread, with tear gas used at several schools. Shooting and sniping continued so that an entire city block went up in flames; because of the sniping the firemen were unable to contain it. Then the National Guard was ordered on duty; some were posted at the Landing. The sisters could look out their windows at the eerie sight of armored cars rolling down Meyer Boulevard. On Holy Thursday, April 11, the chronicler noted: "How vivid the liturgy becomes in this setting of a war-torn city!" Instead of the usual crowded chapel, there were only twenty people at the Mass of the Lord's Supper that evening.

Before leaving for the second session of the Chapter in February, 1969, the indefatigable Mother Bernard set up an exercise room for the sisters. She asked their opinions about painting the first floor hall, along with their bedrooms, in brighter colors. She also introduced a "complaint night," so that they could air and heal their grievances. On her return from the Chapter she reminded the community of Mother Pascaline's urging: "If ever we needed to grow stronger and closer, it is now!"

When Bishop Helmsing came for a visit in April, the sisters asked his opinion about the modified habit they were wearing. Diplomatically, he refused to comment, saying he tried to refrain from telling sisters how to dress. Then the bishop went on to ask the sister-seamstress to modify his own episcopal robes, removing the tassels from his cincture and the buckles from his official slippers.

At this time there was ongoing discussion in the community about the possibility of making altar breads that looked more like bread. Diocesan liturgy committees were pleading for this. Mother Pascaline went deeper in her May letter to the sisters quoting St. Augustine, "Christians receive the body of Christ that they may become the body of Christ!" She urged them to "make real efforts to become the true body of Christ," reminding them of Fr. Godfrey Diekmann's statement: "We really have not practiced the Eucharist."

SAN DIEGO

As this turbulent decade opened, the sixteen sisters in the monastic community on San Diego Avenue were aware that their city was now one of the twenty largest in the nation. Largeness was something they would have appreciated in their cramped quarters. When friends brought loads of fresh flowers, the sacristan, according to the chronicle, "walked the floors" looking for a place to take care of them. The water pressure in the house was very low, with only a trickle for baths. The sisters devoutly hoped that soon the hill north of Balboa Avenue

196

would be crowned with their new monastery, its 100 foot tower, a "beacon light over the Pacific," as Mother Carmelita liked to refer to.

Old and new friends continued to take a lively interest in the small community. The Pruett family supplied them with fresh eggs. The Kilroys were always available to shop for the sisters. A Navy chief petty officer donated family furniture and later a large ship's bell. Mr. Threinen spent many a Saturday working on the lawn. Mr. Gos and Mr. Branzstet could be counted on for any service on their time off, even to setting up vocation displays. It was friends who brought fish who at times posed a problem. There was the one hundred and ninety pound marlin that had to be sawed in half for the deep freeze. Mrs. Santo often came with fresh-caught tuna. One midnight two huge fish arrived, too large even for the laundry tubs.

By March 1961 Sr. Paschalia Noser was able to go over the plans for the new monastery with the sisters. She told them that a Kansas City construction company had been hired to work with the plans and building. This was a mistake that was to be deeply regretted later. The midwest firm believed that it never really did rain in California, with the result that most of the pipes were inadequate to the demands on them. Leaks during the rainy season were a regular feature of community life for some time to come.

As the sisters began taking trips out to see the site of the new building, anxiety about nuclear bombs engulfed the country. The papers were full of articles about fall-out shelters. On November 1 Governor Edmund Brown unfolded a plan for California, "if the bomb drops." A more immediate concern were the worst forest fires in southern California's history, with those in the Los Angeles area destroying eleven thousand acres.

On August 15 the community came to their new site for the cornerstone laying. A Navy band played for the crowds as Bishop Buddy officiated. The sisters were delighted that now they could begin to store things in the basement there to relieve the floor-to-ceiling excess at the older house. Some weeks later, the community said goodbye to Bishop Buddy as he left for the first session of the Ecumenical Council, equipped with a gift of thermal underwear from Mother Carmelita who knew how damp Rome could be in the fall. The sisters followed the opening of the Council with great fascination. They marveled at Pope John XXIII's opening address, in which he referred to those "persons who have learned nothing from history which is the teacher of life. We feel we must disagree with those prophets of gloom who are always forecasting disaster as though the end of the world were at hand." The Pope went on to add that: "The substance of the ancient doctrine of the deposit of faith is one thing and the way in which it is presented is another." He told a group of fifteen thousand pilgrims in the first general audience after the Council opened not to worry or be impatient if things went slowly, for "Go slowly, go far!"

That October, 1962 the community's good friend, Mr. Latour, brought a radio over so the sisters could keep in touch with the Cuban crisis. On October 22 President Kennedy had told the nation that he had clamped a tight naval and air blockade on arms shipments to Cuba. He disclosed that Russia had established bases for one thousand mile nuclear missiles on Castro's island. By November 2 the sisters were storing an extra altar in the air raid shelter of the new building in case of an emergency. A contrast to this worry was a beautiful clear day on November 10 when the sisters at 2610 San Diego Avenue could see from their back porch the new monastery with its shining steeple. By then some of the community were at work on drapes for the windows of this building. All such work was set aside on November 29 to welcome their new prioress, Sr. Eulalia Wagner and her sub-prioress, Sr. Raymond Roos.

Most of January, 1963 was spent moving things from the Old Town house to the permanent monastery. There were twenty-four sisters now, so it was a real blessing when on February 3, Bishop Buddy led a caravan of cars, complete with motorcycle escort, to transfer the Blessed Sacrament to the new building where the majority of the sisters had already moved in. After more than one session of all-night work, the chapel was ready to be dedicated on March 25. Bishops Buddy, Helmsing and Green were there, along with Abbot Anselm of Conception Abbey. Five hundred people received communion during the Eucharist. The tired sisters were happy that night to reflect that for the fourth time in thirty years a new sanctuary had been established.

Much of the sisters' time the rest of the year was spent setting up the various departments: altar bread, church sewing. Outside they were busy planting trees and shrubs, with much help from friends, who often gave up their Saturdays to plant twisted juniper, black pine and myaporum for hedges. The Knights of Columbus donated a tall flagpole for the front lawn. With all this, the sisters were scarcely aware that President Kennedy had visited San Diego in June where he inspected the great carrier, the "Kittyhawk." In early September, the new co-adjutor bishop Francis Furey arrived. San Diego now had forty-thousand Catholics, one hundred and sixty-one parishes, with four hundred and fifty-nine priests and six hundred sisters.

In March 1964 the sisters heard about the dedication of the new Sea World amusement park, where visitors could watch the antics of whales and dolphins and Japanese pearl divers. Along with other Californians, they were alarmed by the violent earthquake in Alaska on March 27, which sent a tidal wave to their coast, after wrecking the town of Anchorage and leaving two thousand people homeless.

In May 1965 Mother Cecilia decided to close the vestment department in the Clyde monastery and transfer this work to the San Diego house. Sewing on chasubles, stoles, surplices and altar linens in their multi-windowed room with its view of Mission Bay, the sisters prayed for the safety of Edward White who made America's first space walk, easing himself out of his Gemini capsule on June 4 that year to float for "twenty eerie minutes in the chilling void of space." Equally chilling was the news on June 16 that eight thousand Marines from nearby Camp Pendleton were being sent to Okinawa, ready for an emergency in Vietnam. The sisters heard that now there were more than one hundred thousand GI's in Vietnam as the situation worsened steadily.

By that August it was the race riots in Los Angeles that the sisters were praying for. National Guardsmen with fixed bayonets marched into the no man's land that was the Watts district, where looters and arsonists were totally out of control. Flying bullets killed civilians and police. The business district was an inferno of raging flames. Newspaper reports described the scene of frenzy with men, women and children chanting: "Burn! Burn! Burn!" It was three days before the rioting was brought under control and only then could trucks of food from St. Vincent de Paul begin arriving with tons of supplies.

On November 21, 1965 Mother Thiadildis Kraus was appointed prioress of the San Diego community with Sr. Pascaline Coff as her assistant. Younger assistants were part of Mother Cecilia's quiet effort to bring new life into leadership. The newcomers marvelled that December at a courtyard full of calla lilies, with orange and lemon trees beginning to show their ripening fruit and scarlet poinsettia reaching to the second floor windows.

The rich Advent liturgy took on a deeper meaning for the sisters as they prayed in English. "What a joy," notes the chronicle, "to understand what we are singing and praying!" By now the sisters were used to Mass facing the people, to the prayers of intercession and to receiving communion standing. Another joy was the glorious climax to the Second Vatican Council, when on December 7, 1965 Pope Paul VI handed the Greek Orthodox metropolitan a declaration which invalidated the excommunication that had led to the break nine centuries before.

As the year 1966 began, the sisters were holding lively discussions on their revised constitution, along with the Constitution on the Church of Vatican II. Some were reading Louis Evely's popular book, "That Man is You." Others were deep into the fine set of volumes on the Fathers of the Church, which a friend of the community had given them for Christmas. Still others enjoyed the new basketball equipment.

As they prepared to help Mother Dolorosa celebrate her sixty-seven years of monastic profession, the sisters were horrified to hear about the Buddhist monks and nuns who burned themselves to death to protest the Ky regime in Vietnam and the American presence there. It was a relief to think instead of Mother Dolorosa: "She exemplifies the spirit of aggiornamento," wrote the chronicler, "although she is now the second oldest in our Congregation, she understands the problems of young people."

In August the sisters were praying that a movement in California to liberalize the state abortion laws would be defeated. The Los Angeles Tidings carried a report that Bernard Haring, the renowned moral theologian and expert at the Council, was urging an all-out effort on the part of Catholics to protect the life of unborn children. On November 8 the community learned that Ronald Reagan had been elected governor of California. Later, news reports told them of his claim that Americans were growing tired of "big government," as well as his belief that the U.S. must deal with communism from a position of strength.

That Christmas was a happy one. Gifts of food, flowers and candy came in the front door, while at the back door the sisters were giving out clothing and food to the poor. Many in the community liked to go to the roofdeck after dark to "view the city which looks like one large Christmas tree. The whole skyline from Mission Bay to the top of Mt. Soledad is framed with colored lights."

Under Sr. Pascaline's energetic guidance, vocation weekends were a regular feature of the San Diego monastery's life in 1967. At the first one in February, eighteen young women discussed religious life and toured the various departments in the house. What they enjoyed most was talking with the sisters about how they had come to enter monastic life. In June, the diocesan vocation director held open house at the Benedictine monastery for some sixty young women. In October the sisters had another open house for fifty girls. They put up a display in the assembly room showing "a day in the life of a Benedictine sister."

That March the community elected Sr. Pascaline as their representative on the committee to revise the constitution. She was not destined to return to San Diego, but remained in the St. Louis monastery as postulant director. Sr. Rosalita Jones replaced her as the San diego community's subprioress. The sisters were so involved with learning more and more English hymns for the Mass and hoping that the American bishops would soon allow the canon in English as well, that they paid little attention to the news that in San Onofre, not far from San Diego, nuclear heat would be generated in the big power plant to be officially opened in January, 1968.

Further discussions on the revised constitution that fall left the sisters energized and hoping, according to the chronicle, "for a new Pentecost." December was a busy month. On the 3rd there was an Advent Bible Vigil for thirty young women. On the 12th the sisters watched television as Bishop John Quinn was installed as auxiliary bishop of San Diego. As the Christmas rush increased, only a few heard from their friends that in far-away Cape Town, South Africa, the first successful heart transplant had been made.

Early in February 1968 Mrs. Rose Bucher, wife of the commander of the seized U.S.S. Pueblo, came to ask prayers for her husband and the crew captured by the North Koreans. Later in March, the sisters were happy to learn of a partial halt to American bombardment of North Vietnam; Hanoi having agreed to talks with the U.S. They were more personally happy to welcome their new prioress, Mother Aloysia (Kathleen Margaret) Gorman with her subprioress, Sr. Bede Luetke-meyer, later that month.

Dialogue, lectures, workshops now became the order of the day. Daily papers were made available. There was a suggestion box for ideas for their community meetings as well as long discussions on the meaning of such things as collegiality and subsidiarity. Sr. Benita Luetkemeyer came to help the community learn how to sing the new Liturgy of the Hours for Lauds and Vespers. This continued on into 1969. There were lectures on communication and feminine psychology; talks on health, hygiene, even on manners and charm. They had group dynamic sessions and encounter groups. The liturgical climax of the year came on September 3 with the consecration of their chapel. Mother Pascaline and Sr. Carmelita were present to see Bishop Quinn officiate at the ceremony.

Chapter Thirteen
1970–1982

As 1970 began Catholicism in the United States had become part of the mainstream, due to some extent to the brief Kennedy presidency. Catholics were now visible, articulate and influential. The "Catholic" vote was extensively courted. Despite all this, an increasing number of Catholics realized the injustices suffered by those who were out of the mainstream. As the decade progressed, more and more lay Catholics, clergy and religious mobilized their efforts for the cause for peace, justice and human rights. Names like Dorothy Day, Mother Teresa of Calcutta, Theodore Hesburgh of Notre Dame were familiar to Catholics and non-Catholics alike.

In the church itself lay Catholics were becoming increasingly involved in ministry. They were directors of religious education, members of pastoral teams, eucharistic ministers and lectors. Lay movements such as the Catholic Charismatics, the Cursillo and Marriage Encounter spread rapidly. Hispanics began making their presence felt. However, it was in religious communities of women in the U.S. that the call for reform and renewal had its greatest impact. Community after community held renewal Chapters which resulted in vigorous and costly changes in the inherited pattern of European religious traditions. For the first time American religious life began to be genuinely American. Monastic life was similarly affected.

For the Benedictine Sisters of Perpetual Adoration this decade meant a deepening of their personal prayer, continuing experimentation with liturgy, a more individualized approach to their spiritual and community lives, a broadened sharing with other religious and more exposure to the influences of the culture in which they lived. This was evident one weekend in January 1970 when eight sisters from other communities were either making a retreat in the St. Louis monastery or studying the life there with a view to founding houses of prayer in their own congregation. It was also evident in the week-long course in "psychology for contemplatives" offered to all the sisters that month, as well as in Brother Ron Fogarty's travels throughout the congregation. This Marist Brother from Australia gave the sisters dynamic presentations on renewal and communication, lecturing and counseling far into the night. Then Mother Johnette Putnam, O.S.B., of the Covington, Louisiana community, came to speak to the sisters about the struggle to integrate Catholic parochial schools in the south. Fr. Francis McNutt, O.P. lectured on Catholic pentecostalism.

On May 4, 1970 the community heard with horror about the four students at Kent State in Ohio who had been shot and killed by National Guardsmen. At this time alienation between the generations was at a peak. The Nixon administration genuinely feared the campus unrest which culminated in this violence. The sisters had no way of knowing then how these killings were going to affect the national consciousness, even helping to end the Vietnam war, while showing the students that there were limits to social revolution. By September the sisters were praying about two other issues that loomed large: drug addiction and abortion. The Equal Rights Amendment was also stirring controversy. Some of the community read about President Nixon's speech in Kansas City decrying terrorism and campus violence: "It's time to draw the line . . . no course can justify resort to lawlessness." The chronicler's attention was on another matter: that of communion in the hand. "This is startling. There has been a movement to legalize the practice of the priest putting the Host in the hand of the communicant, who places it in her mouth. Our Cardinal is taking a poll to see how many want this."

Early in 1971 the sisters were busy preparing for the Chapter of Affairs which began in February. Mother Pascaline's opening talk referred to the need "for more courage to face the questions that must be asked." The sisters in general felt the need for a better balance of prayer and work in their lives, so the Chapter appointed various committees to investigate further the different elements of monastic life. It also set up regular meetings for the council and the prioresses, to be held in turn at the monasteries of the congregation. Slowly new perceptions of basic values were being discovered through sharing with one another. There was also the increasingly urgent question of how best to care for the elderly and retired sisters. The Chapter approved of thirty-day retreats and various aids to prayer, like those found in yoga and zen techniques.

On August 25, 1971 the congregation lost one of its precious links with the past in the death of Mother Dolorosa Mergen at the age of 92, after seventy-three years of monastic profession. She had entered the community at Clyde only twenty-three years after its founding. Mother Dolorosa's faith, charity, patience and winning humor had sustained her and those she led through many difficulties.

After deciding that the periodical *Spirit & Life* would be issued only ten times (and eventually six) a year, Mother Pascaline and her council had a more serious decision to face: the need to close one of the monasteries for lack of personnel. After wrestling with these, it was a relief to help the novices plant fifty seedling fir trees on the St. Louis monastery grounds and then to welcome some students from Glennon Preparatory Seminary. They came to sing Christmas carols with guitar accompaniment. The chronicler described them as "curly-locked and casually attired young men."

As 1972 began the Benedictine sisters were not alone in their concern about numbers. More and more teaching sisters were being forced to withdraw from parish schools to the dismay of the pastors. The February meeting of the council and the prioresses of the congregation resulted in the decision to initiate a six-month in-depth study of membership and finance. Those at the meeting took time out to note President Nixon's historic trip to China on February 17th. They also prayed about his projected trip to Moscow in May to sign the SALT agreement, which would limit nuclear arsenals for five years.

In May the community in St. Louis had its annual retreat directed by Ambrose Wathen, O.S.B., an authority on the Benedictine Rule. This was followed in July by a two-week course on the psalms given by Carroll Stuhlmueller, C.P. Then there were the goal-setting workshops under the auspices of Management Design Incorporated with its energetic founder, Dave Ruhmkorff. He worked with the sisters of the congregation on goals and objectives, leadership, communication and financial management. The sisters learned to identify significant events in their history, to consider the best and worst possibilities of any given decision and to establish goals.

In the summer the sisters were saddened by the horrifying slaying of Israeli athletes at the Olympic games in Munich. A few of the sisters noticed an article in the daily paper that fall which said that Nixon was concerned about reports accusing some of his aids of political spying and sabotage. Most of the community was more interested in Mother Pascaline's account of the regional meeting of religious superiors with Cardinal Carberry and the bishops of Missouri. All at the meeting had agreed that more such meetings would lead to a better understanding, as communities moved out in truly Christian witness.

The year 1973 began for a dozen sisters of the community with a Zen retreat. The Zen master explained to them that "zen does not teach; it points. It is not thinking, but being." Some other sisters attended a course at St. Louis University on mysticism which was given by Sr. Jose Hobday. At this time Srs. Dolores Dowling and Helen Barrow were traveling around the congregation gathering data and opinions on the "future thrust" of the Benedictines of Perpetual Adoration. With other Americans, the sisters gave thanks to God on January 27 when President Nixon announced "peace with honor" in Vietnam. The Secretary of State, Henry Kissinger, called this "a fragile peace" at the end of two million lives and four years of negotiation.

By this time it was five years after the congregation's renewal Chapter of 1968. Now it was quite common for the sisters to direct as well as make retreats. They gave Scripture courses in their monasteries; a few were principal speakers on prayer and liturgy at meetings of other religious. Another congregational outreach was the A.I.M. Secretariate established in 1973 by Mother Pascaline and her council, which would be under the energetic direction of Sr. Tharsilla Noser in the St. Louis monastery to aid third world monasteries.

That June there was a variety of renewal events to hold the sisters' attention. The last of the age-group meetings was held in the Clyde monastery. From the sharings of this 35–50 age group came the suggestion that adoration during the night be on a congregational rather than individual monastery basis, each house being assigned specific nights. Many felt that Christ's presence in the community was also a very real one and that this needed to be emphasized. Back in St. Louis several sisters attended a lecture given by the California healer, Kathryn Kuhlman, and reported that more than four thousand people had been in the hall with several apparent cures taking place.

In September Mother Pascaline left for Europe to attend the World Congress of Benedictine Abbots in Rome as an observer, along with Sr. Joan Chittister of the Erie, Pennsylvania Benedictines. It was late in October that the first mention of "Watergate" occurred in the St. Louis monastery chronicle. Back in 1972 the Democratic national headquarters had been broken into. The *Washington Post* reporters, Woodward and Bernstein, came up with their story of political sabotage on behalf of Nixon's reelection. In February a Senate investigation committee was appointed. By April Nixon was admitting responsibility for what happened and by August there was talk of impeachment. Closer to home, the sisters worried more about the critical gas shortage and the long waiting lines to get some.

1974 brought one of the coldest winters in St. Louis' history. For the sisters the month meant in-depth preparation for the August Chapter. This preparation consisted of a "dialogic process" which some humorists began to call a "diabolic process," as it went on and on and on. Early in March Mother Pascaline had other things to tell the community: five sisters had permission from the council and the prioresses to begin an experiment in "simple monastic living." After traveling extensively to find a place for this experiment, its leader, Sr. Helen Barrow, settled in Payson, Arizona with the other four sisters.

In St. Louis before the sisters had finished praying for the kidnapped heiress, Patty Hearst, they had reasons for prayer closer to home. On April 3 a hailstorm with tornado-like winds smashed all the southwest stained glass chapel windows, sending streams of water over the floors and filling the pews with glass fragments. It took three hours to mop up the water and five months to replace the windows.

On August 8 that year the delegates, who had gathered in the St. Louis monastery for the General Chapter, watched the first President in American history to resign offer his farewell to the nation. On the following days Nixon was forgotten as the delegates went about their own business. On August 12 Mother Audrey Jones was elected the fifth prioress general of the congregation. In response to a feeling that consolidation was needed, Mother Audrey was a more low-key and cautious leader. The Chapter's main concern was to discuss another complete revision of the provisional constitution and to approve some prudent experimentation with simpler forms of monastic life, a concept which remained stubbornly hard to define. The Chapter also appointed a team to continue the investigation of the personnel and other resources.

On September 5, 1974 the congregation celebrated its centennial year in the U.S. Cardinal Carberry was the principal celebrant of a festive Eucharist in the chapel with Dr. Mario Salvador at the organ. Advent that year was marked with increasing concern over the violence in the middle East, as almost daily Palestinian attacks followed by Israeli reprisals turned that part of the world into a time-bomb. With many other religious, the Benedictines decided to remember their benefactors that Christmas with donations in their name to peace efforts and to the poor. This was emphasized by Pope Paul VI in his New Year call for "the active pursuit of peace." "Peace," said the Pope, "must be invented." On January 1, 1975 all the sisters received new emblems, the first change since the original ones forty-nine years before. Sr. Denise McMahon designed the new emblems as a Benedictine cross with chalice and loaves superimposed. It was in this month also that a three-month preparation for final vows was initiated. The other end of the age spectrum was acknowledged by the establishment of a retirement fund for the elderly sisters.

By August the chronicler was writing about the refugees who "arrived in St. Louis with their meager belongings in cardboard boxes, their children in their arms . . . refugees from a country that no longer exists." These were Vietnamese coming to start a new life in the U.S., as America's thirty-year involvement in Indo-China finally ended.

In September Sr. Marietta Crahan was at St. John's University in Collegeville, Minnesota, working toward a degree in liturgy. In Tucson Sr. Clarita (Rita) Downey continued her degree work in counseling at the University of Arizona. It was in October that fall that Mother Audrey and her council discussed plans for a new health-care facility, hoping that a wing could be added to the first floor of the south side of the monastery. Then the council went to the Clyde monastery to check with each of the sick and infirm sisters about where she wished to live. The bedfast and those requiring supervisory care were transferred to the St. Louis monastery. Here Sr. Paula Thompson took care of them until the new unit was ready. She hired lay nurses for the night hours and by November 30 there were sixteen infirm sisters settled in temporary quarters on the second floor.

Early in January, 1976 Srs. Gladys Noreen and Bede Luetkemeyer began preparing a course for the congregation on the pre-monastic and early Fathers of the Church. They had study outlines, books for reference and the agreement of several sisters in each monastery to present the first classes. This two-year course was a great success, heightening appreciation of lectio, and deepening the sisters' understanding of their monastic heritage. As word of it spread, several other monastic communities of men and women asked for the outlines.

On June 25 Sr. Pascaline left for her long-awaited trip to India. Almost a year earlier she had requested permission to spend a year in India, chiefly at the ashram of Bede Griffiths, O.S.B. There she hoped to experience a deeper prayer, with the plan of returning to the congregation to begin a foundation which would bring the benefit of the highly-developed psychology of eastern prayer to western monasticism.

Four sisters of the congregation attended the 41st International Eucharistic Congress in Philadelphia that July. Back in Missouri, Mother Audrey went to Clyde on August 6 to help inaugurate the Rickenbach Center of Spirituality. This was an experiment in a simplified form of monasticism, intended to be a companion to the large community. Seven sisters with Sr. Kathryn Neville as their leader, initiated the venture, using the renovated former canning building as the center. They hoped to reanimate the Clyde press by doing research into the patristic writings and eventually publishing small tracts in a popular style. Apart from the morning Eucharist and late afternoon Vespers celebrated with the larger community, they lived and prayed together at the Center, sharing their life with guests who came seeking monastic peace and greater solitude.

As Jimmy Carter won the presidential election in Washington, the Benedictines in St. Louis were involved in the final transfer of all the patients into the new St. Benedict's Health-Care Center. Some of the sisters were reading conflicting reports about the Detroit "Call to Action." This was the culmination of a series of hearings sponsored by the bicentennial committee of the bishops' conference on the general theme of liberty and justice for all. The problem seemed to be that lay delegates took positions well in advance of some of the hierarchy, approving married clergy, women's ordination and the restoration of remarried Catholics to the Eucharist.

The winter of 1977 was an extremely cold one, yet thermostats were to be set no higher than 65 degrees because of the continuing fuel shortage. Summer meant the usual exodus for home-visits, workshops and retreats. Sr. Matthias Igoe was at Catholic University in Washington doing some work on patristics under Quasten. Sr. Pascaline came back from India and began a series of lectures throughout the congregation on eastern monasticism. In July Fr. Juan Lozano, C.M.F. gave a workshop in the St. Louis monastery on the meaning of monastic charism. At that same time many of the sisters were working on a questionnaire from the Leadership Conference on Women Religious, dealing with the proposed new code of canon law for religious. Few were satisfied with the canons on monastic life.

In September Sr. Joy Ann Wege was appointed administrator of the health-care center, while Sr. Clarita Downey became prioress of the local community. It was at the fall meeting of the council and prioresses that the decision was made to close the Mundelein monastery. As Mother Audrey said: "When buildings and persons are to be considered, then persons must come first." Cardinal Cody agreed to this closing, telling them that he had had to approve the closing of fifty parishes, schools, and religious houses in the archdiocese.

Late in January, 1978 Mother Audrey wrote to all the monasteries to tell them that Sr. Pascaline Coff was to be secretary of the East-West board of A.I.M. She would also begin searching for a location for the small monastic ashram she wished to found after the Chapter in August. The rest of the months until June seemed to speed by as the congregation prepared for the first General Assembly in its history. On June 2 all but the very infirm and bedfast sisters left the St. Louis monastery for Clyde. This eight day assembly marked the first time since the founding of the Mundelein community that all the sisters gathered in one place. The days were filled with special liturgies which each monastery in turn provided, festive meals and much sharing and good fun. Serious preparations for the Chapter went hand-in-hand with the festivities. There were long discussions in small and large groups. The evenings were a show-case of talents in music, dance and drama. On June 9 the delegates elected Mother Audrey to a second term as prioress general. They would choose her council at the actual Chapter in August. On the last day of the assembly a symbolic service of reconciliation marked the desire of all present for unity in their dedication to the Eucharist. Some sisters felt strongly that a change of emphasis was needed, while others wanted no change whatever.

As the delegates assembled in the St. Louis monastery for the formal sessions of the Ninth General Chapter, Pope Paul VI was very ill. He died on August 6 after a pontificate of fifteen years. It was on August 12th that the Chapter delegates voted to end the Rickenbach Center experiment. Ironically enough, they elected three of the sisters who had been part of that experiment as councilors three days later:

Srs. Kathryn Neville, Matthias Igoe and Ramona Varela. At its conclusion the Chapter set up a program of monastic revitalization to be carried out in each monastery under the direction of the local prioress. It also approved a new formation directory and mandated a complete revision of the constitution to be completed by the Chapter of 1982.

That December after the excitement of two papal elections in the space of two months, some of the sisters were also excited by the National Coalition of American Nuns, who had rebuked the failure of the Bishops' Committee on the Liturgy to remove sexist language from liturgical texts. More sisters were reacting with horror as further details of the grisly massacre at Jonestown in Guyana became public. In January 1979 the Shah of Iran fled, leaving his country to the iron rule of the Ayatollah Khomeni. By June the economy was reeling from increased oil prices imposed by the OPEC group. The sisters heard President Carter's plea for the Salt II treaty with the Soviet Union. "The truth of the nuclear age is that the U.S. and the U.S.S.R. must live in peace or we shall not live at all." In Nicaragua the Sandinista party brought an end to the tyranny of Somoza and began the difficult task of reuniting and rebuilding their country. No wonder one of the older sisters said soberly: "There surely is no lack of things to pray for in this world!"

The community on Morganford Road was happy to welcome Bede Griffiths, O.S.B. on July 12. He was an English Benedictine who had spent years in a Christian ashram in southern India. Fr. Bede told the sisters he felt the Church had reached a culminating point in her westward movement and needed now to turn to the east, to reach out to the third world, to learn how to express the Catholic faith in the language and culture of India. A few days after this, Mother Audrey received a letter from another far-away land. The prioress of a Dutch-founded Benedictine community in Tororo, Uganda in Africa, wrote asking for help in the areas of formation and liturgy. After consulting her council, Mother Audrey asked Sr. Lillian (Lenora) Black to offer her competent help to this struggling monastic group.

By this time there were sixty sisters in the St. Louis community. Sr. Lupita Barajas, the vocation director, did her best to explain to them the changing vocation scene at the end of the 70s. At a recent vocation directors' meeting in Denver she told them, there had been two major issues: minority vocations and a call to a more collective vision to encourage commitment. In a workshop toward the end of that same month, Fr. Norbert Brockman, S.M. stressed the cenobitic aspect of the Benedictine charism as dominant, the cenobium being the realization of the "communion of saints." He also emphasized lectio, pondering the Word, and study as preparation for prayer. According to Fr. Brockman, sharing insights on faith and prayer are part of the notion of cenobitic life, which is a radical turning to God in community. The

210

sisters talked about this long after he left, especially his insistence that there is a rhythm to monastic life, that the prioress is to be an animator, not a guru, and that sharing community life is an apostolate for the monastic person. That is why hospitality is so important in a monastery, because it is rooted in the gospel value of evangelization.

In early October everyone's attention turned to Pope John Paul II's visit to the U.S. The sisters watched his arrival in Boston on television, his speech at the U.N. and the Mass celebrated at Yankee stadium, where 10,000 young people greeted him. On October 5 Sr. Clarita Downey went to Washington D.C. to represent the community as the Pope addressed women religious. There she heard Sr. Teresa Kane, R.S.M. appeal for consideration of women being admitted to full ministry in the church. Sr. Clarita said the Pope seemed a little taken aback.

A group of sisters from the St. Louis monastery attended a Pax Christi meeting in Atchison, Kansas on October 19, where the topics were international peace and spiritual strategies for the nuclear age. Speaker after speaker stressed the need for non-violence. It was all the more distressing to learn after this about the storming of the American embassy in Tehran, which resulted in sixty Americans being held hostage.

Benedictines all over the world celebrated 1980 as the sesquimillenium year of St. Benedict's birth. The year began ominously enough with the movement of Russian troops and bombers over Afghanistan. A happier event was the appointment of Bishop John May of Mobile, Alabama as the new head of the St. Louis archdiocese.

On February 9 a television crew came to the St. Louis monastery to do some filming for a documentary on modern Benedictine life, sponsored by the Benedictine confederation for this 1980 celebration. The crew was fresh from St. Meinrad's Archabbey in Indiana, having already filmed sequences in Ampleforth, Westminster and Stanbrook Abbeys in England. On April 27 the community had its first showing of this documentary, "Worship and Work." It depicted the legacy of St. Benedict in scenes from Subiaco and Monte Cassino in Italy, as well as Metten and other European abbeys, along with the American ones. Another celebration was the workshop on centering prayer that Dom John Main gave the sisters in St. Louis on February 10. Dom John was an English Benedictine who had spent years in the east before founding his small, contemplative monastery in Montreal, Canada where a combination of eastern and western prayer-methods were used.

On March 24, 1980 the sisters were shocked to hear that Archbishop Oscar Romero of El Salvador had been murdered by right wing government forces while he was offering Mass in his cathedral. This shock was intensified on December 5th that year when news of the brutal rape and murder of five women, four of them Catholic sisters, came from the same country. In St. Louis the sisters had read that political violence had left 8,500 people dead in El Salvador that year alone. Ambassador Robert White was said to have been at the scene when the women's bodies were exhumed from a common grave. According to reports in the press, he was furious; one newsman heard him say: "They won't get away with it!"

Friends were reminding the community to keep the economy in their prayer because inflation had reached unprecedented levels. Gold had been selling earlier in the year for $600.00 an ounce. Then came the reports on Mt. St. Helens in the state of Washington stirring to life late in March for the first time in one hundred and twenty years. On March 28 it throbbed with explosions, belching gas and volcanic ash four miles high. There was another eruption on May 18, which led to the evacuation of more than two thousand people from the area.

With all this it was an appreciated touch of humor when one man called to ask what time the Easter Vigil service would be held. He was told it would be at 3 a.m. "Only an idiot would get up at that time!" he responded. "Then we won't be seeing you there?" "Oh yes, I have a house full of idiots here." Another happy event was the May–June issue of *Spirit & Life* which commemorated its 75th year of publication.

Early in May the sisters were reading about Pope John Paul II's trip to Africa, to be followed two months later by a journey to Brazil. Some were more concerned about the pontiff's ban on priests in public, political office. Robert Drinan, S.J., who had been in Congress a number of years, said he would obey and leave the political scene. It was in May also that Sr. Clarita Downey accepted another term as prioress of the St. Louis community with Sr. Hildegard Zerwas as her assistant.

That June the Benedictines in St. Louis sponsored a joint celebration in the cathedral. Cardinal Basil Hume of London was the principal celebrant and homilist. The monks of Pevely and the St. Louis Priory, the Benedictine Sisters of Columbia, Missouri, and the Morganford Benedictines all shared in planning the day. Archbishop May, with Bishop Helmsing and Bishop McAuliffe of Jefferson City, Missouri, were among the fifty concelebrants. Afterward all the Benedictines went out to Pevely on the banks of the Mississippi for Vespers and a picnic supper. In the intense heat Cardinal Hume could be seen roaming among the guests in his t-shirt.

The celebration continued in June when eleven sisters from the congregation attended an institute on the origins and contemporary forms of monastic life at St. John's Abbey in Collegeville. Before this, the American Benedictine prioresses came to St. Benedict's community, a few miles from St. John's, for a week of meetings, with talks by Cardinal Hume, Victor Dammertz, the Abbot Primate, Archbishop Rembert Weakland and Sr. Joan Chittister.

To commemorate the sesquimillenium, Mother Audrey began a

series of reflections on the Rule, which she sent around the congregation. By July each sister had received a first copy of the proposed new constitution, which was to be carefully studied to see if it clearly expressed the congregation's charism in a way realistic enough to be lived. That September Mother Audrey, with Sr. Kathryn Neville, set off to Rome to attend the Abbots' Congress from September 17–22. She attended as an observer, along with other presidents of the American federations of Benedictine women. Mother Audrey wrote back to the St. Louis community on September 21 to describe a trip to Monte Cassino, where the Pope arrived via helicopter to celebrate Eucharist with them. Later all five hundred were served dinner in the huge monastic refectory.

That November the sisters stayed up late to watch Ronald Reagan sweep even traditionally Democratic regions to become the 40th president of the U.S. Of more personal concern to the community was the news that Sr. Lillian Black would be returning sooner than expected from Uganda as her health was seriously affected by the strain of life in that revolution-torn country. On November 7 Colman Grabert, O.S.B. of St. Meinrad's arrived to give a workshop on the Rule. A less successful attempt to commemorate the year was the introduction of a seven-week old puppy to the house. At first they named him "Sesqui," later changed to the more manageable "Pepper." Unfortunately, Pepper was not all that manageable; he became the object of a certain amount of controversy, which led to his departure after the visitation in the fall of 1981. More appreciated was the promise of the special 1980 edition of the Rule as a Christmas present to each sister who wanted one.

The entire community joined in prayer for the delicately balanced negotiations to release the fifty-two American hostages still in Iran in the first week of January 1981. When this was finally achieved on January 11 the sisters exulted with the rest of the country. Though they did not consciously understand it, they realized in some way that this return of the hostages to American soil could be celebrated with a joy the nation had not been able to muster when the Vietnam agony finally ended.

In St. Louis the sisters shivered on February 11 at the 55 below zero wind chill factor. Later in April tornado alerts sent them to the basement to await the all-clear signal. Spring brought a series of shocks: the assassination attempt on President Reagan on March 30, the serious wounding of Pope John Paul II on May 14. When later in the fall Anwar Sadat, the Egyptian statesman-president, was shot and killed, the community began to wonder if the apocalypse was indeed at hand. Sr. Clarita had another shock for them in her report of the meeting of the council and the prioresses. She told the sisters that the possible relocation of the Kansas City community had been discussed. It was becoming evident that the congregation would be smaller in the future. The maintenance of their large buildings was becoming too taxing. The "Future Projections" workshop made long-range planning necessary so the council had decided to hire the Pearce Corporation, a firm specializing in management programs for land and buildings.

April was a month of workshops in the St. Louis community. There was one for the vocation directors of the congregation, who worked on the formation directory. They stopped long enough to watch the safe landing of the two-manned space shuttle on April 14. "It looked," wrote the chronicler, "like a bee flying on the screen and then a big, white bird, until finally it took the shape of an aircraft." At the end of the month, Fr. Hugh Tasch of Conception Abbey was with them to lecture on the meaning of Easter in a liturgical spirituality. Early in June Sr. Augusta Raabe, O.S.B. came to join two monks of the St. Louis Priory for another workshop on the Rule.

That summer the sisters lost their faithful friend, Gregory Bockius, who died on June 24. As he was a Benedictine Oblate, his funeral was held in the sisters' chapel. On July 22 their beloved Sr. Edith Marie Kraus also died. She had been a prioress in the congregation for more than thirty years, serving in all the monasteries. Later that same month Sr. Clarita spent time explaining the RENEW program to the community. Modern parishes, she told the sisters, were too large for any real community relationships. The church needed smaller group-ings of people for parishioners to be able to understand and appreciate their faith. This program intended to help parishes enkindle a more living faith.

That fall each monastery held the election of delegates to the Chapter which would take place the following August. The Pearce Company as part of the preparation for this Chapter began an evalua-tion of each house from the standpoint of management feasibility. Mother Audrey gave a series of conferences to the sisters in October as part of her effort to raise consciousness in the congregation about the horrors of nuclear stock-piling and the immorality of first-strike weapons. In November the St. Louis community took part in a nation-wide fast for nuclear disarmament. Later they listened to two Sisters of St. Joseph explain the Catholic lobbying organization in Washing-ton, D.C. called "Network," which worked for social justice by looking for the moral and social implications of national legislation. It was to Poland that the sisters' attention turned before Christmas that year, fearful for the brave Solidarity leader, Lech Walesa, in the mass arrests by the communist government.

There were sixty-three sisters in the St. Louis monastery as the year 1982 began, twenty-four of these in the health-care center. For the Sunday Eucharist there were eleven wheelchairs in the chapel. The number of lay employees kept growing, with a cook, nurses and maintenance workers. At least the sisters felt they were helping the nation's unemployment rate, which was steadily escalating to the highest it had been since 1941. At the end of January there was a blizzard with a reported seventeen inches of snow, all roads blocked, train and air-travel disrupted and no priest for the community's Sunday Eucharist. By February the sisters, along with others, were increasingly concerned about the news from Central America, where right-wing terrorists, some of them supported by the U.S., were responsible for torture and death in appalling numbers. Some of the sisters wrote letters of protest when the press reported that President Reagan supported covert action against the government in Nicaragua.

It was a relief to turn to happier news, like Bishop Joseph Hart's invitation to the congregation to make a foundation in his diocese, which embraced the entire state of Wyoming. He told them he had only fifty priests in the diocese, and some eighty sisters. Visiting the Bishop in Casper, Wyoming, Mother Audrey wrote back to the community in St. Louis that the beauty of the state lay in its expanse of plains. The bishop, she told the sisters, really wanted a monastic presence in his diocese. His formal invitation arrived on June 9 with the statement that his priests were enthusiastic about the possibility and that this would be "a major event in the life of the church in Wyoming."

That Pentecost Sunday the sisters took part in a special day sponsored by the Leadership Conference of Women Religious, symbolizing the Catholic sisters' intention to concentrate on world peace and disarmament as an issue of extreme importance to them. Many felt that this witnessed to a conversion in the church, a conversion to peace. Despite this yearning for peace, the press told them that seldom had so many wars been going on in the world. In Lebanon the Israelis were attacking the Palestinians. Britain and Argentina were fighting over the Falkland Islands. Iran and Iraq had been battling for more than a year. In El Salvador government troops were struggling with the guerillas. In Afghanistan freedom-fighters battled the Soviet troops. Cambodia was fighting the North Vietnamese. To symbolize the monastic presence in this struggle for human liberation, two of the sisters from the Benedictines on Morganford Road took part in a peace march from St. Louis University to the riverfront with two thousand other concerned citizens.

Mother Audrey wrote a paper on the charism of the congregation in June 1982 which she presented in each of the monasteries. She reminded the sisters that the codification of canon law had forced religious communities to fit their unique charism into the mold required by the Code. Vatican II acknowledged that this mold had had the detrimental effect of obscuring the original charism. Then Vatican Council had asked communities to return to their origins to rediscover their fundamental identity. Mother Audrey felt that their own congregation was engaged in discovering a devotion to Christ in the Eucharist which would accord with their original charism, yet recognize the far more developed eucharistic theology of today.

Later in June Srs. Ramona Varela, Benita Luetkemeyer, Marietta Crahan, Gregory Cushing and Daniel Minor set off with nine other Benedictine liturgists and musicians for a tour of selected Benedictine abbeys in Europe. They were to present their liturgical music and learn from the European experience. The group visited Montserrat in Spain, Einsiedeln and Engelberg abbeys in Switzerland, Metten in Germany, Nomberg in Austria, Sant Andre in Belgium and Tyburn convent in London. Sr. Ramona, whose idea and planning were chiefly responsible for the tour, was well satisfied with the results.

On August 4, 1982 the 10th General Chapter of the congregation opened. Sr. Kathleen Margaret Gorman was able to present the assembled delegates with a third volume of her labors on the early history of the congregation in a collection of letters and biographies of the pioneer sisters. This was an excellent source of material on the spirit and identity of which Vatican II had spoken and much appreciated in formation efforts. Then the delegates got down to business. They accepted the revised constitution, voted unanimously to make a new foundation, with Wyoming as the first possible site, decided to move toward closing the Kansas City monastery and to reduce the number of buildings on the Clyde property. On August 14 the delegates elected Sr. Maureen Truland as the sixth prioress general of the congregation. She immediately told them she would not use the title "Mother," but remain "sister." Two days later the delegates elected the general council: Srs. Benita Luetkemeyer, Dolores Dowling, Matthias Igoe and Rosario Martinez. One of the final acts of this Chapter was a commitment to social justice.

SAND SPRINGS

On her return from India in the summer of 1977 Sr. Pascaline was ready to begin what she dreamed of doing, and by Christmas she was able to formulate her request to Mother Audrey and the council: "A child begs to be born," she wrote. Pedro Arrupe, S.J., the general of the Jesuits inspired her with his words to the Montreal Religious Conference of November 1977: "Frugality and austerity of life emerge as absolutely necessary for the material and social survival of the human race ... The greatest service religious can offer ... today is to give irrefutable witness against consumerism by a life that is austere and frugal."

Sr. Pascaline saw her proposed ashram as a place set apart for intense spiritual activity, where the knowledge and experience of God was primary. In her letter to the council she asked to "initiate in communion with our congregation and in behalf of it, a small community of simplified lifestyle, apart from present structures." In such a setting a small group of sisters could "begin to realize a life of deeper prayer and poverty . . . to create and share the needed natural contemplative setting and monastic atmosphere with God's holy people." For this purpose, "buildings, furnishings, schedule, work, meals, clothing would be geared to their top priority: contemplative prayer. Liturgical prayer, though important, would need to be flexible, less structured and more oriented toward contemplation."

On January 6, 1978 the North American Board for East-West Dialogue, sponsored by A.I.M., held a meeting at Rickenbach Center in Clyde. This Board was to promote interreligious dialogue with Asian monks and religious, as requested by the Roman secretariate for non-Christian Religions. Sr. Pascaline was elected secretary with a yearly stipend for her work. It was on this same date that Mother Audrey and her council granted Sr. Pascaline's request for a new foundation, feeling that this could be "a new and unique way for us to express the Eucharist."

By March 10 Sr. Pascaline had written to many bishops about this project and had already interested three sisters in joining her: Srs. Christina Bonneau, Priscilla Trost and Monica Sanders. Soon Sr. Trinitas Nordhus also asked to become a member. At the end of April Bishop Eusebius Beltram of Tulsa, Oklahoma was the first to respond, saying he would be open to such a foundation in his diocese. Two days later a letter came from Fr. Jim Conners, O.C.S.O., who was then on a study sabbatical at Berkeley, California, to say that he would be very interested in joining the group as chaplain. Fr. Jim had been a novice at Gethsemani, Kentucky, while Thomas Merton was novice director.

At the end of May Sr. Pascaline had met Bishop Beltram who helped her look for a suitable property in the environs of Tulsa. During the Chapter Sr. Pascaline reported to the delegates on her venture. The delegates voiced much support for this simplified monastic lifestyle and some of the Mundelein monastery's furnishings were set aside for the Oklahoma house. After the Chapter Mother Audrey suggested that the five sisters to make up this foundation move to Tulsa, as Sr. Anita Gilpin of the Tulsa Benedictines had been kind enough to loan them the use of a building belonging to her community. Sr. Anita with her sisters welcomed the little group warmly on September 22. This began a time of almost daily searching for a suitable permanent location. At first a large property in Pawhuska looked promising, but was later thought to be too far from Tulsa to be accessible. The bishop told them that some of his priests were saying: "Don't let them go out that far!"

Even as they searched, the sisters were busy reflecting on and discussing the guidelines for their community life; they set aside time for faith-sharing to work out a philosophy for the balance of east and west in their lives. Both Srs. Pascaline and Priscilla had spent some time at Fr. Ed Hayes' "Shantivanam" in Easton, Kansas. This was a prayer and retreat center, an experiment in Christian communal living, sponsored by the diocese under the guidance of Fr. Hayes. The sisters used this as a partial model for their own project. They began a new form of adoration, a communal experience both morning and evening when darkness changes to light and light to darkness. They discerned as a group who would be welcome to join them from among the congregation, as there were already sisters wanting to come. They also decided to be open to sisters of other congregations joining them for a time.

Sr. Pascaline was busy at this time arranging the itinerary of Fr. Bede Griffiths' lecture tour of American monasteries for 1979. As secretary of the North American Board, she was also editing the bulletin for the East-West dialogue. Then Mother Audrey and her council arrived late in October to look at various properties. They found that even with austerely simple cabins and a common house for a chapel, kitchen and laundry, utilities and a roadway would be extremely expensive in most of the areas.

At this time eastern Oklahoma was full of reservoirs, clear lakes and hiking trails. The sisters were told that the name "Oklahoma" means "land of the red man." This land had been wrested from the Indians first by grain farmers from the midwest, then mountaineers from Appalachia. These were succeeded by cotton-growers from the south and oil-drillers from the east. The discovery of oil in 1905 turned Tulsa from a village into a major metropolitan center in less than twenty-five years. The city went on to become the headquarters of many oil companies. It was in the oil fields near Tulsa that J. Paul Getty and H. Sinclair got their start. The sisters also discovered that the highest concentration of non-reservation Indians lives in eastern Oklahoma. One of the state's best known citizens began his career as the "Cherokee Kid" — Will Rogers.

On December 12, 1978 Sr. Pascaline was at Columbia University in New York attending the Merton Commemoration. She chaired the session on the state of East-West dialogue, besides presenting a paper on the influence of eastern spirituality on women of the western church. A highlight of this trip was a visit with Robert Muller, Undersecretary of the U.N., in his 29th floor office, as well as visits with the Little Brothers and Sisters of Jesus and to Lindisfarne in Manhattan. "Gifts everywhere!" as Sr. Pascaline wrote to the sisters.

By this time Fr. Jim Conners, O.C.S.O. was living with his own sister in Tulsa, coming regularly to the sisters' temporary house for Mass. He shared their community sessions to help spell out their call to radical gospel living. While waiting for a permanent location, Fr. Jim was appointed administrator of a parish in Bristow, about thirty-five minutes' drive from Tulsa. Early in 1979 he began to share with the sisters his notes from a course in mysticism Merton had taught at

Gethsemane in 1961. That February the sisters were with Fr. Jim at his parish helping him clean and renovate.

In March 1979 Sr. Trinitas left the community to return to the Kansas City monastery. The sisters would always remember her gifts of a beautifully designed wooden cross and tabernacle for the chapel. In May Bishop Beltram told them about some property in the Sand Springs area which was close to Tulsa. It was deeply wooded, included two canyons near Shell Creek Lake and would be peacefully secluded among areas of oak trees. On June 12 Sr. Matthias Igoe of the council was with them helping them to hunt for "the perfect spot." Two days later, just before the feast of Corpus Christi, they found a place in the Shell Creek West area where all the utilities were already in. Was this, finally, what they had been searching for?

After other members of the council had seen the property, they made the decision to buy 40 acres. Then the five sisters of the small community had to leave for the Clyde community to take part in Fr. Bede Griffiths' workshop given at Conception Abbey. Just before this, they had received a special gift in "Nandi." Nandi was a three-week old puppy, part German Shepherd, part Doberman Pinscher, who was to become the indispensable watch-dog of the "Forest of Peace." Fr. Bede and Sr. Pascaline had a moving reunion with much to share. He returned to Tulsa with them to see the site of the proposed Osage monastery and to celebrate Eucharist with them. Fr. Bede was impressed with the place, but also with the heat. "It's hotter than India," he admitted later. "In fact, I think it's hotter than hell!"

From then on it seemed to the sisters, it was building plans and more building plans. They wanted a simple chapel in the main house. Besides this, there were to be six cabins for the sisters themselves and five for those who came to make retreats. Fr. Jim suggested the design for a "sundance pit" in the chapel, symbolic of native American worship. Together the group planned to emphasize their values: a simple setting for deeper prayer must take priority in any building.

In January 1980 cement was poured for the common house and by February 1 carpentry work could begin. While the cabins were being painted that April, the Osage Chief, Sylvester Tinker and his wife, Alice, paid the sisters a visit. After imparting a special blessing, he promised to return for the dedication. Later that month, Brook Reed, a former member of the congregation, sent them a beautiful little altar table she had carved. May 24 was moving day. A priest friend got four trucks to help move beds and trunks. The first Mass in the chapel was offered that Sunday, and on their first night in the forest the whip-porwills sang the sisters to sleep, with Nandi objecting occasionally from Sr. Priscilla's porch. Early in the mornings it was not uncommon to see deer on the gravel roads near the cabins. Every day truck loads of furnishings arrived. By June 6 the unique light fixture for the chapel, a large wagon wheel, could be hoisted to the ceiling and the tabernacle hung. More than two hundred and fifty people came for the blessing and dedication on June 8. Bishop Beltram with six concelebrants presided at the Eucharist and led the procession into the woods where he gave Benediction on this feast of Corpus Christi.

On August 21 Sr. Helen Barrow arrived to join the community just in time for Fr. Jim's classes on mysticism. Later in September Sr. Rachel Ronquillo, who had been novice director for the congregation, also became part of the core group. The sisters began their day with adoration, followed by Lauds and Eucharist. Dayhour was prayed at noon with a fifteen minute period of silent prayer. After dinner, work and lectio occupied the afternoon, with periods of silent time in the sisters' individual cabins, which were scattered in the forest north of the main house. They prayed Vespers at 6 p.m., and then had supper and a faith-sharing. Another time of adoration ended the day at 8:30 p.m.

That November, 1980 Sr. Pascaline with Fr. Jim and Sr. Helen went to Holyoke, Massachusetts for the East-West symposium, where they heard presentations and made plans with the Trappists: Armand Veilleux, Basil Pennington and Sr. Myriam Dardenne, along with Raymundo Pannikar and Euart Cousins. Then it was Advent and the sisters' first Christmas in the Forest of Peace. It began with Midnight Mass celebrated while the full moon shone in the east windows of the chapel. The *Tulsa Tribune* of August 28, 1980 had described this chapel for its readers: "The striking circular chapel faces east. A shallow pit in the middle represents the American Indian sundance circle — the traditional gathering place for worship of the Plains Indians . . . It contains a stylized crucifix, an American Indian statue of the Madonna and a Hindu statue."

By January 1981 there was a steady stream of sisters of the congregation coming to make retreats at this Osage ashram. Others also came: sisters from various congregations, priests, people of various faiths. The guest cabins were rarely empty. Many told the small community how much they valued the peace of the forest setting, the utter simplicity of the life, the lack of noise from television and radios. On January 14 the sisters, who used their television set only once a day for the evening news, watched President Carter's farewell address and heard him stress three things: the nuclear threat and our responsibility as a people — the need to be good to the earth and preserve her resources — the important place human rights must have in the nation. It was only a few days later that Sr. Christina Bonneau left the community to return to the Kansas city monastery. The sisters were sorry to lose one of their pioneers.

That March Sr. Monica and Fr. Jim were busy making graveled paths between the cabins and planting dogwood, redbud and holly trees in the clearing around the common house. The community was delighted to welcome Fr. Ed Hayes that same month. He told them he felt religious needed three new vows: contentment, communion and contemplation. During Lent the community shared together on the works of Henri LeSaux, the French Benedictine who spent years in India, becoming an expert on eastern prayer. The sisters also worked at improving their interpersonal relations with the help of a Tulsa psychologist. They took a "solitude" week, one of whose highlights was a zen-type Eucharist early one morning on the peak of a canyon. Another topic of discussion was the wearing of some kind of tunic, since they did not have the customary black and white dress or veil of the congregation.

In June while the rest of the group went to St. Louis for Harold Grant's workshop, Sr. Pascaline flew to Paris for the A.I.M.-sponsored meeting about dialogue between east and west monasteries. Later in the month, Sr. Lioba Hanley arrived to spend six weeks with them as a possible preparation for joining the group after her year of monastic study with Terrence Kardong, O.S.B. At the Naropa Institute in Boulder, Colorado, the sisters heard a fine presentation on Zen by Eido Roshi and Sr. Pascaline had a meeting with the Dalai Lama, who spoke of Thomas Merton as a bridge between east and west.

David Steindl-Rast, O.S.B. was with the community in September giving conferences on monastic mindfulness. After this, Fr. Jim shared notes from Merton's unpublished "Inner Experience." Guests continued to come. In November three young men visited from a nearby Catholic Worker house which they had opened. Several sisters of the congregation came to make a three-month preparation for final profession. Sr. Pascaline and Fr. Jim were kept busy with spiritual direction and retreats. But there was time to go out walnut picking and enjoy days of solitude. As the year ended, the sisters regretted Sr. Rachel's departure from the congregation and were concerned about Sr. Helen's hip surgery. Christmas was a peaceful time in the forest with white candles in each window to show solidarity with the Polish workers.

On January 21, 1982 Bob Sellers, who had already done so much for the group, had his men clearing the area for a new craft-house. Sr. Pascaline returned from the pre-Chapter in the St. Louis monastery on a bus that had to crawl over highways that were sheer ice part of the way. On February 12 northeast Oklahoma had a snowfall that closed all the Tulsa schools, blanketing the forest in white. By March, however, the forest was a spring delight, with crocuses, jonquils, iris and Sr. Monica's tulips pushing up amid the dead brown leaves. Squirrels were busy with their nut supplies, cardinals called from the oak trees and meadow larks from the pastures, while little inch-worms dangled from branches, something of a threat to those with a vow of non-violence. Non-violence was one of the themes of Fr. Jim's Holy Thursday homily. "Jesus girded himself with a towel. Gird usually

221

means to prepare for battle; it has a warlike meaning. But Jesus was preparing for service. He was defenseless."

At the end of April, that ever-peripatetic monk, Jean Leclercq, arrived from the Philippines for a brief visit. Later in May Sr. Lioba came to join the community and helped keep an all-night vigil for peace on the eve of Pentecost. June and July brought the first temporary lay members to the sisters for a three month period. Late in July they experienced a Vipassana retreat, which included conferences interspersed with sitting and meditative walking. On the last day of the retreat they were accompanied by both Nandi and a female dog called "Sakti," who had recently given birth to six puppies who bore a suspicious resemblance to Nandi. The retreat ended on July 30th with eight hours of "sitting." At the end of August Sr. Pascaline was happy to return from the General Chapter to report that the delegates had unanimously approved their continuance as a monastic ashram under the supervision of the general council.

CLYDE

As the new decade opened at the Clyde monastery, it had been four years since the council and novitiate had moved to St. Louis. Many of the Clyde sisters were still feeling the shock. For them the mother-house in northwestern Missouri would always be the center of the congregation. These sisters developed an attitude very protective of Clyde, seeing this house as THE center of true monastic life. Clyde, they felt, had the space needed and the rural calm for contemplation. It had the beloved chapel with its decades of adoration and liturgy. It had the changing seasons which became part of the life and prayer of all who lived there.

There was the spring with the heavy fragrance of lilacs and the strawberries growing apace. Later, peonies lined the roadways while roses bloomed languidly in the courtyard. May 30, 1979 brought something unusual to this courtyard: an enormous swarm of honey-bees gathered on the statue of the Virgin Mary. The sisters hastily summoned the beekeeper from Ravenwood, Missouri. He had been dealing with bees for more than forty years and said he had never seen a swarm to equal that one.

Summer at Clyde meant evening meals outdoors for those who chose, as well as occasional picnics at the Platte River or a fish-fry down near the pond. It meant fresh vegetables, cherries, plums and melons. It also meant a draining heat and humidity. In July 1977 a summer storm felled the beloved old cottonwood tree by the pond. Generations of sisters had sat beneath its shade on the little bridge or watched the reflections of the leaves in the water. The heat wave of July, 1980 occurred when the Clyde and Conception communities were celebrating the sesquimillenium of St. Benedict's birth. The temperature reached 105 degrees that day. More than once, the sisters joined local parishes in outdoor processions to pray for rain. They knew that farmers in the area were hauling water long distances for the cattle, while tugboats on the Mississippi could scarcely navigate so low were the waters.

Autumn brought exotic colors to the Clyde landscape with leaves of gold, tangerine and scarlet brilliant against the evergreens. It also brought thousands of apples. One day in September, 1979 the sisters picked 113 crates of apples. When the cost of wages for workmen, watering, spray and other hidden factors were totaled up, not everyone was sure that the apples were all that profitable.

Then there was winter. "Snow! Snow! Snow!" wrote the chronicler for January 23, 1973. On January 14, 1979 there were eight-foot drifts in places, to the point where no chaplain could get over from the Abbey for Mass. This was further complicated on January 18 by a freezing rain which sent power lines down laden with ice, so that the sisters had to grope their way to bed with candles until Srs. Lucy Carter and Andrew Faber could get the diesel generator going. The weather held everyone's attention again on January 10, 1982 which was, said the chronicler, "the coldest day of the century." All that night howling winds kept the house contracting with short, sharp explosions, while the wind-chill reached 72 degrees below zero. After this, the sisters tacked plastic over the chapel windows to reduce the drafts, since those in charge of maintenance were "exhausted trying to keep us and the pipes thawed out."

Animals were also part of the rural atmosphere of Clyde. In the early spring the baby lambs came. One April day in 1981 five fox cubs were discovered behind the old hog shed. "They looked like small kittens," noted the chronicle, "and are very playful." There were always cats about: a mouser for the altar bread building and a series of kittens who lived royally in the printery. Dogs, too: Clyde was a dumping-off place for unwanted puppies. In January 1971 there were three of them to delight the sisters with their antics. Later a beautiful part-Husky, named "Lady" appeared. At night those of the community whose bedrooms faced the south and west could hear the cows bawling for their calves. When the wind blew from the east, it was obvious to all that the hogs were still on the property rented to Mr. From.

In the fall of 1981 a series of five monks began to rotate the duties of chaplain for the Clyde sisters. Before this, Frs. Hugh Tasch and Aelred Rosser had offered them much help with the new liturgy. Back in the fall of 1970 Conception College had opened its classes to the sisters: and one class a semester was taught at the sisters' monastery for some years. Later, postulants and sisters went to the college for various classes in scripture, theology and music. Before the monks gave up their school of theology because of reduced enrollment, the seminarians regularly came to the sisters' chapel to lend solemnity to the services. Abbot Kevin McGonigle was there to help them celebrate their centennial in September, 1974.

For the bicentennial celebration of the nation in May, 1976 at Conception Abbey, Sr. Jean Frances Dolan, the prioress, represented the Clyde community. About twelve thousand people attended, with all fifteen of the Nodaway County churches represented as well. There were displays in the auditorium of each church's books, ledgers, and sacred vessels. One of the features of this event was the presentation of certificates to twenty-seven families who live on "centennial farms," farms which had been handed on in the family for a hundred years or more. Later in the fall of 1976 the Clyde sisters welcomed thirty Vietnamese seminarians for dinner and recreation one evening. These students were among the four hundred and fifty Vietnamese seminarians settled in the area, who used one of the Conception Abbey's empty buildings for their studies.

The monks and sisters joined forces to celebrate the 1980 festivities, sending out three thousand invitations for a Eucharist in the Kansas City, Missouri cathedral, with Bishop John Sullivan as principal celebrant and Abbot Jerome Hanus as homilist. In the course of his homily the abbot told those present that "This celebration is a commemoration of the past, but even more important, it is a recommitment for the future." Before this, on the feast of St. Scholastica, most of the monks had been with the Clyde sisters for a family celebration which featured a hilarious skit, "A Sesqui is nothing to sneeze at."

The Clyde community experienced the workshops, lectures and seminars that the other monasteries of the congregation had. Brother Ron Fogarty was there in 1970. The M.D.I. firm worked with the community in 1972, encouraging goal-setting, discussions on deaneries, as well as a study of the press operations in hopes of better management. In June 1973 a 30-day retreat was held at Clyde directed by a team of Jesuits, with Sr. Trinitas Nordhus of the community also helping to direct. At this time other members of the community were also involved in retreat work and spiritual direction; among them Srs. Mary Jane Romero, Lioba Hanley and Lupita Barajas. Sr. M. Jane had written a short paraphrase of the Rule of Benedict, called "Seeking," which was to be very popular. It was published by the Liturgical Press in September, 1972. The well-known liturgists, Fr. Godfrey Diekmann, O.S.B. and Fr. Gerard Broccolo came in 1977 and 1979 to lecture. In 1981 Fr. Terrence Kardong, O.S.B. gave the community retreat on the theme of monastic spirituality. The previous year Dr. Harold Grant had come to Clyde for his Meyers-Briggs Personality Indicators workshop, which left the sisters talking about being thinkers or feelers, intuitive or sensate.

There were frequent discussions in the community so that the sisters were kept abreast of congregational concerns during this decade. In 1970 the Eucharist was the chief topic. The chronicler felt that Pope Paul VI's encyclical, "Mystery of Faith," was a basic and solid foundation for thinking about this sacrament, although "others take some of the more modern, speculative views." They also discussed television: was it dangerous to their contemplative life? There were divergent opinions, although all agreed to move Compline back so that those who watched the Lawrence Welk show could do so in peace. Mother Pascaline was in Clyde in 1972 to talk about the needs of the congregation and the possibility that one monastery would have to close. In May 1975 it was Mother Audrey who spoke to the community about the number of aging members and the growing concern about maintenance of six large buildings. Members of the general council were there again in 1982, with representatives of the Pearce Corporation to discuss possibilities for the Clyde buildings and maintenance. "Since part of this proposed plan dealt with the demolition of some of our outlying buildings, as well as the infirmary and south wing of the monastery itself," the chronicler noted with some understatement, "tension was experienced."

The novices of the congregation annually came to Clyde in the summer to get in touch with the roots. In 1975 the postulancy was established there. Before this there had been a happy reunion of some thirty former sisters of the congregation at Clyde. In 1982 Sr. Lupita directed the first "Monastic Experience" there. The young women who participated shared in the prayer-life of the community, as well as in daily periods of work and lectio. They discussed Benedictine spirituality with some of the sisters. The chronicler felt that "one of the highlights of recreation times was a picnic and tour of the abbey and an evening hayride."

The movements which circulated through religious communities during the 70s affected the Clyde community as well. The first was the small-group movement. Brother Ron Fogarty had insisted on the need to belong to a "primary group." One such small group was begun after his workshop but faded away before long. There was another attempt in 1972 when several sisters experimented with living together at the guest house, sharing meals, prayer and recreation. The most organized attempt was the one at the "Rickenbach Center," which was begun in 1976 and ended at the Chapter of 1978.

A different type of small-group experiment involved the older sisters. It began with a craft and hobby room for them. Sr. Clarita Downey worked with the sisters in weaving, making hooked rugs, crocheting afghans. There were other kinds of occupational therapy and mild exercise sessions. Sr. Paschalia Noser followed her as director. For the sick sisters an infirmary team had been set up consisting of nurses, nurses' aids, the cook and later a coordinator. In December 1973 Sr. Benita Luetkemeyer, the prioress, and Sr. Paula Thompson, the nurse, proposed a sub-priory for retirement-age sisters. There would be a separate, more relaxed schedule for them. Mother Pascaline agreed to this early in 1974, appointing Sr. Margaret Mary Bielinski as superior of what was to be known as the "St. Mary's Group." Fr. Alphonse Sitzman, O.S.B. was their chaplain. Observing his continuous concern and affection for these elderly sisters, the community could understand the young Conception Abbey monk who said that in case of fire the first thing he would save would be Fr. Alphonse. The St. Mary's experiment continued until the general council decided to move the sick sisters to the St. Louis monastery in 1975. They were concerned about the quality of life at Clyde with its diminishing number of able-bodied sisters. The energy crisis also had to be taken into account: to save heat it seemed necessary to close off parts of the large building. That December wooden partitions were put up to effect this conserving of fuel. Many of the sisters were upset by this, referring to the partitions as the "Berlin walls."

In the spring of 1978 another decision reversed this: the partitions came down and the large refectory and main kitchen were once again in use. By May, with the general assembly only weeks away, the entire house was scrubbed, the floors waxed and windows washed. The fuel crisis of 1979 led to the closing of the guest house, the chaplain's former residence and Rickenbach Center for the winter months. In April 1981 the long-debated decision to move the laundry to the basement of the main monastery building was finally made. That September both the 100-foot smokestack and the old laundry were demolished.

The Clyde press underwent some major changes during the 70s. The gradual disappearance of the Catholic sub-culture, from which the majority of the sisters had come, and to which the majority of the magazine and booklets' readers belonged, greatly influenced these changes. Subscriptions to *Spirit & Life* fell off; there was little demand for the booklets. The move to St. Louis meant a diminished work-force for the press. In the fall of 1971 the press staff met to talk over these problems and later M.D.I. made suggestions about improvement. Early in 1973 a new arrangement was tried when Srs. Rosario Martinez and Paulette Marie Threinen took charge. Insufficient personnel led to the failure of this effort. Later Srs. Reparata Hopp, Marjorie McManus and Jacqueline Steinbrenner worked as a team. In 1975 the editorial and press staff agreed not to print any booklets and to cut the leaflets down to fifteen titles.

The altar bread making also experienced changes. In the early years of the decade there were experiments with thicker breads. When the Mundelein monastery closed in 1978, the long process of transferring their equipment to Clyde took much thought and time. Between Srs. Lioba Hanley, Karen Joseph and innumerable trips between the two monasteries it was accomplished, so that the Clyde altar bread department was expanded to take on the Mundelein monastery's orders. Sr.

Daniel Minor took charge of the expanded department in 1982, reorganizing and improving management and methods.

Other changes worried the sisters in various degrees during these years. As the saints shifted around in the liturgical calendar, the sisters struggled to learn new hymns and new rubrics. Then there was the vexed topic of clothing. In the entry for May 21, 1972 the chronicler wrote: "We have permission to wear white now. Some are wearing this today, but most of us prefer our black habits. Thank God for this!" The next year in an entry for June 10, she noted: "Some who went on a picnic wore no veil and slacks!" Then in a more philosophical vein she added: "So very much now is left to the responsibility and accountability of each one." The chronicler had more sympathy for those who had joined a boycott on coffee which had risen to $3.50 a pound in 1977. "This is a distinct hardship for those sisters who find coffee almost indispensable, especially early in the morning."

In many ways the most significant change came in 1981 when Sr. Marietta Crahan, Clyde's prioress, replaced the large standing monstrance with a smaller chalice-monstrance, such as the Tucson community used. Sr. Marietta had studied liturgy at St. John's University in Collegeville for several years and used all her expertise to help the sisters understand the reason for this change. It would provide a better link between exposition and the action of Eucharist. More important still, was the link between adoration and Christ's desire to give himself as food. The chalice-monstrance was a clearer symbol of this, she explained to the community. Despite all this careful preparation, some of the sisters could not bring themselves to accept the change.

In many areas life went on as usual at the Clyde monastery during this decade. One of the highlights occurred in September 1973 when the sisters held a "Water Festival" to aid in building a well for the Benedictine Fr. Mayeul de Dreuille's mission in India. There had been an enduring drought there and water was desperately needed. The sisters worked like trojans for this outdoor bazaar, mailing letters to friends far and near. Their faith was sorely tested when it rained the morning of the festival, but by noon the skies had cleared so that booths and stands could be set up. With great satisfaction the community counted the proceeds that night, amounting to some eighteen thousand dollars for the well. At this time the sisters hosted weekend Marriage Encounter groups of twenty to thirty couples. Sr. Gertrude Gross coordinated these groups for the community. Many other such groups, both Catholic and Protestant, used the Clyde facilities during this decade.

Sr. Lucy Carter's golden jubilee of profession in 1976 was an important event for the community. Later that same year the sisters gave the use of a large room on the first floor of the guest house for a "Well Baby Clinic," where young mothers could come to learn how to take care of their babies. In September the community held another auction. Old beds, mattresses, chairs, pictures, kitchen equipment, antique dishes and silver, long stored away in attics and cupboards, were auctioned off. Some of the ancient tin plates used in the early days sold for $5.00 each. Lucky Strike cans brought $9.00 apiece. An old gramaphone went for $300. For the two days of the auction there were more than one thousand people milling around the grounds.

Many of the sisters thought that Fr. James Jones' homily at the golden jubilee Mass for Srs. Flora Schuster and Ernestine Lagemann in August 1981 summed up the state of affairs at Clyde quite accurately: "A characteristic of this community has always been and is, charity. Here forgiveness comes readily . . . There is hard work in this community . . . Your barns are cleaner than our monastery . . ."

MUNDELEIN

In April 1970 Sr. Audrey Jones was appointed prioress of the Mundelein community with Sr. Juliann Wolbert as her sub-prioress. With the rest of the sisters they enjoyed the solemnity which several seminarians added to the services in their chapel. The third-year theologians could always be counted on for this and also liked to come for an occasional recreation with the sisters. They dialogued together about the relevance of contemplative life in modern times, played guitars or spoke about their own hopes for ministry.

That summer there were outings to a cabin on Lake Petit, loaned to the sisters by the Chicago Benedictines. The chronicler noted that the Mundelein sisters were in the boat, "fully clothed and in an upright position, quite a contrast to others who went on the lake." During the summer Fr. Gerald Broccolo came to speak on the liturgy and later Brother Frank of the Taize community was with them to talk about his work in Chicago.

In January 1971 many of the sisters were taking a course in hatha yoga. The Little Sisters of Jesus came to explain their life of contemplation amid the very poor in Chicago. Fr. John Egan spoke to the community about ecumenism, suggesting books they could read and encouraging them to have Lutheran and Episcopalian pastors come to talk to them about their vision of faith. A volunteer from the Peace Corps told about her experiences in India. Fr. Edward Schillebeeckx was at the seminary in May that year and attracted a large number of the Mundelein sisters to his lectures.

In the summer months the sisters used the seminary pool every Thursday afternoon. Sr. Daniel Minor went to St. John's in Collegeville to study liturgy, while Sr. Carmela Rall began to exhibit her paintings at art fairs and local banks. It was a real satisfaction for the sisters who looked after the apple orchard to know that 650 jars of apple sauce were safely canned in the fall of 1972. Before they could draw breath, it seemed to many of the sisters, it was 1973 and the beginning of Chapter preparations, though they did have time to welcome Srs. Pat Haines and Carol De Fiore of the Notre Dame de Namur Sisters. They came to spend a year as a preparation for establishing a house of prayer.

After the General Chapter when Sr. Audrey Jones was elected prioress general, Sr. Corona Boylan became the prioress with Sr. Regina Arnold as her assistant. One of their first duties was to plan the celebration of the congregation's centennial. Cardinal Cody was the principal celebrant of the festive Eucharist on September 5, 1974, along with twenty-five other priests and a crowd of friends.

Soon after 1975 began, Sr. Matthias Igoe arrived to share the general council's growing concern about the numbers of aged and ill sisters and the lack of vocations. Mother Audrey reinforced this in her June letter which said: "Holding to any building as our treasure, our security, is to betray the deep purpose of our life." Early in August Sr. Matthias was there again with Sr. Miriam Humbel, the congregation's treasurer, to place before the sisters as plainly as possible the reality of the situation facing them. The fact that at this time there were three young women with the community observing the life as possible future candidates may have reduced the impact of these warnings on the sisters. Later that same month the sisters were much involved helping a Vietnamese family settle into the community's guest quarters for a few weeks, while their sponsors found them housing and jobs.

In January 1976 Sr. Agnes Cunningham, the patristic scholar who taught at the seminary, gave the sisters a brief workshop as an introduction to their own congregational study of the early Fathers. Indirectly this was the cause of a project initiated by Sr. Romanus Penrose. She began a series of booklets with short excerpts from the Fathers to be published by the Clyde Press. The series was called "Seeds of Hope." Later that year Sr. Corona told them about her meeting with Mother Teresa of India at a workshop in the area. More of the sisters were involved in welcoming the eighteen hundred women of the Chicago Council of Catholic Women who came to their chapel in relays as part of a pilgrimage for vocations.

Throughout the early months of 1977 the general council in the St. Louis monastery struggled with the awareness of an increasing need to close one of the monasteries. Sisters in each house were requesting this, due to constant understaffing in their various departments. When Mother Audrey met with Cardinal Carberry, she told him about this and felt his real understanding, since the archdiocese had been forced to close one school after another for lack of sufficient sisters. In the summer the council began weighing the pros and cons of each monastery. The Kansas City house was in a deteriorating neighbor-

229

hood. Many of the sisters in the Tucson monastery were in poor health. The San Diego house with its beautiful location might be easiest to sell. The Mundelein building was the oldest, except for Clyde, and would soon need extensive, costly renovations. There was also talk of closing the seminary, which would create a problem about chaplains.

Finally in August the council came to the reluctant conclusion that the Mundelein monastery would close. On August 22, 1977 Sr. Mary Jane Romero, who had only recently been appointed prioress of the community, had to tell the sisters this sad news. It came as a shock. Somehow the concern about closing a house had not affected this oldest daughterhouse as it had the others in the congregation. There was much pain and grief to work through, but the reality became more and more clear, especially after the meeting of the prioresses of the congregation with the council there in early September.

On September 8 Sr. Mary Jane Romero and Mother Audrey had a meeting with Cardinal Cody. By the 21st of the month both the local and Chicago papers carried stories about the proposed closing. Earlier, a television crew had filmed shots of the chapel and grounds, which appeared on the six o'clock news. Friends began dropping by to express sympathy and regret. By the end of the month Srs. Lioba Hanley and Jacqueline Steinbrenner had worked out with the sisters in Clyde a method of transferring the altar bread orders. Then the sisters began to take inventory of the contents of their monastery. A truck arrived from Clyde in mid-October to take all of Sr. Carmela Rall's art supplies, since she was transferring there. Next various interested parties began touring the house and property. Despite all this, several of the sisters took time out to drive to Marmion Abbey to hear the renowned expert on the Benedictine Rule, Adalbert de Vogue, O.S.B. speak on lectio. The discussions in preparation for the General Chapter also continued.

Early in 1978 the Franciscans from Marytown in Kenosha, Wisconsin sent some of their members to inspect the building. Before them, a representative of the Opus Dei group had been there. Next an architect and builder toured the place to see its possibilities for a low-cost housing development. Cardinal Cody was proving obstinate about any sale to a religious group, since he said he did not need any more religious in his archdiocese. Parts of the monastery were now closed off to conserve heat. Tension mounted as beds, mattresses and the sisters' personal belongings were packed. Some of the sisters had lived here for more than forty years. At the end of January novices from the St. Louis monastery came to help clean and sort for the spring garage sale. Other furnishings were set aside for the different houses of the congregation who had asked for them.

By February many people in the area were coming to buy tables, chairs and other items, like the hundreds of fruit jars which had accumulated over the years. As the chronicler wrote: "This was an exodus experience." Srs. Mary Jane, Lioba, her sub-prioress and Sr. Paschalia Noser worked late into the night with the sisters to inventory, pack, sell and set aside what had been requested. Some of the seminarians came down regularly to help carry the heavier things to the garage for the sale. Furniture and boxes galore lined the halls. "There is no time now to be fussy about dusting and cleaning," remarked the chronicler laconically.

The sisters who were transferring to other monasteries began leaving, so that the adoration chapel was open only on Sundays and feasts with the small Sorrowful Mother chapel used during the week. By the end of March so much had been sold, sent to the other houses or given away, that the house felt empty. The eleven sisters who remained were using folding chairs and tables and other makeshift furniture. They wondered if the Marytown Franciscans would be the buyers, since they seemed the most interested. It was on April 15 that the Franciscans agreed to buy the property, if Cardinal Cody would give his consent to the sale, which he finally did the following month. The sisters held a last Eucharist on April 22, a Mass of thanksgiving for the nearly fifty years of the community's existence in Mundelein. Eight hundred people came to celebrate and sorrow with them. At the end of the month only seven sisters were left and formal adoration was discontinued.

On May 6 the final van was loaded and a week later the last sale held. Now there remained only one more cleaning as the accumulated treasures of fifty years were disposed of. At the end of the month the seven sisters drove off to the general assembly at the Clyde monastery, while behind them the white spirea blossoms nodded in the spring breeze.

TUCSON

The new decade opened in the Tucson monastery with what seemed to the chronicler to be a ceaseless flow of questionnaires from the St. Louis house. "We are living through apparently endless discussions on the questionnaires," she remarked plaintively on January 7, 1970. More philosophically she went on to note: "Some of the sisters want to be pushed instead of taking initiative. This is, of course, due to past methods of discipline which were calculated to root out any initiative!" Along with the questionnaires came a steady flow of directives about the habit: the veil could be shorter, blouses and skirts could be worn.

The chronicler felt that everyone was interested in Brother Ron Fogarty's workshop at the end of May, though by its finish she was writing: "We all need to unwind and get back to normal!" Brother Ron had talked a great deal about the true spirit of aggiornamento. The chronicler mused about the difficulty some sisters had in accepting the changes: "Either way spells suffering, so why not be open and accept the growth-suffering rather than its opposite?" Aggiornamento was evident in the community's sponsoring of a Prayer Institute that August featuring Fr. Carroll Stuhlmueller, C.P. The following years this Institute continued with speakers like Brother Frank of Taize, James Carroll, C.P. and Brother David Steindl-Rast, O.S.B. In the early 70s priests and sisters thronged to the Institute.

On September 9, 1970 Sr. Matthias Igoe introduced a topic destined to change the congregation's century-old method of exposing the Blessed Sacrament. In an interview with Bishop Green, she had presented her idea of using a chalice-type monstrance. The bishop agreed that exposition under a simpler form would probably appeal to young people. Sr. Matthias explained to the community that the basic reason for suggesting the change was the development in eucharistic theology, which now stressed Christ's presence to the sacrament as food. On November 7 the following year the chalice-monstrance was used for the first time. It was a large wooden chalice with a lunula attached to a gold paten, so that the Host would stand upright above the chalice. The sisters had mixed feelings about this. Architecturally it was not well suited, since the chapel had been designed to feature a large monstrance. Yet many felt that it was simpler, closer to the meaning of Christ's presence. By the end of that decade two other monasteries of the congregation had adopted this form of exposition.

Late September saw another innovation in the Tucson community. For the first time a profession was held outside the central house. Sr. Cathleen Marie Timberlake's health required the Tucson climate at this time, so with Mother Pascaline there to receive her vows and a carful of San Diego sisters to help her celebrate, she made first profession in the Tucson chapel. The following May there was the ceremony of final vows for Sr. Evangelista Lange. She had been an Oblate sister for many years, but now according to the congregation's policy of only one status for all members, she made final profession in her 78th year.

In late fall a group of the sisters had an outing to the great Kitt Peak observatory, stopping off later to visit the Franciscan sisters at Topawa who worked with the Papago Indians. The sisters annually took food and candy to children on a reservation near Tucson at Christmas time. It was a few weeks before Christmas that year that the chronicler summed up her impressions of the community meetings, "Looking back at our previous agenda meetings and seeing the number of matters, big and small, which we have decided upon ... we realize what a growth has taken place in our outlook. It is encouraging ... as we struggle through the stormy waters of post Vatican II religious life."

Early in January 1971 the retired Abbot Anselm Coppersmith arrived to be the community's chaplain. He was with them until July

1974, his understanding and strong Benedictine spirit a real help to the sisters, although he himself never did learn to like the desert. On February 14 they learned that Sr. Dawn Vercellino would replace Sr. Kathryn as their sub-prioress. She helped them adapt to the greater freedom of those days in things like dress, outings, and the use of television. Two groups made a trip to the Grand Canyon that summer, while others enjoyed the use of the swimming pool at St. Mary's Hospital. All the sisters were praying for rain most of that summer, as Arizona suffered one of the worst droughts in its history. By August seeding the clouds was resorted to, which did produce a good rain on the 3rd.

The chronicler noted two signs of the times in March 1972. On the 10th a group of sisters drove to Phoenix to hear a lecture by Cardinal Josef Suenens, "a very controversial figure." On the 23rd nine sisters enrolled in a car maintenance class. Once again in April the chronicler was fascinated by the moon walks. "Our astronauts were on the moon's surface for seven and one half hours today and are more and more enthralled by the beauty of it all." It was not the moon they were worried about that summer but the air-conditioning: it was either breaking down or so cold that some of the arthritic sisters took to wearing gloves in the chapel. Once on a trip to Phoenix the car's air-conditioner broke down when the temperature registered 105 degrees. But heat or not, the sisters rejoiced with Sr. Lucina Thompson when she completed her L.P.N. course and became the community's in-firmarian.

On July 9 a goal-setting workshop left the chronicler convinced that "if we drag our feet there is only one end for us — oblivion." She forgot about this in the general concern about Sr. Matthias' health at the end of the year. It was touch and go with the prioress until almost Christmas. This was followed, as often happens, by a number of other illnesses, falls, broken bones and back trouble. By mid-February, 1973, the sisters' attention was free to turn to the altar bread depart-ment's relocation into what had been the community room.

As some sisters went to see "Jesus Christ, Superstar," and others watched "A Man for all Seasons" on television with its moving por-trayal of St. Thomas More, the chronicler was more interested in the political scene. "Aren't there any honest people left?" she asked about Vice-President Agnew. President Nixon's speech on August 15 left her unmoved: "The man thinks he's a demi-god!" Both these were rele-gated to the background in April when the community was able to move back into their renovated chapel. It had been carpeted through-out with movable choir-stalls arranged near the portable altar, set closer to the people. A complete repainting made the chapel attrac-tively light and airy.

Meanwhile in northern Arizona the Payson venture was underway. The chronicler could not detect much enthusiasm for this experiment in a more simple, contemplative lifestyle, except in the San Diego and Tucson communities. "Ah well, little plants must demonstrate their ability to survive the early winters." When the group disbanded in mid-June 1974, she was not dismayed: "While some may feel the venture failed, many of us do not consider it in that light. It was a brave and generous attempt. Others see it as a wonderful hope for the future ... to withdraw from everyday life for a period of time and discover in what ways they are permitting unnecessary things and plans to dominate their lives to the at-least partial exclusion of Christ."

On August 16 that year the chronicler notes: "Much happiness at Sr. Dawn Vercellino's appointment as prioress." She was installed on August 21 along with Sr. Trinitas Nordhus, her sub-prioress. The two went with some of the sisters to visit the new Holy Trinity monastery at St. David's, some sixty miles from Tucson. This was an attempt by some Benedictines and lay Oblates to live the Christian life as described in the Acts of the Apostles. Then it was time for the sisters to celebrate the congregation's centennial, along with the fortieth anniversary of the community's existence in Arizona. Bishop Green was the principal celebrant of the Eucharist, together with thirteen others, one of whom was the retired Bishop James Davis of Santa Fe, who had preached the homily at the opening of the little chapel on Main Street, back on November 7, 1935.

In February 1975 the chronicle speaks for the first time of what was to be a six-year project: feeding the poor who came to the back door of the monastery. From their arrival in the city the sisters had never turned away anyone who came asking for food. Gradually over the years this had grown until now the lines coming for food caused the police to patrol the premises from 10 to 11 in the morning and 3 to 4 in the afternoon when sandwiches and coffee were distributed. The chronicler was dubious about some who came, referring to "a poor class of hippies." On March 2 she noted: "Sunday is the only day we can feel free really to enjoy our own garden because of the presence of hippies looking for food on other days." Many of those who came for sandwiches were on drugs; they often spent time lying around the grounds.

On May 16, 1975 the sisters had a community meeting to discuss this issue. They learned that in four months they had served 7,000 meals of sandwiches and coffee. Most of the sisters agreed to continue the project, although some still felt uneasy about the drug-taking and the loss of privacy. Tucson's mayor and council members called Sr. Estell Schaffer to talk over this food program. Sr. Estell was known locally as the "egg lady," since she was the chief supporter of the program, making and distributing the sandwiches. By that December those who helped Sr. Estell were making about one hundred and fifty sandwiches daily. One grocery store in the area gave her all the unsold bread from the previous day. On the other hand, some of the community's neighbors were becoming increasingly disturbed about the youths who lounged around the property.

As 1976 began Sr. Trinitas turned the sisters' attention to another cause when she told them about a workshop she had attended, where the participants declared themselves in favor of women priests and women bishops. "Feelings in the community are mixed about that last one," noted the chronicler wryly. Sr. Trinitas was also attending classes at Arizona University in Tucson for a degree in art, while Sr. Clarita Downey continued working for a Master's in counseling. In the community, classes on the early monastic period were underway. As usual there were some sisters of other congregations staying with the community for health reasons. Something not so usual was the sight of their orange and avocado blossoms covered with an unexpected snow on March 3.

Because of their friendship with the artist Ted De Grazia, the sisters were horrified to learn of his burning one hundred of his paintings, which had been valued at over one million dollars. He did it, he told them, because he feared the inheritance taxes would wipe out his family's finances. After this, it was a relief to enter into some quiet days of retreat directed by a team of their own sisters, Bede Luetkemeyer and Virginia Ann Argenziano, with Bruce Willmer, O.S.B. who was studying at the University. Then it was time for the community to host a meeting of the congregation's liturgists, with representatives from all the monasteries. They studied the 1975 Directory on the Opus Dei as requested by the Abbot Primate, Rembert Weakland.

The Tucson sisters appreciated the U.S. bishop's approval of communion in the hand in 1977, since twice before this permission had been refused. However, their main concern that year was the fear that their monastery might be the one to close. Sr. Rosario Martinez, whom the sisters had elected as their delegate to the General Chapter the following year, pointed out the inescapable fact that the congregation had more to be done than it had people to do it. Personnel could be stretched no farther, while maintenance of their large houses continued to be a heavy drain on the sisters. On July 8 the community held a brain-storming session to try to surface ideas on how to maintain the Tucson monastery. Could they live on a smaller income, with a much-reduced altar bread department? Were there alternatives to closing their house? "A dark future looms before us," wrote the chronicler with foreboding.

Optimism revived when Sr. Dawn was reappointed their prioress, choosing Sr. Hope Rodenborn as her assistant. A general sigh of relief could be heard when a phone call from Sr. Dawn at a meeting in the Mundelein monastery assured them that it was not their house which would close. On her return the lengthy discussions on their eucharistic charism continued. The chronicler noted that this troubled some: "How difficult it is for those trained to see perpetual adoration as more important than monasticism to accept the greater emphasis on the latter now." As the General Chapter drew nearer, these discussions lengthened: "Will we ever return," fretted the chronicler, "to a meeting-free routine of daily living!" Many did take time out to watch the television presentation of the "Holocaust," with its shocking depiction of the horrors of the slaughter of the Jews in the Nazi era. Another relief from discussions was Jim McMullen's workshop on the Eucharist. This Jesuit would drop into the lunch-room for a coffee break with the sisters, where they had friendly debates on "the whole gamut: celibacy, women priests, permanent deacons, church leadership." Then it was time for the exodus to the general assembly at the Clyde monastery, with only a few of the elderly sisters remaining in the house cared for by Sr. Cathleen Marie's parents. Chapter followed in August and then it seemed the rest of the year flew by.

At the end of January 1979 the Arizona Mental Health Center invited Sr. Estell Schaffer with her companion, Sr. Laurann Weis, to a banquet at the Plaza Hotel, where they presented her with an award "for her quiet support of needy people in Tucson." The chronicle had a sadder notation for May 25: "The second execution in the U.S. (since the reinstatement of the death penalty) took place in Florida. We can only pray that he was surprised by the mercy on the other side." The chronicler went on to pay attention to the gas shortage that summer, writing on July 4: "People have been assured of sufficient gas for their needs over the holiday, but the gas crunch is keenly felt. Some of the newspapers carry pictures of the reduced traffic lines." She was relieved on another account on July 12, when Sky Lab II fell "into a watery grave off Australia with pieces scattered far and wide." On the local scene the chronicler observed two little girls who came into the chapel with their ice cream cones and sat down to enjoy them there: "Of such is the kingdom."

All that summer the sisters worked at "Project Clean-Up" which meant going outside when it was cooler to clean up the grounds, weeds and remove the litter left by those who came for food. In October Sr. Bede Luetkemeyer was part of a team giving a workshop to permanent deacons, while Sr. Hope Rodenborn attended her first workshop on liberation theology. As chairperson of the Sisters' Council of the diocese, Sr. Hope also arranged a Day of Prayer with Sr. Jose Hobday as principal speaker. The following March Sr. Hope attended the conference for Vicars of Religious in Orlando, Florida, since the Tucson Vicar felt that a woman should represent other religious women in the city. In mid-March 1980 seven of the community drove to Sonoita for a day of sharing with the Trappistines there on the Rule of Benedict. All the sisters shared in the excitement when their new "spa" arrived. Since they had eight among them with serious arthritic conditions, state-help had aided them to pay for this spa, which even the older sisters began to use regularly.

With the rest of the nation, the sisters were dismayed to learn on April 25 about the failed attempt to rescue the American hostages in Iran. The failure was particularly sad when they heard about the Canadian embassy in Tehran sheltering six Americans for three months and then smuggling them safely out of the country.

On June 11, 1980 the Tucson community became the first in the congregation to choose election rather than appointment for its prioress. On July 17 they elected Sr. Bede Luetkemeyer after a careful discernment process, with Sr. Cathleen Marie as her sub-prioress. As the summer continued, the usual number of sisters were absent on home-visits, retreats and workshops, to the point where the chronicler noted: "We are experiencing all the advantages of small group living with all the disadvantages of a big group set-up!"

That fall Sr. Dorothy Kordick, who was the congregation's Oblate Director, went to Prescott, Arizona, to receive fourteen new Oblates. Then in November thirteen more were received into affiliation, in what seemed to be a genuine renewal of interest in the spirituality of Benedictine Oblates. The chronicler, however, had another interest: space exploration. On November 12 she wrote: "The scientific world is agog with surprise and delight over the pictures which Voyager I is sending back as it draws ever closer to Saturn, ten million miles away from mother earth." She also took account of homier investigations: "We wonder what winter will bring. We hear no hints or prognostications. Are the caterpillars wearing heavier than usual furry coats? Are the squirrels busier than usual storing away nuts? There are no rumors."

By May 1981 the sisters who were working on the theology section of the revised constitution gathered at the Tucson monastery for a session. Srs. Bede, Salome Komar, Mary Jane Romero, Gladys Noreen and Sarah Schwartzberg worked untiringly for many days. They did take time out to help Sr. Bede celebrate her nameday on May 25 with a pancake breakfast in the patio. The oleanders were in full bloom and the sun high in the east, while in the west the moon descended.

Early in August a sister, who was staying in the guest-house of the monastery, returned home late and had to step over the recumbent bodies of three men sleeping on the little porch. This brought the ongoing debate over the food-program to a head, so that finally the decision was made to end it. There were now other agencies in the city which provided food for the poor. An article appeared in the *Tucson Citizen* for October 21, 1981 had this to say: "Last year 34,000 transients grabbed a sandwich from the sisters ... The police will be happy. A knight of the road barely alights at the Southern Pacific yards, according to the cops that work the beat, before he asks: 'Which way to the egg ladies?' The generosity of the sisters is known from

237

coast to coast among hobos, tramps, and hitchhikers. The neighbors will be happy, too . . . People sometimes mill around for hours waiting for a meal . . . Men ring the doorbell at all hours of the night."

On December 1 the sisters were shivering in the cold as their heating system failed. The chronicle refers to them dressing for this arctic climate in "multiple sweaters and woolens, including sox of various shades, disinterred for the occasion." There was more serious concern in the community about economic conditions in the Tucson area. An increasing number of miners were being laid off: one company had let go over six thousand men. January 12, 1982 brought happier news when the sisters learned that Bishop Manuel Moreno would be their new ordinary. He was the fifth bishop of Tucson, which now had a Catholic population of 280,000. Sixty-nine percent of these were Mexican-Americans in a diocese which covered thirty-seven percent of the total land in the state. According to Bishop Green, Bishop Moreno was a man of the people, whose father had been a "wetback." For the new bishop's installation on March 11 that year, Sr. Irene Pauline Revering made fourteen huge banners for the cathedral and three more for the altar of the Community Center, where the Eucharist had to be celebrated since the cathedral was too small.

By that March the sisters were hearing about the pastor of the Southside Presbyterian Church, Rev. John Fife, who offered his church as a sanctuary for undocumented Central Americans escaping from their own countries. His was part of a nationwide protest of the tough U.S. immigration policies toward Central American refugees, particularly those from El Salvador. The Rev. Fife said the church has a long and proud history of providing sanctuary to the politically oppressed and that the Salvadoreans today certainly fall into that category. Later in the month several of the sisters participated in a procession and ecumenical service in solidarity with the refugees.

On April 13 William Lynch, S.J. was with the community speaking on imagination. A week later Basil Pennington, O.C.S.O. followed him to give lectures on centering prayer. On the 19th of the month it was Sr. Bede who reported to the community on a recent meeting of the American Benedictine Prioresses, during which they had discussed the possibility of federation with the monks of the Order. As the chronicler understood the matter: "The monks want the sisters to be subject to taxation, but with no active share in their meetings or voting rights. Shades of our own war of independence from that same situation!"

April 18 was the beginning of Ground Zero week in Tucson, a week of public education about the dangers of nuclear war. The community kept an extra night of adoration and a fast day to pray for peace. April 25th was "Freeze Sunday," with petitions for a freeze on nuclear arsenals circulating in the chapel vestibule. Many were convinced that Tucson would remain a primary target in case of war, despite the removal of the Titan missiles, since these were being replaced with the MX. It was a relief to turn attention to the General Chapter coming in August and to celebrate Sr. Euphrasia's diamond jubilee of profession with a lively mariachi band.

KANSAS CITY

In the winter of 1970 the sisters in the Kansas City community experienced two attempts to break into their chapel, while one day the sacristan was horrified to catch two teen-agers sniffing glue in the sacristy. There were also several incidents of purse-snatching in or near the chapel. It was somewhat better in the summer months, which brought Brother Ron to them as he continued his rounds of the congregation. Mrs. Cecilia Franklin was giving voice lessons to some of the schola members, while other sisters took art lessons and a few learned square dancing. Everyone suffered from the 100-degree heat in August.

Then Mother Pascaline made an announcement which challenged them: their prioress, Mother Bernard Vidal, had decided to resign, feeling she had given all she could to the community. She wished to resign before her term expired, so that her successor would have time to become acquainted with the sisters before the General Chapter the next February. Mother Pascaline appointed Sr. Miriam Humbel to fill out the term until this Chapter. It was Sr. Miriam who became the prioress after the Chapter, choosing Sr. Lucilla Scurlock as her sub-prioress. Both took note of the place where a variety of sisters were taking lessons in guitar, piano, bookkeeping and typing: the Jewish Community Center. Another sister was learning to drive at this same time. The sister who was teaching her took her to a local cemetery to practice, which Sr. Susan Huppe felt might be something of a reflection on her ability. Everyone in the community, which then numbered thirty-four sisters, got the point when, to illustrate what she meant by "plurality" — one of the catchwords of the early 70s — a sister dressed two dolls: one in the traditional habit, the other in a bathing suit.

The spring of 1972 brought Mother Pascaline with Srs. Audrey Jones and Regina Arnold to give the Kansas City sisters a workshop on goal-setting and leadership, according to the M.D.I. methods. There were other lectures as well: on the crisis in Vietnam, the lettuce boycott, the lay missionary movement in South America. The sisters were also eucharistic ministers at this time. By 1974 their ministry at St. Luke's hospital had become a real involvement for some.

With the rest of the congregation the sisters on "Holy Hill" were busy with discussions in preparation for the General Chapter of 1974. After this Sr. Pascaline Coff was appointed their prioress with Sr. Lucilla continuing as her assistant, until she left to become the St.

Louis monastery's prioress. During her year in Kansas City, Sr. Pascaline was much in demand as a retreat and spiritual director. Several of the sisters in the community also took advantage of nearby Rockhurst College to have Jesuits as their spiritual directors. That fall Sr. Esther Therese Peth left for Chicago where she studied Scripture under Fr. Carroll Stuhlmueller. An important day that fall for the entire community was the consecration of their chapel on October 8.

In the spring of 1975 Sr. Pascaline was in Norfolk, Nebraska with the other Benedictine prioresses. From this meeting, under the leadership of the dynamic Sr. Joan Chittister, O.S.B., they issued the first of a series of statements on American monastic life. This first document was called "Upon This Tradition," and dealt with monastic values in the lives of American Benedictine women. Dom Jean Leclercq continued to emphasize these values in the workshop he gave at the Kansas City monastery some time later. As that year ended the sisters were surprised by Sr. Pascaline's announcement that the following June she would be leaving to spend a year in India studying eastern monastic life, especially its prayer forms, at Bede Griffiths, O.S.B.'s ashram.

In June 1976 Sr. Benita Luetkemeyer accepted the appointment as prioress of the community. As a former prioress of the Clyde house, she recognized the ministry of hospitality that the sisters in the Kansas City monastery had cheerfully exercised over the years. The comings and goings were constant, as a notation in the chronicle makes clear: "A very quiet day on the home front. No one came or went!"

With the rest of the congregation, the sisters in the Kansas City house prayed about the possibility that one monastery would have to close. Then their interest turned to the arrival of their new subprioress, Sr. Josetta Grant, and the news that Bishop Helmsing was retiring. In the fall interest centered on practicing for a special celebration of the feast of Christ the King. They had trumpets, a bass viol and a director for the singing, Sr. David Marie, S.C.L., a friend of the community. At this time some of the community were also involved in writing letters of protest to their congressmen about the violence in El Salvador.

1978 opened for the sisters with a retreat given by the scripture scholar, Eugene LaVerdiere, S.S.S., whose conferences on the Eucharist were taped by V.C.R. cassettes. By this time the community numbered forty-five sisters, some other sisters having come when the Mundelein monastery was closed. After the General Assembly in June, the sisters spent some time in consciousness raising about social justice issues. They had a speaker explain the equal rights amendment, and a parole officer came to talk about prison reform. That Christmas they took cookies and sang for the prisoners at the local jail.

In the summer of 1979 Sr. Lillian Black left for her third session at Creighton University in Omaha, while Sr. Esther Therese Peth completed her scripture studies with a six-week stay in the Holy Land. At this time a number of the sisters were holding weekly contemplative prayer sessions with friends outside the community. Still others went to Des Moines, Iowa that October to catch a glimpse of Pope John Paul II in rural America. It was Sr. Lillian who left for Uganda, Africa the following year as part of the congregation's aid to third world countries. The sisters at home felt that Uganda could not be much hotter than Kansas City in July. They did forget the heat long enough to welcome the arrival of new altar bread equipment, stoves designed by George and Mark Schorr, after many years of patient experimenting.

On October 27, 1980 the council and prioresses of the congregation met at the Kansas City monastery. There was a very sober discussion of the future of this house because of increasing concern over the neighborhood, the number of robberies in the area and the fear experienced by some of the sisters. It was a relief for several sisters to travel to the Sand Springs ashram to make retreats there in the peaceful forest and pray in the seclusion of the little cabins. They had a disaster to pray about on returning to the city in the summer of 1981 when they heard of the collapse of the catwalk in the new Hyatt Regency hotel, which killed more than one hundred people and injured scores.

Early in 1982 the sisters were able to enjoy their new sanctuary furnishings, an altar, chair and lectern, all hand carved in wood by John Noll of Kansas City. On January 25 it was time for the Chapter delegates: Srs. Benita, Josephine Marie Roos and Lillian Black to leave for St. Louis and the pre-Chapter. Three days later the community was host to six Buddhist priests and one nun on their cross-country peace march. Later in May the community offered hospitality to two Little Sisters of the Poor, who stayed with them for some time while supervising the building of one of their homes.

All during that spring and summer the sisters spent time discussing the Chapter proposals, one of which was the closing of their own monastery. Naturally, most of them were opposed to this, although some could appreciate the reasons it was suggested. It was obvious from the investigations of the Pearce Corporation that one house should be closed. The Kansas City monastery had been under consideration for some time. Bishop John Sullivan was understanding of the necessity. There was the additional reason that the building would soon need extensive repairs. Nevertheless, it came as a blow when the Chapter decision was made: the Kansas City monastery would be closed as soon as this was feasible. The sisters, some of whom had been there from their novitiate days, felt it very keenly; the heart tends to root itself in well-loved places.

SAN DIEGO

As the decade began, the sisters in the San Diego community were praying, along with other Americans, for peace on the college campus. More and more rebellions flared over Nixon's sending additional troops to Vietnam. The sisters were also receiving letters asking support for Caesar Chavez' United Farm Workers in their efforts with the non-union grape pickers. Another letter came from Governor Ronald Reagan to say that California now had 20 million citizens. The sisters felt they knew something about the population explosion when fifteen sisters of different communities made retreats with them that Easter.

In September the sisters were worrying about the forest fires raging in the San Diego area, as the city filled with smoke from an enormous fire to the southeast. The sun was overcast, the air heavy and the community on the alert to evacuate if necessary. The fires were forgotten the following February when Sr. Kathryn Neville arrived as their new prioress with Sr. Virginia Ann Argenziano as her assistant. Sr. Kathryn and Sr. Rose Regina Kessler were the first women in the San Diego diocese to be eucharistic ministers. Sr. Kathryn approved of the plan to build an attractive little wooden summer house on their back lawn, a refreshing place to pray or read when the warm Santa Ana winds blew.

In the spring of 1972 Sr. Angela Toigo's little book "God and a Mouse," poems about a small mouse called "Topolito" who talked to God about his adventures and misadventures, was highlighted in *Arizona Highways*. With its whimsical illustrations by Ted DeGrazia, the book became an immediate success so that the first edition sold out in a few weeks. It continued to be popular, going through edition after edition, with translations into German, Spanish, Italian and Finnish. Sr. Angela wrote another such book in 1979 called *Caves and Canyons*.

That summer some of the sisters attended a workshop on Teilhard de Chardin, a theologian whose influence was steadily increasing. In the fall more of the sisters were at the preparatory meetings for the diocesan synod. This was a three-year plan with massive consultation of clergy, religious and laity. At home others of the community watched Kenneth Clarke's magnificent television series "Civilization" every Sunday evening.

Early in January 1973 everyone in the monastery was involved one way or another in making ready for the Benedictine Prioresses' Retreat which was to be held there in February. The community moved beds, scrubbed floors and washed windows. The sisters moved out of their bedrooms to accommodate the sixty prioresses. After Dave Ruhmkorff's workshop on goal setting, the Abbot Primate arrived to conduct the actual retreat. In an article in the March 3 edition of the diocesan paper, the *Southern Cross*, the Primate was reported as

saying that he was responsible to twenty-one congregations of Benedictine monks, numbering approximately 11,000 men and had a
coordinating office for the 21,000 nuns and sisters of the Order.
According to this article, his major concern for the Benedictine sisters
was: "How these courageous women will be able to care for their aged,
and at the same time permit their younger recruits to have the
freedom to develop. We don't want the younger sisters suffocated by
this responsibility." The prioresses assembled at the "lovely Paducah
Drive convent" were, said Rembert Weakland, "courageous, profound
and more serene each time I see them."

For Easter that year the sisters arranged more than two hundred
calla lilies in the sanctuary of the chapel. Then it was time for those in
the 35–50 age group to get ready for their workshop at the Clyde
monastery. They returned in June full of enthusiasm. Describing
their experience to the other sisters, they told them of the talks they
had heard on the problems to be expected at their ages, the need to
accept limitations, integrate their "shadow" side, the need to have
intimacy and their right to fail. In their conversations with each other
at this meeting it had become apparent that many desired less structure in the adoration program, more emphasis on the real presence of
Christ in the community. They had asked each other: "Have we
internalized our eucharistic orientation? Do we truly 'put on Christ' in
our adoration?"

The rest of the summer there were other workshops for those
interested, including one on the psalms as Christian prayer by Alonso
Schoekel at the University of San Diego. Others went to hear the
NASA-sponsored lecture by the anthropologist, Margaret Mead, who
outlined the three options she felt were left to humanity in the nuclear
age. By the end of summer the sisters were busy turning the auxiliary
chapel into a warmly inviting prayer room, which was to become a
favorite place for meditation and centering.

Late in January, 1974 the community hosted one hundred and fifty
sisters of the diocese who were dialoguing together on the role of
women in the Church as part of the preparation for the diocesan
synod. Again in March they had a group of their own sisters with
them, those who were planning a small new foundation, where they
hoped to live a simplified monastic life-style. The place chosen by Sr.
Helen Barrow, their leader, was in Payson, Arizona, about seventy-
five miles northeast of Phoenix in a timberland of pinon and ponderosa
pine.

That March the San Diego community spent some time examining
its own "thrust," coming to the conclusion that their goal would be to
stress prayer and community, with a particular emphasis on hospitality. The ever-increasing number of groups using the facilities they
offered, bore witness to this thrust. Among these was a Zen group with
their roshi, who did their sittings in the assembly room and were only

243

seen by the sisters when they walked processionally around the back lawn, clad in their black robes.

In August the delegates left for the General Chapter. On the 23rd of the month the community learned that its next prioress would be Sr. Dolores Dowling; her assistant Sr. Jane Mary Weisbrook would arrive in November. Soon the community began having Dayhour in common rather than in separate groups so they could share on the scripture readings together. Late in October they decided to bring the large monstrance to rest on the altar itself, moving the tabernacle to the prayer room.

Early in February, 1975 Sr. Dolores, with nine of the sisters, agreed to give instructions on the Catholic faith to Marriage Encounter couples, at the request of Fr. Mike French, one of the chaplains of the movement. He became the sisters' chaplain that March. Then the community discussed what more could be done for the Benedictine Oblates, deciding to have monthly meetings for them at the monastery with spiritual instruction as well as social activities. The combination of the sisters' hospitality, Fr. French's presence and homilies, and the efforts of many individual sisters led gradually to the formation of an extended faith community around the monastic one. Hospitality was in fact becoming evangelization.

Each year the sisters had a "quiet" month, one in which they concentrated on building their own community, shaping their identity, trying to affirm one another. They shared in small groups and read the early chronicles of the congregation to deepen their sense of its history. They took time for outings to Valyermo, a monastery founded in California by Belgium monks after they had been expelled from China. Fr. Vincent Martin, O.S.B., the sub-prior, had known Teilhard de Chardin in China. He told the sisters of his belief that monasticism today represents the humanity of Christ: a response to the Father in keeping the covenant. There were other kinds of outings: to the harbor to see the great ships, like the USS Dixon, with its crew of more than one thousand men. In December the sisters went to the roof-deck of the monastery to watch the annual parade of boats on the bay, their sails outlined in colored lights.

The early months of 1976 found the sisters involved in the Monastic Studies program. In July they decided to reintroduce the Hour of Vigils on Saturday evening as a preparation for the Sunday liturgy. Another community meeting brought the idea of experimenting with one "free" Saturday a month, on which there would be a minimum of community exercises. This experiment was found to be good for letting off any accumulated steam. It was Sr. Salome Komar in 1977 who suggested a small monthly allowance for each sister, out of which she could purchase personal items, pay for phone calls and the like. This was a novelty in the congregation at the time and had to be defended at congregational meetings. Many of the sisters felt that it did more to teach them about choice and accountability than abstract theories about monastic poverty.

Sr. Gladys Noreen began a popular series of scripture classes for wives and mothers once a week at a morning hour which they could be free to attend. In February a group of sisters started a weekly Centering Prayer session with some of the laity. There were also less contemplative activities. One such was a trip to see the famous swallows return to Capistrano in March. The carful of sisters who went returned to report that they had seen four thousand people and two swallows. It was that Easter that the sisters celebrated the Easter Vigil at 4:30 a.m., gathering outside the chapel under the stars for the blessing of the paschal fire and walking out again into the sunrise when the Vigil ended.

One July morning in 1977 the community gathered on their roof-deck with a few guests to celebrate Eucharist there, all praying for San Diego, as Fr. Mike held the Host up over the city. Their liturgical activities for the year ended with the decision to follow Sr. Bernard Vidal's plan to place the Mass altar in the transept aisle of the chapel. This would be a new, smaller altar which the sisters would face as they sat nearer the people who came to celebrate with them.

As 1978 began there were twenty-seven sisters in the San Diego community. They were all involved in the on-going preparations for the general assembly in June. At meetings they asked each other questions such as: What does it mean to be a sister of this congregation? How do I see my congregation manifesting the Lord? How do I experience using — or not using — my gifts for the Church? Then Sr. Dolores asked the sisters to begin changing the sexist language in their choir books to a more inclusive usage. This took some persuasion as consciousness about the women's issue was only gradually rising. Late in May as the last car pulled out of the driveway to take the sisters to the airport for their flight to the general assembly, Sr. Dolores listened to the echo of her footsteps in the empty building as she locked the door behind her. Ten days later they were all back from the experience, happy to be welcomed by those who had looked after the monastery for them and by friends like the Froelicks and Sheltons, who greeted them with a festive supper and a mariachi band.

July brought them the news that the diocese was finally to be divided as Archbishop Jean Jadot, the Apostolic Delegate, announced that San Bernardino and Riverside counties would now form a diocese with some eighty-five parishes. San Diego, which had been created from the Los Angeles diocese in 1936, had eighty-seven parishes. Most of the sisters were more interested to know that Sr. Gladys Noreen had chosen to make her profession of final vows in the San Diego monastery, the first time such a ceremony had taken place there.

When Pope John Paul II made his first visit to Mexico City early in 1979, the sisters prayed for the success of the important Puebla regional conference. They were involved in their own celebration at the end of March, which was the 25th anniversary of their arrival in San Diego. Music for the festive Eucharist was provided by the choir of St. Brigid's church with its well-known director, Jerry Witt. Over four hundred guests came to help celebrate and hear the St. Brigid's handbell choir.

Early in May eleven of the sisters undertook a class in Spanish, as a small way of witnessing to the church in the area with its many Hispanic people. These classes stopped for the summer, which gave Sr. Gladys more time to work on her book, a commentary on the Rule of Benedict, which was published that fall with the title, "Notes and Comments." In July the community was involved in an arts and crafts workshop. They welcomed sisters from each of the monasteries, who came to learn something about advertising, pricing and selling their crafts from the experts in these fields, whom Sr. Bernard had contacted.

When the year 1980 began, some of the San Diego sisters were busy planning for the sesquimillenium celebration. The various Benedictines in the far-flung state got together from Woodside in the Portola Valley near San Francisco to the Valyermo monks in the high desert; from the Sunnymeade and Glendora sisters near Los Angeles to the Oceanside monks and the sisters on Paducah Drive in San Diego. There was time, though, for some of the sisters in late January to make a voyage with the Chabot family on their cruiser to watch for the migrating grey whales off Point Loma. Eleven sisters were lucky enough to see several of these giants frolic in the blue waters.

On February 22 Fr. Alan McCoy, O.F.M. arrived to lead a workshop on the vows, sponsored by the Sisters' Senate of San Diego, of which Sr. Gladys was president that year. With March came more rain, some of the heaviest rains in the city's history. It also brought more workshops. Fr. Basil Pennington spoke to the sisters on centering prayer on the 16th. Sr. Dolores left for San Francisco later to represent the community at the official opening of the 1980 celebration in the cathedral there with Archbishop John Quinn officiating.

The sisters in the sewing room were kept busy at this time with orders for robes for eucharistic ministers. These came not only from Catholic churches, but from Lutheran, Methodist, Presbyterian and Orthodox as well. The entire community was busy that May with a discernment process regarding the election or appointment of their next prioress. Sheets of newsprint hung on the walls, the community's important events were historicized; there were lengthy discussions about goals and needs. On July 19th the community elected Sr. Paula Thompson. She was installed on August 20th. Sr. Dolores left for a year's study at the Institute for Spirituality and Worship in Berkeley, California. Sr. Gladys also departed to take up the role of administrator of the St. Benedict Health Care Center in the St. Louis monastery.

In February 1981 a number of sisters, along with some hundred other religious women of the diocese, attended a memorial Mass for the five churchwomen murdered in El Salvador. After this, it was time to welcome the prioresses and sisters from all the congregation, including nineteen from the Tucson monastery, to Dr. Harold Grant's workshop. The Paducah Drive monastery was filled to capacity with some sixty-six sisters. June was a month for celebrations. On the 7th Sr. Wilmarie Erhardt began her term as sub-prioress. On the 20th two sisters who had long served the community celebrated their golden jubilee of profession, Srs. Meinrada Dietrich, a pioneer member of the community who had been there since Old Town days, and Mary Frank, the community's infirmarian.

On January 1, 1982 the sisters wakened to the sound of rain, the first in months as 1981 had been the driest year in decades. Later that month they enthusiastically inaugurated a specially equipped exercise room. Sr. Paula had commissioned Sr. Trinitas Nordhus to decorate the walls with murals of clowns, dancers and yoga exercises. The sisters who attended Sr. Teresa Kane's talk to the Sisters' Senate in March were even more enthusiastic. The chronicler noted: "All were impressed by the vision, simplicity, honesty, compassion and dedication of Sr. Teresa."

That Lent the sisters made special efforts at prayer and fasting for the poor. There were particular days when only bread and soup were served, so that increased gifts of food, clothing and money could be sent to the Mexican sisters who ran the orphanage and dispensary in Tijuana. Perhaps because of this the joy of Easter seemed all the more vivid. They lit the paschal fire on the front lawn, so that all could see its flame. A full moon kept appearing from behind the clouds to shine on the service. During the Eucharist the sun burst forth gloriously. After the thanksgiving of the Vigil Mass there was an interpretive dance. The chronicler described the dancer in white who moved like a "great butterfly," so that even some of the men present were "touched to tears in a real resurrection experience."

In June the community experienced the sorrow of the death of one of their members. Sr. Rose Regina Kessler, long a victim of cancer, died while visiting her family in Ohio. In mid-July the sisters welcomed Willigis Jaeger, O.S.B. who spoke to them about contemplative prayer in the western tradition and about Zen spirituality. A Zen master himself, this monk had spent years in the Orient and was now director of a retreat house in Warzburg, Germany, which was a center of prayer in both the eastern and western tradition.

Later that month Srs. Paula, Wilmarie and Salome Komar left to take part in the Chapter at the St. Louis monastery. The sisters in San Diego prayed for the delegates and rejoiced in the election of Sr. Maureen Truland as prioress general. They had mixed feelings about losing their bookkeeper, Sr. Rosario Martinez, who was elected to the general council.

Chapter Fourteen
Epilogue

As this story of the Benedictine Sisters of Perpetual Adoration shows, the journey of the Maria Rickenbach sisters from a plateau in the Alps to the plains of Missouri was a pilgrimage of the spirit as well as of space. Mother Anselma Felber came to America with the firm conviction that prayer was far more needed in her adopted country than either teaching or preaching. The generations which followed her have retained that conviction.

The changes lived through from 1874 when the sisters came to the United States, until 1982 when this story ends, have been as vast and varied as any century ever witnessed. Through them all the singular tenacity of the monastic search for God endured. A 6th century Rule still acts as a catalyst for 20th century American monastic women. Reflected on, it still helps us harmonize the signs of the times with a return to the sources, self-renewal with self-transcendence, flexibility with stability. It still helps us believe that the discipline of prayer and silence can open us to wholeness.

In an age of unparalleled individualism like our own, the Rule of Benedict works to ensure that decisions of faith can be brought to bear on contemporary issues. It does this by encouraging a certain reflective distance from the imperatives of the present, recalling to us that some of our absolutes will turn out to be relative.

As American Benedictine women we share that hunger for commitment that also characterizes us as a nation. As Benedictine Sisters of Perpetual Adoration with a "distinctive dedication to Christ in the Eucharist,"[1] we find in this paschal meal of God's people the source and constant reminder of the Lord's presence in His Church, in the community. With St. Augustine, we know that "we are what we receive" by the grace of redemption. We struggle daily to discern the body which is the church, before we recognize the Body in the gifts of bread and wine. That is why we commit ourselves to adoration as intercession for the church. That is why we choose to live together in

249

community, believing with Benedict that "community becomes . . . the central metaphor for the experience of God."[2]

The pilgrimage from the concept of adoration which Mother Anselma brought with her from Switzerland to the eucharistic theology of our own day has been long and at times painful. Enriched by the fidelity of generations of sisters, we strive now to take the thanksgiving and reconciliation of the Mass and live these out hour by hour all the day long. Adoration is a way of life far more than it is a program.

Our Constitution reminds us that the daily praying of the Liturgy of the Hours not only sanctifies time, but forms us by the Word, shaping and expressing our faith. This corporate celebration of the Hours is both "remembrance and invocation."[3] Here the monastic search for God is made manifest. Here we hand on to one another the revelation of God's wonderful works, helping "the tradition which comes from the apostles to develop in the church."[4]

Nourished like this by Eucharist and the corporate celebration of the Hours, our personal prayer is deepened by lectio and that silent contemplative search that helps us live in humble hope, "in the tension of what we are and what we are becoming."[5]

From this ministry of prayer flows our hospitality. Listening to those who come to us for retreats or spiritual direction, learning from and with them, we try to foster their own seeking of God. We offer them space and solitude. We share scripture with them or Oblate programs. There has always been a quiet kind of evangelization in monastic hospitality, for ultimately it makes room for God in life. "The intensity of the contemplative vision in any monastic community can perhaps best be reflected in and nourished by its spirit of hospitality."[6]

When Mother Anselma and her pioneer sisters came to America, they faced a different and uncertain future. Today we face one that seems even more uncertain. The future may be for us what the desert was for early monasticism: a place dangerous, unmapped, full of mystery. But monastic prayer, biblical prayer, has always reached out to bless the future, trusting that life as God gives it to us is basically good. "Nothing is more mysterious than the unknown future; nothing carries more potential for threat to mortal beings. But the future contains also the messianic fulfillment and the victory of God's saints. To praise God for what has been is good prayer; the perfect prayer is to praise God for what will be."[7]

THAT IN ALL THINGS MAY GOD BE GLORIFIED

NOTES

1. Constitution of the Benedictine Sisters of Perpetual Adoration (1985), p. 13.

2. Nathan Mitchell, O.S.B., "Eucharistic Orientation in Benedictine Life" (*Benedictines:* XXXV:2, 1980), p. 164.

3. Conference of American Benedictine Prioresses, *Of Time Made Holy* (Erie, PA: Benet Press, 1978), no. 18.

4. *Dogmatic Constitution on Divine Revelation, #* 8.

5. Constitution of the Benedictine Sisters of Perpetual Adoration (1985), p. 16.

6. Conference of American Benedictine Prioresses, *Of All Good Gifts* (Erie, PA: Benet Press, 1980), no. III.

7. Demetrius Dumm, O.S.B., "Benedictine Hospitality" (*Benedictines*, XXXV: 2, 1980), p. 71.